Joan D. Atwood, PhD
Frank Genovese, PhD

Therapy with Single Parents
A Social Constructionist Approach

D0160889

Pre-publication
REVIEW . . .

"This book is a valuable resource for anyone working with single-parent families. It provides a well-rounded overview of the basic constructs of the single-parent family and details guidelines for developing and sharpening skills in conducting therapy with this specific type of family group. It is refreshing in its balance concerning issues of resiliency, viewing single-parent families as viable, healthy family forms. As people have typically been socialized to view two-parent families as the norm, the authors address various therapeutic strategies to help single-parent families overcome feelings of inferiority and despondency. It is a book that incorporates a focus on the strengths, rather than deficits and problems.

Treatment strategies for effectively dealing with a variety of family issues are presented. Commonly reported experiences of single parents are described and current research findings are utilized to suggest intervention strategies. Case examples are used to clarify such concepts as assessing families on a systemic level, understanding resilience/competence of children, and forming/redefining relationships.

The authors describe how social construction theory and therapy can be applied in therapeutic settings with families. Through this model, they demonstrate how families can be assisted in writing new scripts and constructing new stories and healthy solutions to challenges."

Sanna J. Thompson, PhD
Associate Professor,
School of Social Work,
University of Texas at Austin

Therapy with Single Parents
A Social Constructionist Approach

HAWORTH Marriage and Family Therapy
Terry S. Trepper, PhD
Senior Editor

Marital and Sexual Lifestyles in the United States: Attitudes, Behaviors, and Relationships in Social Context by Linda P. Rouse

Psychotherapy with People in the Arts: Nurturing Creativity by Gerald Schoenewolf

Critical Incidents in Marital and Family Therapy: A Practitioner's Guide by David A. Baptiste Jr.

Clinical and Educational Interventions with Fathers edited by Jay Fagan and Alan J. Hawkins

Family Solutions for Substance Abuse: Clinical and Counseling Approaches by Eric E. McCollum and Terry S. Trepper

The Therapist's Notebook for Families: Solution-Oriented Exercises for Working with Parents, Children, and Adolescents by Bob Bertolino and Gary Schultheis

Between Fathers and Sons: Critical Incident Narratives in the Development of Men's Lives by Robert J. Pellegrini and Theodore R. Sarbin

Women's Stories of Divorce at Childbirth: When the Baby Rocks the Cradle by Hilary Hoge

Treating Marital Stress: Support-Based Approaches by Robert P. Rugel

An Introduction to Marriage and Family Therapy by Lorna L. Hecker and Joseph L. Wetchler

Solution-Focused Brief Therapy: Its Effective Use in Agency Settings by Teri Pichot and Yvonne M. Dolan

Becoming a Solution Detective: Identifying Your Client's Strengths in Practical Brief Therapy by John Sharry, Brendan Madden, and Melissa Darmody

Emotional Cutoff: Bowen Family Systems Theory Perspectives edited by Peter Titelman

Welcome Home! An International and Nontraditional Adoption Reader edited byLita Linzer Schwartz and Florence W. Kaslow

Creativity in Psychotherapy: Reaching New Heights with Individuals, Couples, and Families by David K. Carson and Kent W. Becker

Understanding and Treating Schizophrenia: Contemporary Research, Theory, and Practice by Glenn D. Shean

Family Involvement in Treating Schizophrenia: Models, Essential Skills, and Process by James A. Marley

Transgender Emergence: Therapeutic Guidelines for Working with Gender-Variant People and Their Families by Arlene Istar Lev

Family Treatment of Personality Disorders: Advances in Clinical Practice edited by Malcolm M. MacFarlane

Unbecoming Mothers: The Social Production of Maternal Absence edited by Diana L. Gustafson

Therapy with Single Parents: A Social Constructionist Approach by Joan D. Atwood and Frank Genovese

Family Behavioral Issues in Health and Illness by J. Lebron McBride

When Adoptions Go Wrong: Psychological and Legal Issues of Adoption Disruption by Lita Linzer Schwartz

Therapy with Single Parents
A Social Constructionist Approach

Joan D. Atwood, PhD
Frank Genovese, PhD

The Haworth Press
New York • London • Oxford

For more information on this book or to order, visit
http://www.haworthpress.com/store/product.asp?sku=5540

or call 1-800-HAWORTH (800-429-6784) in the United States and Canada
or (607) 722-5857 outside the United States and Canada

or contact orders@HaworthPress.com

Published by

The Haworth Press, Inc., 10 Alice Street, Binghamton, NY 13904-1580.

PUBLISHER'S NOTE
The development, preparation, and publication of this work has been undertaken with great care. However, the Publisher, employees, editors, and agents of The Haworth Press are not responsible for any errors contained herein or for consequences that may ensue from use of materials or information contained in this work. The Haworth Press is committed to the dissemination of ideas and information according to the highest standards of intellectual freedom and the free exchange of ideas. Statements made and opinions expressed in this publication do not necessarily reflect the views of the Publisher, Directors, management, or staff of The Haworth Press, Inc., or an endorsement by them.

Identities and circumstances of individuals discussed in this book have been changed to protect confidentiality.

Cover design by Jennifer M. Gaska.

Library of Congress Cataloging-in-Publication Data

Atwood, Joan D.
    Therapy with single parents: a social constructionist approach / Joan D. Atwood, Frank Genovese.
        p. ; cm.
    Includes bibliographical references and index.
    ISBN-13: 978-0-7890-0294-5 (hard: alk. paper)
    ISBN-10: 0-7890-0294-9 (hard: alk. paper)
    ISBN-13: 978-0-7890-0407-9 (soft: alk. paper)
    ISBN-10: 0-7890-0407-0 (soft: alk. paper)
    1. Family psychotherapy. 2. Single parents—Mental health. 3. Single parent families—Mental health. 4. Children of single parents—Mental health. 5. Constructivism (Psychology) 6. Social psychology.
    [DNLM: 1. Single Parent—psychology. 2. Divorce—psychology. 3. Family Therapy. 4. Psychotherapy. 5. Single-Parent Family—psychology. HQ 759.915 A887t 2005] I. Genovese, Frank. II. Title.

RC488.5A92 2005
616.89'156—dc22

                                           2005017057

To all the single parents who over the years have shared their experiences, both joyful and painful: This book is a tribute to your strength and courage.

J.D.A.

To the memory of Dr. George Krupp, mentor, colleague, and friend

F.G.

ABOUT THE AUTHORS

Joan D. Atwood, PhD, is the Director of the Graduate Programs in Marriage and Family Therapy at Hofstra University in Hempstead, New York. She is also the Director of the Marriage and Family Clinic, located in the Saltzman Community Center at Hofstra, and President and CEO of L.I.F.T., the Long Island Family Therapists, an organization devoted to the empowerment and wellness of individuals and families. Dr. Atwood is past President of the New York State Association for Marriage and Family Therapists and was awarded the Long Island Family Therapist of the Year award for outstanding contributions to the field. She has published eight books, including *Counseling Single Parents,* and more than 100 journal articles in the field of marriage and family therapy.

Frank Genovese, PhD, is an Adjunct Assistant Professor of Health Professions and Family Studies at Hofstra University in Hempstead, New York. He has published several articles and book chapters dealing with bereavement processes and with adolescence, and is the co-author of *Counseling Single Parents.*

CONTENTS

**PART IV: SOCIAL CONSTRUCTION THERAPY
WITH THE SINGLE-PARENT FAMILY**

Acknowledgments

We would like to thank the following people for their help, support, and assistance:

Our students, Stephanie Edelson, Danielle Macri, Yassiel Celin, and Emily Klucinek for their tireless efforts in researching materials for this book

Our families for their love, encouragement, and support

Introduction

For years professionals and the public have been warned by experts in the field of therapy about the pathological effects of disrupted bonds of attachment. Psychological theories and research served to validate the view that divorcing individuals have failed and that they and their children suffer psychologically from this trauma. In so doing, therapists everywhere focused their therapy sessions around the "emptying out" of feelings of anger, pain, sadness, and guilt. Today the term *divorce* still holds connotations of failure and shame for many Americans. Emery, Hetherington, and DiLalla (1984) believe it is crucial to keep in mind that social and political views affect both lay and professional opinion regarding the effects of divorce on adults and children.

The socially constructed definitions about divorce and the ensuing psychological reactions in terms of its negative connotations can be traced to an era in the United States before the Industrial Revolution when the two-parent family system was the norm. However, evidence is accumulating slowly showing that social definitions are changing. In the past decade the use of the term *broken home* has gradually shifted to the more neutral term *single-parent family*. This newer term, however, still does not accurately depict the family situation because for the most part in cases of divorce two parents are present. They simply live in two different locations. Yet this shift in attitude does reflect in part the public's recognition and acceptance of the dramatic rise in the divorce rate, which has cut across all socioeconomic classes such that in many primary, middle, and high schools today at least half of the students come from homes headed by one parent. In terms of incidence, the consensus is that most youth will spend some time prior to age eighteen in a single-parent household (Demo and Acock, 1988). Norton and Glick's (1986) analysis projects that 60 percent of American children will live in a single-parent family before reaching age eighteen.

A changing view of marriage also has contributed to the decline of the judgmental attitude toward divorce (Morawetz and Walker, 1984, pp. 5-6). Although expectations about marriage are changing slowly, at the beginning of the twentieth century the average age of death was approximately forty-five years old. This meant that individuals were married for about twenty to twenty-five years. Today, with the average life span over age eighty for women and close to eighty for men, it is possible that couples will be married for sixty years or in some cases even longer. It may not be reasonable to expect couples to remain married for such a long period of time. It might be a more viable option to be married to one person during the child-rearing years and to another for the post-child-rearing years. It appears that this is beginning to happen, as evidenced by the serial monogamy picture of marriage that has recently emerged in American society. Another factor clearly affecting the changing values around marriage is women's entry into the labor force due to economic need. The result is that wives are no longer as financially dependent on their husbands as they once were.

The media also plays a very important role in this change of attitudes. Early images of the family resembled *Little House on the Prairie.* In the 1950s and 1960s, we all wished for homes similar to those of *The Adventures of Ozzie and Harriet* or *Father Knows Best.* Few bothered to question why our mothers did not wear aprons while standing over the stove as *Leave It to Beaver*'s June Cleaver did, or why the men on these shows never ventured into the kitchen except to offer some worldly bit of advice.

The 1970s showed a change in values and attitudes with regard to the image of family structure. And society shifted to a reality that had not been there before. *One Day at a Time* was a television show that depicted a single mother raising two children. Although she suffered some setbacks, it was a lifestyle she chose. In fact, early in the show's run, she rejected a marriage proposal because she wanted to remain a single parent.

In the 1980s, the shift in family structure continued. Families became more open, actualized, and experienced at expressing their feelings. *Kate & Allie* depicted two single mothers pooling resources to raise three children in New York City; *Who's the Boss?* portrayed a reconstituted family of a male housekeeper, his daughter, and a female corporate executive and her mother and son. All lived together as a family. *Diff'rent Strokes* showed a single white man adopting two young black children.

While all of these situations were alternatives to the more traditional marriage or the result of the death of a spouse or divorce, the 1990s brought us *Murphy Brown,* who made a conscious choice to be a single parent, even though she had the opportunity to marry the father of the child.

This book, while providing the reader with a thorough, in-depth exploration of the single-parent family system, will also explore the four societal assumptions underlying the Intact Family Myth. They are as follows:

1. Staying together in long-term relationships is good; short-term relationships are bad. In other words, marriage "should" be forever.
2. A society in which people will live to age seventy-five can operate with the same relationship commitments as a society in which people live to age forty-five.
3. The traditional family is the basic social unit and should be strengthened. This assumes the traditional family model of mother, father, and children.
4. Only dysfunctional adults divorce, and this results in dysfunctional children.

Single persons are found in every age group and represent hundreds of thousands individuals in American society. Within the category "single," there are two major avenues to reach this status: never having married and having been divorced. A third possibility, death of a spouse, is the most common avenue among people past middle age. Those who fall into the "never having married" category are represented by the single parent by choice and the single parent not by choice. Those in the first section, the "Murphy Browns," are generally women who have not married for a whole host of reasons yet, usually around age thirty-five, decide to have a child. These women are generally financially secure and involved in their careers. As single parents, they face many of the same problems other single parents face; however, there are differences. Often they do not experience the feelings of failure that divorced women experience or the loss that widowed women experience. They also do not experience the psychologically uncomfortable identity transition that these women face as they move from the married world to the world of singles. This is not to say that motherhood is easy for these women. Many have thought through the decision to have a child and the transition to parenthood is smooth, but for others, the enormous responsibility of caring for a child is overwhelming.

For the second group of women, those who become mothers not by choice, usually in their teenage years, the picture is not as rosy. Although the rate of teenage pregnancy in the United States has been declining, it remains the highest in the developed world—approximately ninety-seven per 1,000 women ages fifteen through nineteen years old. One million American teenagers become pregnant each year. The majority of these pregnancies, 78 percent, is unintended (AGI, 1999). Teens that give birth are much more likely to come from poor or low-income families (83 percent) than are teens that have abortions (61 percent) or teens in general (38 percent) (AGI, 1994). This represents approximately 1 million young women in the United States (nearly 11 percent of this age group) who become pregnant every year (Hayes, 1987). Thirty-nine percent of these premarital pregnancies end in abortion, 12 percent end in miscarriage, and just under 50 percent result in live births. Of these premaritally conceived births, approximately 184,000 are legitimized by marriage and roughly 261,000 end in out-of-wedlock births (Hayes, 1987).

The rate of teen childbearing in the United States has fallen since the late 1950s, from an all-time high of 96 births per 1,000 women ages fifteen through nineteen in 1957. Birth rates fell steadily throughout the 1960s and 1970s; they were fairly steady in the early 1980s and then rose sharply between 1988 and 1991 before declining througth the 1990s. In recent years, this downward trend has occurred among teens of all ages and races (Boonstra, 2002).

Despite the decline of pregnancy rates in the United States, young women of color continue to be disproportionately affected. In addition, adolescent pregnancy does not affect all communities in the same way. For example, although African-American teens have experienced the greatest recent decline in pregnancy rates, those among Latina teens have not declined as significantly (Ventura et al., 2001).

The consequences of teenage pregnancy are often disastrous. It increases the health risks to both mother and child. The maternal death rate for teens under age fifteen is two-and-a-half times greater than that of mothers aged twenty to twenty-four (Morris et al., 1993). They are also liable to have numerous health problems and are at high risk for abuse and neglect of their children (Alan Guttmacher Institute, 1976). Single adolescent mothers have a lesser chance of getting married than their peers and a much greater chance of divorce if they do. Among girls who keep their babies (90 percent), only two out of ten marry the father (Furstenberg, Brooks-Gunn, and Morgad, 1987; Glick and Norton, 1979; Hayes, 1987). The teenage fathers often prematurely leave school to go to work to care for their families.

The baby also faces increased risks. Babies born to adolescent mothers are more likely than babies born to older mothers to have low birth weights, neurological defects, and childhood illnesses, all of which are major causes of infant mortality (Bolton, 1980). The social and economic consequences can be enormous. Adolescent mothers are twice as likely to drop out of school, less likely to be employed, and more likely to depend on welfare. Fully half of all payments made under the Aid to Families with Dependent Children program (AFDC) go to women who bore children during their adolescent years (Gilchrist and Schinke, 1983).

This book is not about either of these populations. Although single parents of all types share similar experiences, the experiences of the two groups just discussed represent unique segments of the single-parent population. Although segments of this book are relevant to each of these groups (for example, Chapter 9 on "Single Parents, Work and Welfare," would be very relevant for those therapists working with adolescent women), to cover their uniqueness in one book would be an impossible task, and other sources do justice to their situations (Atwood, 1992; Atwood and Kassindorf, 1992; Atwood and Donnelly, 1993). Further, this book does not include differentiation among cultural groups. We believe that although culture is a critical therapy consideration, economic status is probably more relevant. As stated, Chapter 10 describes community and social resources available to those who are financially disadvantaged, this chapter serves to direct therapists to the resources available to their financially disadvantaged clients and enables them to competently assist them in procuring these services.

This book is also not about men. Although some sections certainly apply to the single-parent father, more than 90 percent of single parents in the United States are women and it is to them that we direct the majority of our comments.

Basically, then, this book is directed toward helping those therapists who work with white, middle-class, divorced, and widowed clients—those individuals who would be most likely to seek the services of mental health therapists in private practice. This is where our expertise lies, and it is here that we feel we can make the most appropriate contribution. In no way do we mean to minimize the importance of the other groups; we have simply decided to focus on particular segments of the single-parent population, the divorced and the widowed, in order to provide an in-depth analysis of the single-parent situation rather than a superficial gleaning of all groups fitting into the single-parent category.

What, then, is the uniqueness of the present book? It is unique because it is the first book on therapy with single parents that includes a focus on the strengths of the single-parent family rather than a focus on the deficits, which is more typically seen in the literature. This is not to say that we ignore the psychological problems often experienced by the members in such families; rather, we present a more balanced picture in light of recent, methodologically sound research findings. Our view is that the single-parent family is a viable, healthy family form. Our assumption is that ideas we hold about what it means to be a member of such a family system are socially constructed. We believe that whereas the absence of a parent is obvious in the single-parent family, the prevalence of family values clearly is not, demonstrating that one nurturing and loving parent can produce healthy and productive individuals if society's prejudices do not interfere. As competent professionals it is time that we examine some of these assumptions (as well as our own) in order to provide these families with therapy that will empower them. Our book assists therapists in this questioning process. Thus, it is as much a book for therapists on a personal level as it is for therapists on a professional level.

People who have gone through a divorce or who have experienced the death of a spouse must confront life in a completely new role. Both of these situations create special problems, and both of these situations present new challenges for growth. Simply put, single parents have three major concerns: loneliness, children, and money. Their problems around these issues generally evolve over time, and the pressures of being a single parent build over time. The difficulties of providing for their own and their children's physical, psychological, and social needs may result in task overload and exhaustion. In addition, the single parent's relational-sexual part of life is affected. When, where, and with whom can they have intimacy and sex? Many single parents are reluctant to have their dates meet their children or have a difficult time finding babysitters. Clients who are involved in these readjustments encounter important social and psychological issues as they try to find a new place for themselves as social and sexual beings. As for the children, many of them grow up "faster" than their peers in two-parent family situations. Although these children have many competencies and resources and tend to be quite resilient, in some cases they experience responsibilities beyond their capabilities. This book assists therapists in exploring both of these experiences.

Thus, the first focus of the book is to specifically describe the most commonly reported experiences reported by single parents. These experiences are examined from the single parent's perspective and also from the child's perspective. In this way, the professional therapist can understand the many and often overwhelming problems that are faced by their clients. These considerations are addressed primarily from a social-psychological point of view, in that a major task of the single parent is to redefine social roles. These social redefinitions have psychological consequences, which are also described and discussed in detail.

The second focus of the book is on therapy with this type of family. The book not only teaches interventive strategies relevant to treating specific single parent family issues but also takes into account current research findings. In so doing it provides a deeper understanding of the single-parent family system. The book proposes specific therapy strategies throughout, assisting the therapists in therapeutic direction. The theoretical orientation of the book is primarily systemic, looking at persons in context, whether that context be intimate relationships, the family as a system, or larger, outside systems such as school, the workplace, or social services.

For the most part, this book will impart technical knowledge in a nontechnical language. It is based on many years of experience. All case material is real but disguised, originating from the authors' clinical practices. Throughout the book there is a progressive deepening of the reader's knowledge and awareness of the special issues faced by these two populations, along with a presentation of the therapy issues and strategies in more depth. The implications for reflective psychological therapy during the process of intimacy dissolution are explored, as is a presentation of psychological stages of the separation and remergence process. Suggestions for facilitating growth at each of these stages is given so that this life-cycle transition can eventuate a time of freedom, challenge, exploration, and growth.

The third focus of the book is on deepening the complexity of therapeutic understanding. For example, initially therapy strategies are presented from a more traditional family therapy model utilizing structural family therapy assessment and techniques. Next, there is a focus on the internal dynamics of individuals in this type of family, focusing on attachment bond dissolution and the ensuing feelings of loss. Throughout the book, social constructionist assumptions are alluded to, and this culminates in Chapter 10, " The Single Parent Family and Social Constructions," where a new model for working with this type of family is presented. Thus, the goal is to deepen the therapist's understanding of the therapeutic process. In so doing, the therapist's own assumptions around the therapy process and what it means to work with this type of family are challenged.

Chapter 1 primarily explores one segment of the single population—those who are separated or divorced. The focus is on the typical psychological problems, adjustments, and social issues faced by this growing population. Here the objective is to assist the therapist in understanding the experiences of these individuals. Chapter 2 explores the special category of widowhood. In so doing, the psychological and social issues surrounding this life stage are examined. Differences between psychological responses to divorce and widowhood are examined in detail, with an emphasis on presenting problems and emotional responses. Once the problems and the associated feelings are presented, therapeutic considerations for empowering clients are discussed in detail.

Chapter 3 describes a detailed case history, clearly depicting many of the special concerns of this population. The case history illustrates specific areas of concern for the single parent, demonstrating specific therapy techniques by example. Therapy with the family is approached using structural family therapy assessment and techniques.

Chapter 4 discusses children of divorce and presents a picture of the flip side of the coin, or the competent divorce. In this chapter, evidence is presented on factors that are predictive of the good divorce, which provide for positive outcomes in children and their parents.

Chapter 5 discusses a major component of the readjustment process after divorce or widowhood: redefining relationships. Here issues such as establishing relationships with the ex-spouse, in-laws, and extended family, as well as dealing with "ghosts," are described. In addition, redefining relationships with friends is presented—both for single and coupled friends. There is a section on the role of the professional therapist, including descriptions of the typical problems presented by clients around these issues and the potential for growth. Therapeutic assessments and interventions are presented from a more psychodynamic theoretical base.

After considering the socially constructed definitions and psychological experiences of the single parent, the next area of concern is dating and sexuality. Chapters 6 and 7 present the relational and sexual issues of the divorced and widowed single parent in more detail, illustrating the complexity of these family systems. The chapters explore the typical situations that single parents face in this area and present information that will facilitate the therapy process in assisting clients with values clarification. Chapter 7 also educates professional therapists about HIV/AIDS (human immunodeficiency virus/acquired immunodeficiency syndrome). It examines the impact that AIDS had on sexual behavior in the 1990s and discusses the special worries and concerns of divorced and widowed persons who are sexually active. In addition, it describes how therapists can best educate their clients so that they will be better able to protect themselves. A discussion of high-risk behaviors and psychosocial concerns is presented, along with a thorough investigation of therapy strategies.

Often times, single parents and their children are hurt by the attitude of school personnel. It is not unusual for educators who are insensitive to the single parent's plight to further add to the emotional devastation of the single-parent system. Chapter 8 explores how the professional therapist can assist the single parent in dealing with school personnel. Research on children of divorce indicates that some children experience academic problems when a disruption occurs in the family system; others do not. Chapter 8 describes the many ways that therapists can educate parents about school personnel issues and how therapists can best mobilize the competencies and strengths of parents and their children with regard to these issues.

Chapter 9 deals with the single parent and larger systems. First there is an examination of issues around returning to work. Most single parents, whether single from divorce or from widowhood, experience serious financial distress. In this chapter, the problems arising from decreased finances are explored, along with the problems which can arise when a newly single person decides to return to work. The psychological reactions to problems and the role of the therapist in terms of provider of psychoeducation are discussed here, along with details for uncovering strengths. Next, we explore how changes in lifestyle after divorce or widowhood often necessitate the single parent's dependence on social welfare agencies. Here professional therapists must be familiar with all social service resources available to single parents. This chapter describes ways in which professional therapists can facilitate this process for their clients through education.

Chapter 10 deepens the therapist's understanding of the therapeutic process in working with single-parent families. Recently, concepts from social construction theory have entered the field of marriage and family therapy. Social constructionists believe that how we know what we know is *not* through an exact pictorial duplication of the world: "The map is not the territory." Rather, reality is seen experientially, in terms of how we subjectively interpret the constructions. In this sense, we are responsible for what we believe, feel, and see. This chapter explores how these notions can be applied to therapy with the single-parent family and presents a model of therapy that creates an environment for change.

Chapter 11 summarizes some of the points made throughout the book, giving additional suggestions for therapists.

PART I:
SOCIAL AND PSYCHOLOGICAL
EXPERIENCES OF THE SINGLE AGAIN

Chapter 1

Single Again Through Divorce

The offices of professional therapists are filled with persons who are thinking about divorce, are divorcing, or have divorced. The high rate of divorce and the complexity of the emotional reactions to divorce lead many to seek professional help. To understand the complexity of the single-parent family system, it is first useful to examine the divorce rates and propose certain hypotheses about the composition of this group. This chapter examines the incidence of divorce in the United States and explores the divorce process from social and psychological frames of reference, describing how our social definitions of divorce influence our psychological reactions.

HISTORICAL DIVORCE RATES

The divorce rate (number of divorces per 1,000 marriages) began to increase in the United States early in the twentieth century. It seemed to peak after World War II and then to drop back a bit. However, it has been rising again in recent years (Ditzion, 1978). By the middle of the 1960s, however, the incidence of divorce started to increase and it more than doubled over the next fifteen years to reach a historical high point in the early 1980s. Since then, the divorce rate has modestly declined, a trend described by many experts as "leveling off at a high level" (Goldstein, 1999). Most of this increase in divorce during the 1970s was among younger couples. In 1975, 460 divorces occurred per 1,000 marriages. Since then, this rate has been rising, and current estimates indicate that approximately 500 divorces occur per 1,000 marriages, or approximately 1 divorce for every 2 marriages. Each year, approximately 2.2 million marriages and 1.1 million divorces take place in the United States (United States Bureau of the Census, 2000). As a result, more than 1 million persons yearly return to single status. The divorce rate is higher for nonwhites than whites and is generally higher among lower-class than middle- and upper-class whites (United States Census, 2000). The average age at divorce from first marriage in the United States today is twenty-seven for females and twenty-nine for males. Divorce appears to have become so common that 60 percent of Americans who get married today report that they do not expect the marriage to last the rest of their lives (Yankelovich, 1981).

In addition to the already divorced, a sizable number of people are in between marriage and divorce. At any given time, individuals who are separated from their spouses constitute a very large population. In March 2000, the U.S. Census reported 2.04 million men and 9.68 million women who were single parents (United States Census, 2000). The same report indicates that 27 percent of all family groups were headed by one parent in 1998. Clapp (1992) says, "Based on current trends, Sandra Hofferth of the Center For Population Research at the National Institute of Child Health and Human Development recently made the startling projection that 70 percent of white children and more than 90 percent of black children born in 1980 will spend sometime living in a single parent home before their 18th birthday." However, it should be noted that these figures probably represent underestimates inasmuch as an unknown number of persons report that an absent spouse is "visiting relatives." It is basically impossible, then, to measure separation, either through agreement to separate or desertion, since no formal reporting techniques exist, except for the few couples who go through the formalities of legal separation.

Current figures (U.S. Bureau of the Census, 2000) indicate that more than 19 million people in the United States are divorced and more than 1 million more join the ranks each year. Divorced people make up more than 40 percent of the U.S. population. One-quarter of all children growing up today will have more than two sets of parents by age eighteen. Eighty percent of divorced people remarry. Sixty percent have more children. Forty percent of second marriages end in divorce in the first four years (http://www. divorcemag.com).

These statistics mean that American society has the highest divorce and/or separation rate of all industrial countries and that most of this population involves children. Thus, from both the available divorce statistics and from the estimates of separations, it is clear that a large segment of the population is confronted with the task of readjusting to postmarital life.

INTERPRETING DIVORCE RATES

It is obvious that a growing number of marriages are ending in divorce. How to interpret such figures is less obvious. Rising divorce rates are a common topic in the popular media, and such rates are often interpreted as a sign of societal rejection of the institution of marriage. This explanation, however, is questionable. First of all, available divorce statistics are not necessarily an entirely reliable indicator of the current state of marriage. Although it may be true that fewer people value the commitment of marriage, it is also possible that expectations of marriage are higher than they were historically and that people are more easily disappointed. In the days of arranged marriages, many people tolerated unhappy or unsatisfying situations and adjusted to them. Now, fewer people are kept from divorce by religious prohibitions, legal barriers, and social disapproval and sanctions. Therefore, couples who are dissatisfied with their marriage are more likely to terminate the union. Divorce is probably also more common now because women have more opportunities economically and emotionally to support themselves and their children and to receive financial aid from governmental agencies. (About one family in seven now has a woman as the head of the household.) Finally, changes in gender roles and gender role expectations may have led to increased dissatisfaction with the institution of marriage in general. However, it is important to keep in mind that the number of divorces may reflect dissatisfaction with a particular marriage more than with the institution of marriage itself; the great majority of people who divorce eventually do remarry, thus indicating that the dissatisfaction may rest with the person rather than the institution of marriage. No simple summation of the positive and negative features of divorced life as compared with married life is available. How postmarital individuals feel about marriage versus singlehood is perhaps best revealed by an interesting statistic. Five out of six men and three out of four women eventually remarry (Cherlin, 1992).

- One-quarter of all Americans have experienced at least one divorce.
- More people are part of second marriages today than first marriages.

Moreover, half of these individuals remarry within three years of their divorce, and divorcees of all ages are more likely to wed than are their peers who have never been married (May, 1988).

Meanwhile, the probability of remarriage among divorced women was 54 percent in five years—58 percent for white women, 44 percent for Hispanic women, and 32 percent for black women. The likelihood that divorced women will remarry has been declining since the 1950s when women who divorced had a 65 percent chance of remarrying. Data for 1995 show that women who divorced in the 1980s only had a 50 percent chance of remarrying (Bramlett and Mosher, 2002).

Although a majority of divorced persons eventually remarry, the growth of divorce has led to a steep increase in the percentage of all adults who are currently divorced. This percentage, which was only 1.8 percent for males and 2.6 percent for females in 1960, quadrupled by the year 2000. The percentage of divorced is higher for females than for males primarily because divorced men are more likely to remarry than divorced women. Also, among those who do remarry, men generally do so sooner than women (Goldstein, 1999).

Several other factors could have bearing on the way divorce statistics are interpreted. As was mentioned earlier, only half of the states in this country have developed uniform standards for divorce record keeping (Glick and Norton, 1971). This probably means that the records reflect variable data collection procedures. Also, recently many legal aspects of divorce have changed. Thus, the recent rise in divorce rates may result from the increased ease with which divorces are obtained, rather than from an increased dissatisfaction with marriage itself. In recent years, obtaining a legal divorce has become a relatively simple, less expensive legal process. Compounding this is the fact that a significant percentage of the divorce rate is composed of individuals who have had more than one marriage and divorce, which means that a higher percentage of first marriages than is obvious at first glance remains intact. Using most measures, however, the research does appear to indicate that the proportion of marriages ending in divorce has almost doubled since the 1950s, lending support to the idea that a large and still-growing divorced population is confronted with the emotional task of adjusting to new social, psychological, and sexual roles.

SOCIAL DEFINITIONS AND REACTIONS TO DIVORCE

Many social stereotypes of the divorced or separated person exist. Traditionally, the divorced male or female was seen as a social loser, sitting alone in his or her apartment with four or five cats and stacks of newspapers piled to the ceiling. This stereotype invokes the image of the sad, depressed, psychologically devastated victim of divorce, struggling over the trauma of this life change, who experiences devastating problems in his or her interpersonal and sexual relationships. Today, this image has changed. The contemporary divorced single is now typically viewed as a young, upwardly mobile career person without a worry in the world who lives out the sexual fantasies of which others only dream. There is the "gay divorcée" image—the person, who, feeling released from the bonds and burdens of marriage, supposedly lives amid constant parties and entertainment, has plentiful sex (hopefully safe), and experiences general abandonment in sexual and other areas of life. Of course, neither stereotype is completely accurate, but both probably contain elements of truth applicable to many people's adjustment to divorce or separation. Becoming single again for most people falls somewhere between these extreme stereotypes.

Lois, a thirty-nine-year-old social worker, was married for fifteen years. She separated from her husband when she learned that he was involved in a long-term extramarital relationship. Now, five years later, she lives with her eleven-year-old son in a condominium on the beach, realizing her longtime dream. For the most part, she is happy with her life. She is currently dating someone she likes, but reports that at times she feels lonely and misses the sharing and intimacy of married life.

As with almost everything else, individuals report both desirable and undesirable aspects of singlehood. On one hand, for some, it may offer an independence that they feel is rarely obtained in marital relationships. Singlehood also offers time alone when one wants it. It gives the person an opportunity to examine individual needs and desires, a concern of many young people today. For individuals who value privacy and time alone, singlehood is defined as a very positive lifestyle. Individuals can come to know what kind of person they are in the absence of day-to-day life with partners who may be the primary focus of their self-definition. It also offers variety in terms of both interpersonal and sexual relationships. Some people believe that only singles can truly experience the human diversity in interpersonal sexual relationships, an opportunity that many people find rewarding in terms of the uniqueness of each person and each relationship.

On the other hand, many people report disadvantages to being single. Some people define being single as lonely rather than as being alone. Perhaps more important for the average single person, there are many times when the price paid for independence and time spent alone is the absence of intimacy and not having another with whom to share day-to-day living. Individuals report that little things may also be problematic. Such necessary life events as errands during the day, doing laundry, washing the car, and the like, which are necessary to accomplish, must be accomplished alone.

Changing status from being married to being single again may involve varied difficulties in emotional adjustments. "Divorce, as a cardinal turning point in the individual's life, triggers waves in the social circles of those who divorce" (Albeck and Kaydar, 2002, p. 334). Many social adjustments must also be made. Many individuals have established friendships and social relationships as couples rather than as individuals. Albeck and Kaydar (2002) examined the changes that occur with the social networks of divorced mothers after the divorce and as a result of the divorce. They found that intensity in the relationships with the group of friends formed during the marriage decreases. However, the overall network of friends increases, with women experiencing more closeness in their relationship with the group of friends, rather than with the husband's group of friends or friends that the couple shared in common. An individual experiencing divorce may feel awkward partaking in social activities previously enjoyed with the spouse in the company of other couples. At the same time, other couples may not be comfortable including singles in their previously coupled activities. Mutual friendships formed by the marital unit are sometimes lost after divorce. Researchers found that during the divorce process, individuals lose as many as 40 percent of their prior friends (see also Duffy, 1994). Often, then, a sense of security or belonging that accompanies being part of a couple is replaced with sudden autonomy. This may be uncomfortable for many individuals.

Mel, a fifty-four-year-old business executive, divorced Ellen, his wife of twenty-five years, because he wanted to experience other women. Initially feeling secure with his support network of friends whom they both had known for many years, he didn't feel lonely. Over time, however, his friends tended to side with Ellen, and Mel became increasingly uncomfortable in their presence. So he stopped seeing them. Eventually, he began to experience depression—feeling alone and abandoned by his friends. After two years of therapy, Mel eventually began to establish a support network of his own, consisting mainly of persons who were single again like himself.

Males and females experience the divorcing process differently. Initially, men report that they feel relieved—relieved of obligations and responsibilities. Many experience a sense of euphoria. They have more time alone enabling them to leisurely watch television or stay late at work. They are free from the obligation of having to come home on time for dinner or having to help a child with homework. Many women, who more typically define themselves in terms of relationships, experience loss—loss of a husband and loss of the "married" status or the relationship. They take on many of the responsibilities their husbands gave up—financial, parental, and familial. Initially, many women report that they feel overwhelmed, fear for their financial and emotional security, and worry about their future.

Over time, the picture appears to change as men report that they begin to miss the structure that marriage afforded them. The highest rate of suicide is among divorced men. It appears that over time they have more difficulty than women establishing social support networks and creating a day-to-day living structure for themselves. Women, on the other hand, generally have no place to go but up emotionally. They typically find employment outside the home if they had not prior to the divorce, which tends to enhance their feelings of self-esteem and competency. Settling in with the children tends to become systematized and over time their lives, although changed, remain much as they were before the divorce. Durkheim (1951), an early sociologist, was one of the first to believe that marriage gave men the benefits of structure but placed women in "chains." Divorce, he believed, represented freedom from those chains for the women, but threw the man into a state of "anomie," feelings of helplessness and despair. He accounts for the high suicide rate among divorced men in this way. Epstein's (1974) found that women, while initially depressed after divorce, reported higher rates of happiness one year later; while men, who immediately after divorce reported high levels of happiness, plummeted one year later.

Divorcing individuals often need to establish new social contacts, which include new groups of single people. Many cities have organizations through which single people can meet and form new friendships. However, for many individuals, giving up old relationships and seeking new friendships can be a frightening experience.

Divorced men and women undergo a radical change in social role, from "wife" or "husband" (and thus part of a couple) to an unattached person for whom society has established no definite role or expectations. For this reason, recently divorced people often feel anxious and rootless. They may watch helplessly as the friends who saw them as half of a couple drift away. As Ganong and Coleman (1999) point out, Americans have idealized the nuclear model of family life. The nuclear family model has come to be associated with a moral, natural imperative. Other forms of family life are considered to be immoral or, at best, less moral than the Western nuclear family model. Cultural adherence to this ideology helps explain why policymakers can intrude so thoroughly into family life at the time of legal divorce yet be so reluctant to develop ways to support the divorcing parents and their children. The unofficial policy has been that because divorced persons have done wrong, they do not deserve help. This then influences how divorced parents think about themselves and their children. Parents who believe that the nuclear family is the only natural, normal type of family may then have difficulty figuring out new roles and responsibilities when their own family ceases to fit the model. Single-parent families have been called "broken families," and by implication their members were also seen as deficient. Most of the early literature concerning single parenting was based also on the assumption that children of single-parent households were automatically at risk for some form of deviance ranging from weakened gender or sex-role identity to poor self-esteem to social deviancy (Inhinger-Tallman, 1995).

These social definitions, expectations, and assumptions about marriage and divorce, which delineate the appropriate contexts for sociosexual behavior, create the setting within which individuals experience the psychological reaction to the divorcing process.

PSYCHOLOGICAL REACTIONS TO DIVORCE

Although the chain of events leading to marriage is varied, most people do marry with the hope and expectation that the marriage will last. Divorce often represents loss of this hope, as well as other losses: one's spouse, sometimes one's children, possibly a lifestyle, often the security of familiarity, and perhaps most important, part of one's identity. That the single-parent family system is born of loss, either through death or divorce, is the focus of a portion of this book. Although most families successfully negotiate the developmental tasks involved in the dissolution of intimacy bonds, others do not. In these cases, the marital bond appears to persist, regardless of the quality of the marriage. Some feel anxious, fearful, or terrified when contemplating their separated or divorced situation. These individuals often feel trapped and unable to grow.

The disturbances most clients feel at this time are almost always associated with disruption of the attachment bond. Marital dissolution is an extremely disruptive event, not only by ending the accessibility to the spouse but also by changing the client's social role and his or her relationships with the children, relatives, and friends. Psychological reactions to the dissolution of the marriage then become intertwined with reactions to many other disruptions.

The loss of attachment may, however, be seen as the primary cause of the distress that persons experience in single-parent situations. This distress includes the need to reorganize attention around the image of the lost spouse, the working through of the urge to contact the lost spouse, anger or guilt toward the lost spouse, and hypervigilance around issues involving the lost spouse. This feeling is indicated by feelings of fear or panic at the thought of contact with the spouse; this can also manifest in sleeplessness or loss of appetite. Children from single-parent homes also exhibit many of these symptoms. These distress signals are often exhibited in school situations, and they often present as failure to concentrate, drifting off into fantasy, academic decline, withdrawal from social relationships, and/or acting out with peers. Thus, the manifestations of the core problem of loss of attachment can be numerous and subtle. Therapists and families often fail to cognitively connect presenting problems with mourning issues.

The presenting issues are similar for those who are single due to widowhood. Persons experience numbness and disbelief accompanied by feelings of denial, a nonacceptance of the fact that the person is *really* dead. This is then followed by emotional reactions such as crying, psychosomatic symptoms, insomnia, feelings of guilt: "If I would have done . . . , maybe she wouldn't have died." Some clients become immersed in anger: "Why me! Why did this happen to me!" Or "The doctors killed him." Next come the feelings of sadness, loneliness, often incapacitating depression, and loss of usual patterns or habits, for example, not being able to have coffee together in the morning. A variety of persistent grief reactions, such as reconstructing idealized versions of the lost spouse, may be experienced if the person does not express emotion or refuses to deal with the loss. In addition to the more psychologically based issues that single parents experience, very real concrete factors influence the plight of the single parent. Some examples include financial problems, finding new roles, and the disruption of family relationships.

Changing status from being married to being single presents varied difficulties in emotional adjustment. It usually takes two to three years to form a strong attachment to a partner. If separation occurs after this time, it usually involves separation shock for the individual. It is a myth for people to assume that couples who are married thirty years suffer more than couples who are married for seven years. In both cases, many the individuals involved suffer separation shock. Many individuals going through the divorcing process pass through a series of psychological stages. Not all clients go through these stages, and not all clients experience them in a particular order. However, many individuals do report experiencing the stages discussed next, and it is helpful for therapists to be aware of these stages in order to help clients in this sociopsychological process. For purposes of clarity, the four stages are denial, conflict, ambivalence, and acceptance.

Denial

Stage I of the emotional divorcing process, denial, is usually manifested by separation shock. If the individual is experiencing separation shock, he or she experiences relief, numbness, or panic. Relief is often felt when the divorce has been a extended and drawn-out process. The most typical reaction to separation is fear of abandonment. The emotional response to this fear is often apprehensiveness and anxiety.

Linda, a thirty-two-year-old housewife, separated from her husband of eight years because of their constant arguing. For the most part, she was comfortable with her decision. However, about once a week she said that she felt shaky, not on solid ground. During these times, she would doubt her decision to divorce, feeling that she had made a mistake. Often she would go to bed feeling anxious and upset, staying there for days, leaving the care of her children to her mother. Eventually, she would feel a little better and, after a few days, would get up and function as usual. She would be fine for a while; however, after a few weeks, the pattern would repeat.

These anxious feelings may be accompanied by disturbances of sleep or appetite patterns. If there are increases in food intake and decreases in number of hours spent sleeping, the person usually experiences anxiety. Decreases in food intake and increases in time spent sleeping are probably related to depression. In either case, both symptoms are indications of separation shock. Often, during this time, individuals will report that they are unable to concentrate on work activities or carry on conversations with people. They think about other things while people are talking to them, often about old conversations with or memories of their former partners. Each memory brings a different experience, which may result in sudden outbursts of tears or anger. They seem unable to "get outside of themselves."

Linda reported that once she had to leave the supermarket because she started to cry "for no reason." This added to her "shakiness" because she felt she couldn't control or predict her emotions.

Other people report that they often lose control of their anger and, for what later seems to them to be an insignificant reason, explode into sudden flashes of rage.

Jim, a forty-nine-year-old advertising manager, said that he snapped at a waitress in a rage because she forgot to bring him milk for his coffee. The strength of his anger frightened him and precipitated his coming to therapy. He said he felt as if he wanted to kill her.

For many individuals, though, feelings of numbness or the absence of feelings are experienced. Numbness is a way of muting or denying feelings that, if experienced, would be too overwhelming for the individual to handle.

When Linda felt shaky and went to bed, if asked how she felt, she would reply, "I feel nothing. The world feels numb. I don't love anyone or hate anyone. I just don't feel anything."

In this case, Linda is overwhelmed by the reality of the situation and responds with denial, temporarily turning off her psychological system. Often during this stage, the person vacillates between these emotions—feeling first anxious, then angry, and then numb. These emotions are often combined with and compounded by feelings of optimism about their new life. This stage of separation shock can last anywhere from a few days to several months.

Often one partner desires the divorce more so than the other. Typical reactions to the impending divorce depend upon whether or not one initiates the divorce. It is important to be aware of the specific emotional reactions to each situation. For example, the person who leaves is often burdened with enormous amounts of guilt and self-blame, whereas the person who is left potentially feels more anger, hurt, self-pity, and condemnation of the other. The person who requests the divorce may fear being labeled a deserter, whereas the person who is left may feel embarrassment and a fear of being labeled a loser. Both individuals suffer.

Linda requested the divorce. The arguing in the marriage had nearly escalated to physical violence. Steve, her husband, often came home at 2 or 3 a.m. This would enrage Linda. On these nights, she would wait up for him and question him extensively as to his whereabouts because she was convinced (rightly so) that he was having an affair. Then she would feel guilty about arguing and accusing him. During and after the divorce she felt tremendous guilt over depriving him of his family and hurting him.

The process of divorce can have effects far greater than the simple dissolution of an unworkable marriage. Even when the marriage ends because one of the partners has fallen in love with someone else, the partner who asks for the divorce can experience profound pain. In sum, Stage I emotionality involves coming to grips with the fact that the marriage is ending. The emotional task of the person at this stage of the divorcing process is to accept the reality of the separation.

Conflict

Once acceptance occurs, the divorcing person enters into Stage II, conflict. Shortly after separation shock, the individual may begin to experience a multitude of emotions, with moods changing constantly and without warning. One minute people may feel perfectly comfortable with their new lifestyles and the next they may find themselves in tears, reminiscing about their former spouse. Shortly thereafter, remembering a negative event or an argument, they may then feel enraged.

After being in therapy for about six months, Linda started to feel better about herself. She had taken up racketball, she had lost ten pounds, and she had started a part-time job. She reported to the therapist that for the first time since she was married, she was focusing on herself—her own needs, her own wants and desires. She was learning who she was as a person. Before she always focused on Steve's needs, trying to anticipate them to avoid conflict. These feelings of well-being lasted about two weeks, until Linda came to therapy reporting that she didn't know what she was doing; she had "made a mistake; being married and miserable was better than not being married at all." Her feelings had "fooled" her again. Just when she thought she was doing better, she came crashing down.

The only thing that is predictable in this stage is the unpredictability of feelings.

During the conflict stage, feelings of disorganization may occur. One day they may feel that the entire world has turned upside down; the next day, they may feel perfectly comfortable with their newfound freedom. Volatile, explosive emotions may unexpectedly surface during this time. Individuals in this stage typically feel as if they may fall apart at any time. Feelings of guilt and anger become strong. Persons may feel enraged at their spouse and then, a few hours later, feel ashamed and guilty about their angry feelings. They may experience periods of anger at themselves and their spouses for having failed at marriage or at being left alone in their current situation. Along with these feelings they may also ponder whether they should have stayed with their spouse; they may feel as though they made a mistake. At times, feelings of regret may surface. These feelings usually come in waves and they may catch them off guard. This stage is typified by conflicting emotions: at any given time the individuals cannot predict which feeling they will be experiencing.

Also during this second stage of the divorcing period, individuals may do what is called scanning (Krantzler, 1975). In this process, they will reminisce about what went wrong with their marriage, wonder who was to blame, and consider what their own role was in the failure. It also means that they are reliving the best times in the marriage and mourning the loss of its more intimate aspects. Scanning, in many ways, may be a way of preserving the attachment bonds; it may also provide much constructive insight to individuals about their own constructive and destructive patterns in relationships. In this sense it may be a valuable learning experience. This review process may go on for months and is a major contributing factor to the mood swings divorcing persons experience. Each memory and each new awareness causes them to feel different emotions. This process, although emotionally uncomfortable, enables individuals to release their pent-up feelings which might otherwise cause them much distress at later points in their lives.

During this stage, which may be characterized by emotional upheaval, a sense of loss and loneliness may frequently develop. Loneliness manifests itself in many ways. Some individuals may sit in front of the television set for hours. Gradually, they may withdraw from social contacts. Others may experience a more active type of loneliness. Instead of sitting at home, they frequent old restaurants, pass by their former spouse's home, or go from one singles bar to another, desperately looking for solace from their loneliness.

Also during this time, negative feelings and emotions experienced as a child, such as separation anxiety, low self-esteem or feelings of worthlessness, may resurface, causing individuals much distress. Yet at other times, they may experience periods of euphoria. Hunt and Hunt (1977) found that a small percentage of individuals in their sample and after separation felt a sense of relief, increased personal freedom, and newly gained competence, and were able to reinvest emotional energy into themselves—energy which was previously directed toward the marriage. These euphoric feelings tend to appear suddenly and for no apparent reason, causing the person to feel "on top of the world." These happy feelings may last for days or weeks. The danger during this phase is that the person may think that the worst is over, only to suddenly plunge into the depths of depression. Unfortunately, it is usually during this time, when emotions are changing rapidly, that individuals are usually required to deal with lawyers and make major decisions.

In sum, for most people, Stage II represents an emotional seesaw, usually characterized by psychological conflict. The emotional task of individuals at this stage is to achieve a realistic definition of what their marriage represented, what their role was in its maintenance, what their responsibility was for its failure, and where they were "stuck" psychologically.

Ambivalence

Stage III is characterized by ambivalence and involves changes in the person's identity. In many ways, this is the most psychologically stressful aspect of the divorcing process. Being married is a primary source of self-identity. The two individuals involved codevelop identities about who they are as a couple and where and how they fit into the world. They cocreate social definitions that are consonant with the social definition of marriage. When their relationship ends, they may feel confused and fearful, as though they no longer have a script telling them how to behave. Often during this time period, they may try on different identities, attempting to find one that is comfortable for them. At this time, the divorcing people face a major change in self-perception. Instead of a husband and father, a man may find himself living in a small apartment and seeing his children only every other weekend. Instead of a wife and homemaker, a woman may find herself labeled a "divorcée," a term that sometimes means promiscuous and loose to the uninformed person.

Linda again, typifies feelings experienced while going through these emotional stages. As stated earlier, she requested the divorce. She was tired of fighting and felt that she wanted to find a loving relationship. Most days she felt this way. Occasionally, however, she would remember the good times—a party they went to together, a funny instance with one of the children. Sometimes when her husband came to pick up the children, she would feel a resurgence of tenderness. A moment later, she would experience the rage she felt when he would stay late at work after promising he would be home early. Then she would feel certain of her decision once again. The emotions she experienced during a few seconds, however, were extreme. When she felt tender toward him, she also felt guilty about having deserted him. A few seconds later, remembering all the hatred and arguing, she would feel rage at his behavior. These emotional swings would leave her exhausted. She would spend the next few days in bed.

Sometimes, during this period, people go through a second adolescence. Similar to the first adolescence, persons may become very concerned about how they look, how they sound. They may buy new clothes or a new car. Many of the struggles that were experienced as a teenager may reappear, and persons may find themselves trying to decide how to handle sexual advances or when to kiss a date good night. Sexual experimentation may occur as individuals attempt to explore their new sexuality outside of the marital situation. The emotional task for persons at this stage involves making the psychological transition from being married to being single again. This constitutes an identity transformation which, for many, is psychologically the most difficult and stressful undertaking of the divorcing process.

Acceptance

Finally, usually not until after several months or a year, individuals may enter Stage IV. In this stage individuals typically feel a sense of relief and acceptance about their situation (Krantzler, 1975). After a while individuals start to experience a new sense of strength and accomplishment. For the most part, they feel quite content with their lifestyle and no longer dwell on the past. They now have a new sense of awareness and knowledge of their own needs. If, after months of separation, a sense of acceptance of the past is not developing, the person may decide to seek professional help. Hunt and Hunt (1977) and Weiss (1975) feel that the most painful aspects of divorce peak within the first several months of a divorce and then tend to level off by the end of the first year. They believe that the complete emotional resolution of a divorce occurs when the spouses are no longer significantly influenced by the previously described reactions. This, they believe, usually takes between two and four years. Although many of the feelings triggered by divorce are painful and uncomfortable, they ultimately lead toward resolving the loss so that, if the individual desires, he or she will be emotionally able to reestablish an intimate relationship.

In therapy, Linda's feelings eventually began to stabilize. Her feelings of well-being began to take precedence over her feelings of anxiety and anger. She was able to pursue her own interests and put her former spouse and former marriage in a perspective with which she was comfortable. She had started to date someone that she liked and, although she felt he was not the "right" one, she was content in her situation.

Unfortunately, though, not all people go through the stages to experience resolution. Some individuals get stuck. Although most people would benefit from therapy while going through this major life-cycle change, those who get stuck would find therapy most useful.

Terry, an attractive fifty-seven-year-old bookkeeper, couldn't accept the idea that her husband had left her to move in with his young, pretty secretary. After her husband moved out, Terry withdrew from all her friends and eventually they stopped calling her. She spent all her evenings at home alone preoccupied with thoughts of her ex-husband and his girlfriend. All she could think about was the two of them together. Becoming obsessed with these thoughts, she was determined to discover what they were doing in their daily lives. She decided to set her alarm clock for 2 a.m., at which time she awakened, dressed, and drove to their home. She snuck out of her car and stole their garbage. She took the garbage home and examined it on her kitchen table. In therapy, she exclaimed to her therapist, "You'd be surprised how much you could learn from people's garbage. I know when they're sick, what they eat for dinner, when she has her period!"

After two years of therapy, Terry was able to develop her own support structure, become involved in meaningful activities, and begin dating. Eventually, she gave up the possibility of a reunion with her ex-husband.

Under the best of circumstances, separation and divorce represent a major life-cycle transition. Even in mutually agreed-upon, friendly terminations of a marital situation, many significant lifestyle changes occur. The newly single person often faces adjustments in social, psychological, and sexual relationships, financial arrangements, living arrangements, and, in most cases, parenting roles. Most divorces, however, do not occur under the best of circumstances; typically, divorces are not logical or rational agreements. Rather they are emotional, irrational conflicts full of bitter contention. During this time, individuals' self-confidence may be shattered because they believe they have failed at the marriage. In a society where the "family value" is the outmoded and unrealistic two-parent norm, persons opting for divorce often define their situation as deviant. The psychological consequences based on this social definition then ensue. Extensive changes such as these, even if accomplished by the relief of ending an undesirable situation, typically cause stress. Holmes and Rahe (1967) found that divorce and marital separation rank second and third respectively behind death of a spouse as events that produce the highest degrees of stress in individuals' lives.

The stress of divorce shows in many ways. Compared with married (or remarried) people, divorced men and women drink more often, smoke more marijuana, are lonelier and more despondent, and are more likely to feel anxious or guilty (Cargan and Melko, 1982). It is likely that this is why Mohammed said, "Divorce is the most detestable of all permitted things" (Epstein, 1974, p. 19).

Interview and clinical data indicate that most divorced individuals go through a period of social and psychological readjustment as they redefine themselves as single again. For many this is difficult, and for a few, quite traumatic. After this period, however, the person's life settles down into its own pattern.

Chapter 2

Single Again Through Widowhood

PSYCHOLOGICAL DIFFERENCES BETWEEN DIVORCE AND WIDOWHOOD

In divorce, the human factor is involved in the decision making; whereas in death, a life has been ripped from two people. So, in this respect, widowhood has an element of respect that divorce, no matter who is at fault, does not. For many people, divorce represents a unique kind of a loss, called a relationship loss. Reactions to loss are mourning processes. The road back to emotional stability is the healing process. The loss a person feels in divorce is very comparable to the loss an individual experiences when a significant other dies. In both cases, a grieving process occurs. However, there are important differences. In divorce, even though a person is lost, the focus is primarily on the loss of the relationship. In death, the focus is on the loss of the person. In divorce, the lost spouse continues to exist and in many cases continues to interact with the other spouse around legal, financial, and parenting matters. In the case of death, interaction no longer occurs. When the grief is caused by death, social rituals and supports are available that may aid the remaining spouse in his or her emotional adjustment in the mourning process. Hetherington and Kelly (2002) suggest that widows receive greater social support from family, friends, and relatives than do women that divorce. This descrepancy likely involves the social stigma associated with the decision to terminate an intimate relationship. Society as a whole tends to view marriage in terms of success or failure and expects subsequent accountability.

The postmarital adjustment of widowhood is also different from divorce. Widowed individuals typically do not have the sense of having failed at a marriage. In addition, the anger and resentment that often help facilitate emotional separation after a divorce is frequently lacking when a partner dies. The grief may be more intense, and the quality of the emotional attachment to the deceased mate is often quite high. For some, this emotional tie remains so strong that other potential relationships may appear unfavorable or lacking by comparison.

Rathers and Nevid (1983) believe that divorce may require more difficult adjustment than the death of a spouse. They state that when a spouse dies, legalities in most cases are less drawn out. Often, clear-cut dictates in a will or insurance document, specify the wishes of the deceased. In divorce, persons generally experience financial decreases because two households now must be supported. Generally, when a partner dies, insurance monies are available; in some cases, home mortgages are paid off. Divorce may seem to require a ream of legal documents and endless waiting periods. When someone dies, the surviving family remains intact. In divorce, children and others may choose sides and assign blame. For the parent who does not have custody of the children, divorce signals changes in the parental as well as the marital role. After a death, people receive compassionate leave from work and are expected to be less productive for a while. After divorce, people are often criticized. Death is final, but the divorced may nourish "what ifs" and vacillate in their emotions for many years. It is important for the therapist to keep in mind that personal reactions to both processes vary and few typologies or general statements can be made with regard to the trauma suffered by each.

U.S. WIDOWHOOD RATES

Of the more than 22 million people in the United States who are age sixty-five years and older, almost one-half of the women and one-fifth of the men have lost their marital partners (Leslie and Leslie, 1977). Because of the differential longevity of men and women, we can expect an increasing preponderance of widows in the aged population over the years to come.

One out of every twelve women in the United States over the age of fourteen is a widow. There are more than 11.5 million widows and widowers in the United States. The overwhelming majority (by a ratio of five to one) are women. By contrast, there are only 6 million divorced persons, of whom five-sixths are men and three-fourths are women. Widowed men and women tend to be much older than divorced people. More than 43 percent of the women between ages sixty-five and seventy-four are widows (Strong, 1979).

Only 12 percent of the 11 million single people over the age of sixty-five have never been married; 3 percent are separated; 77 percent are widowed; and 7 percent are divorced. Thus it appears that widowhood is shared by a very large number of women. There are about 10.02 million widows in the United States (Bureau of the Census, 2000). This is about 13 percent of all women over the age of eighteen. Growth in the number and proportion of women who are widows is likely to continue well into the twenty-first century. According to the Census Bureau's projections, the elderly population will more than double between now and the year 2050, to 80 million. By that year, as many as one in five Americans could be elderly. Most of this growth should occur between 2010 and 2030, when the baby-boom generation enters its elderly years. During that period, the number of elderly will grow by an average of 2.8 percent annually. By comparison, annual growth will average 1.3 percent during the preceding twenty years and 0.7 percent during the following twenty years (U.S. Bureau of the Census, 2001).

Discussion of Widowhood Rates

By far, the majority of U.S. marriages end with one partner's death. Although a spouse can die during early or middle adult years, widowhood usually occurs later in life. In most cases, it is the man who dies first, a tendency that became more pronounced in the twentieth century. The most current Census Bureau statistics suggest that elderly men are nearly twice as likely as their female counterparts to be married and living with their spouse (75 percent versus 41 percent). Elderly women, on the other hand, are more than three times as likely as elderly men to be widowed (48 percent versus 14 percent). The remaining men and women are either separated, divorced, had never married, or had absent spouses. Thus, while most elderly men have a spouse for assistance, especially when health fails, most elderly women do not (U.S. Bureau of the Census, 2001). Widows, particularly if they are older, tend to be less active sexually. This is more true or widows than for widowers. Older widows are often reluctant to begin new relationships and may be influenced by loyalty to the departed husband and by negative family pressure. Widows and widowers are likely to be older than divorced persons. Since the ratio of widows to widowers is 5:1, the problem of the single widowed woman is complicated because the pool of available men is small relative to the number of women looking for partners. The high ratio of widows to widowers can be attributed to the fact that women live longer than men and tend to marry men who are older than they are. It is also easier for widowers to remarry, and they tend to marry younger women. This reinforces the cultural stereotypes, shared by elderly women themselves, that physical attractiveness is more important in women than men and that aging women are less attractive than aging men.

Currently American women have a life expectancy of seventy-nine years, about seven years longer than American men. If demographic patterns were used to suggest marital arrangements, it would make sense for older women to marry younger men. However, our cultural norms, socially constructed definitions around mate selection, and opportunities are such that the initial mortality differences are compounded by the tendency for women to marry older men. Since only about 5 percent of previous cohorts of American women never married at all, the inevitable result is that ever larger proportions become widows and remain so for an increasing number of years.

Though the modal age for widowhood is above fifty, a recent detailed study by the U.S. Bureau of the Census (2000) shows that the majority of women whose first husbands die are widowed before the age of fifty. The younger the age at widowhood, the more likely a woman is to marry, but overall less than one-third of these widows ever remarry.

SOCIAL ASPECTS OF WIDOWHOOD

Most preindustrial societies have very clear roles for widows. For example, in traditional Indian society, a Brahmin widow was expected to commit suttee by throwing herself on her husband's funeral pyre. If she did not do this, she was condemned to live out her life dressed in a single course garment, with shaven head, eating only one meal a day, and shunned by others as unlucky. Another solution, practiced by many African societies, was an immediate remarriage in which the wife and children were inherited by a younger brother of the deceased or by some other heir, and the widow then became one of his wives in a polygamous family.

Widowhood can thus be defined more by the collapse of old roles and structural supports than by norms and institutions that specify or provide new role relationships and behavior patterns. Lopata (1975) concludes from her data that American society has been phasing out the traditional status role of "widow" as an all-pervasive lifelong identity: "Usually, widowhood is a temporary stage of identity reconstruction, and this is a major problem. The direction of movement out of it is not clearly defined" (p. 47).

The widow in American society and other Western industrialized societies has lost not only a husband but, in many cases, if she is not working, her own main functions, reason for being, and self-identity. In spite of the women's movement most women who become widows today have defined themselves primarily as wives and mothers.

As stated, less than one-third of widows ever remarry, so remarriage is not a likely solution. There are fewer than 2 million widowers in the United States. Less than 5 percent of women widowed after age fifty-five ever remarry (Cleveland and Gianturco, 1976). A woman is likely to spend as much time as a widow as she does raising children. Although in many cases she was socialized all through her early years for the wife and motherhood roles, the whole subject of widowhood is taboo and few women prepare for it ahead of time.

A younger widow is apt to be lonelier than an older widow, who is more likely to have many more friends in the same position. Furthermore, older people might be better prepared psychologically for widowhood because they have had occasions (the death of friends and relatives) to "rehearse" for the deaths of spouses.

"Anticipatory socialization" had not occurred for the forty Kansas widows studied by Gibbs (1979), however. They had little preparation for widowhood, even though all were over fifty years of age. Intensive interviews with widows of three age groups (thirty to forty, forty-one to fifty-nine, and sixty and older) revealed some common as well as some age-specific problems (Wyly and Hulicka, as cited in Rice, 1996). All complained of loneliness and of difficulties in maintaining homes and cars. The two younger age groups also mentioned problems with decision making, child rearing, sex, and money. The oldest widows had trouble learning how to manage money, worried about finding transportation, and feared becoming a victim of crime. Although some younger widows acknowledged that they felt more independent and free than they had been while they were married, the oldest widows saw no advantages to their condition. To some extent, cohort differences were more important than age differences. For example, younger women were more likely to have participated in money management and to have driver's licenses.

Other investigators feel that although younger widows have lower levels of well-being, they are more likely to remarry (Cleveland and Gianturco, 1976). Wyly and Hulicka's (1975) older subjects reported nothing good about their state—but a Los Angeles study (Hulicka et. al., 1975) found that older widows had higher morale than did older married women.

PSYCHOLOGICAL ASPECTS OF WIDOWHOOD

Carr and Utz (2002) explored whether preloss marital quality affected widows' psychological adjustment following the loss. They found that the bereaved yearn most for their deceased spouses when their marital relationship was characterized by closeness and interdependence. Individuals in a conflicted marriage reported less yearning for their deceased spouse. Troubled marriages tended to decrease, rather than exacerbate, grief and mourning. Thus the closer the marital relationship, the more depressed widows and widowers were likely to be.

The death of a spouse is one of the most serious life crises a person faces. The immediate emotional crisis of bereavement, if not fully worked through, may result in psychological symptoms. During the first few days of bereavement, sacred and secular guidelines define the proper mourning role for the widow. However, over the longer term a need surfaces for the restructuring of the widow's life as she often finds herself much poorer, socially isolated, and left without a meaningful lifestyle.

Perhaps at least in traditional situations, because of their greater dependence on the deceased, the stress of bereavement tends to be greater for women than for men. Widowed women who greatly depended on their husbands to carry out household tasks such as home repairs and finances were at a higher risk for anxiety (Carr and Utz, 2002). "These findings suggest a changing picture for bereavement among older couples, as more egalitarian divisions of labor make women less dependent on their husbands for home repair and financial management" (Carr and Utz, 2002, p. 21). Men also seem to accept death more readily than women and find it harder to express grief

(Glick, Weiss, and Parkes, 1974). However, whether the survivor is a man or a woman, the death of a loved one deprives the survivor of various kinds of satisfaction. The deceased served as a satisfier of the physical needs of the bereaved as well as a source of emotional gratification. As a consequence, over the years the bereaved's sense of identity and the meaning of his or her life may have become intertwined with the personality of the deceased. Somehow he or she must now learn to cope with the loss and the resulting stress.

The period of greatest stress for the bereaved is usually immediately after the death of the deceased. This is the time when the reactions of the bereaved are most intense. Among the behavioral reactions observed during the first month of mourning are periodic crying, difficulty sleeping, loss of appetite, and problems in concentrating or remembering. A study of 109 widowed persons found that the emotional disturbances and insomnia associated with bereavement can also lead to dependence on tranquilizers, sleeping pills, and/or alcohol (Clayton, Halikes, and Maurice, 1971).

The emotional reactions of a surviving spouse, who in 75 percent of the cases is the wife, may be so intense that severe physical illness, a serious accident, or even death—occasionally from suicide—occurs. It was found in a study of 4,500 British widowers aged fifty-five and over, for example, that 213 died during the first 6 months of their bereavement (Parkes, Benjamin and Fitzgerald, 1969). The rate of death, most instances of which apparently resulted from heart problems, was 40 percent higher than expected in this age group. Concluding from a series of related investigations that grief and consequent feelings of helplessness make people more vulnerable to pathogens, Seligman (1975) suggested that individuals who have recently lost a spouse would do well to be very careful about their health. He recommended monthly medical checkups during the first year after the loss.

Although anxiety and depression are the most common reactions to bereavement, anger, guilt, and even psychotic symptoms have been observed. Depression is a normal response to any severe loss, but it is augmented by feelings of guilt in cases where interpersonal hostilities and conflicts with the deceased have not been resolved. Anger may be expressed toward nurses, physicians, friends, and family members—any individual the bereaved believes to have been negligent in his or her treatment of the deceased. For various reasons, survivors may also experience anger toward the deceased or relief at his or her death—both of which can lead to feelings of guilt.

The emotional and psychological traumas of grief and mourning involve letting go of the emotional ties and roles centered on the spouse. If this working through of grief is successfully accomplished, the widow can face a second set of problems having to do with building a new life and a new set of role relationships and constructing a new identity.

> Maggie, at forty-six, had been married for twenty-one years. She and her husband, Michael, had three children. The two older boys were away in college and their daughter, age seventeen, was still at home, finishing high school. Maggie and Michael enjoyed their life together. For a while she had worked in his family business, an interstate trucking company which was doing very well financially. But after two years in the firm, she yearned for painting and sculpting, which were her true vocational interests, and she pursued them with great dedication and with Michael's complete support. Her art was exhibited in a few well-known galleries in SoHo. Their life was happy, worry-free, and cheerful. Both were in excellent physical health and went regularly for medical checkups. Michael had seen the doctor just the week before and nothing amiss was found with his health. However, one night he experienced what he thought was indigestion and slight nausea. He went to bed in this condition and he died in his sleep of a massive heart attack. He was forty-seven years old.
>
> Maggie was in a state of shock, unable to function or think clearly. The boys and her older brother, whose family was very close to theirs, took care of all the arrangements for Michael's funeral and burial. Maggie could not stop crying; her speech was incoherent and her whole demeanor made her look twenty years older than her chronological age. Even two weeks after Michael's death, she needed someone—usually her daughter, Chrissie—to watch over her. Otherwise, Maggie would forget to eat, to take a shower, to get out of bed. After a month of this, her brother told the children that he thought Maggie should be seen by a doctor for her depression. She was under psychiatric care for five months.
>
> When we talked to Maggie, about a year after Michael's death, she explained that she still missed Michael very much but she knew she had to focus on the future, not on the past. She thought their happiness together had made them such a close couple that his death made her feel lost, panicked, and helpless. She realized they had not achieved the balance between closeness and separation that she thought they had. Her whole life had not made her ready for being without her husband even though, because of her artistic career, she seemed "independent." She was now organizing a self-help group—not for widows, but for married women. She wanted to prepare women for the possibility of having to cope with the type of circumstances she had gone through.

Bowlby (1980) found evidence for five stages in mourning:

1. concentration on the deceased;
2. anger toward the deceased or others;
3. appeals to others for help;
4. despair, withdrawal, and disorganization;
5. reorganization and direction of love toward a new object.

Relatively little research has been carried out on Bowlby's stages, but it is recognized that not all mourners go through them in the order listed.

Kavanaugh (1974) also described stages in the process of grieving or mourning for a loved one:

1. shock,
2. disorganization,
3. volatile emotions,
4. guilt,
5. loss and loneliness,
6. relief, and
7. reestablishment.

Kavanaugh (1974) also recognized that a particular mourner may not go through all these stages and not necessarily in the order listed.

Gorer (1979) presented a three-stage conception of mourning:

1. Initial shock is the first stage, which lasts only a few days and is characterized by loss of self-control, reduced energy, and lack of motivation. The mourner is bewildered, disoriented, and loses perspective. The person cannot accept the fact that the individual is really dead, gone forever. This numbness often extends for several weeks beyond the funeral.
2. This is followed by intense grief, the second stage. This stage is characterized by emotional reactions such as crying and a confused inability to comprehend what has actually happened, often accompanied by such psychosomatic symptoms as headache and insomnia; feelings of guilt ("If I had done so and so, maybe he wouldn't have died"); expressions of anger ("Why me? It was so unfair!"); hostility or blame ("The doctors killed him"); and often preoccupation with memories and an idealiza-

tion of the deceased. The second stage can last for several months, but it gradually gives way for the third stage.

3. Feelings of sadness and loneliness, which are often incapacitating; depression; loss of customary patterns of behavior and of motivation to try to go in living, constitute the third stage.

This stage is followed by a recovery phase. Here there is a general recovery of interest. During this final stage the mourner accepts the reality of the loved one's death and all that it means. As Glick, Weiss, and Parkes (1974), from their extensive studies on bereavement, have concluded, "the death of a spouse typically gives rise to a reaction whose duration must be measured in years rather than in weeks" (p. 10).

A variety of grief reactions may occur when the mourner does not express emotions or refuses to deal with the loss. These include delay of grief reactions for months or even years; overactivity without a sense of loss; indefinite irritability and hostility toward others; sense of the presence of the deceased; acquisition of the physical symptoms of the deceased's last illness; insomnia; apathy; psychosomatically based illnesses such as ulcerative colitis; and such intense depression and feelings of worthlessness that suicide is attempted (Parkes, 1972; Van Coevering, 1973).

One tendency is for the bereaved widow to reconstruct an idealized version of the deceased husband and of the role relationship with him before the death. Referring to this as "husband sanctification," Lopata (1972) reports that three-quarters of the Chicago area's current and former beneficiaries of Social Security define their late husband as having been extremely good, honest, kind, friendly, and warm. Sanctification is especially likely among women who rank the role of wife above all others. It is an attempt to continue defining oneself primarily in terms of the now-ended role relationship. Lopata (1972) views this as an effort to "remove the late husband into an other worldly position as an understanding but purified and distant observer" (p. 30), so that the widow is able to go about reconstructing old role relationships and forming new ones.

Several factors are related to severe or prolonged grief. Sixty-eight widows and widowers under the age of forty-five were interviewed shortly after their spouses died and again a year later. The researchers found three classes of strongly correlated variables predict continued severe bereavement reactions thirteen months after the death (Parkes, 1975, pp. 308-309):

1. Low socioeconomic status, e.g., low income of the husband
2. Lack of preparation for the loss due to noncancer deaths, short terminal illness, accident or heart attack, or failure to talk to the spouse about the coming death
3. Other life crises preceding the spouse's death, such as infidelity and job loss

It is interesting that a poor income is likely if the marriage relationship was troubled before the death; folk wisdom would have it that the widow would "be glad to be rid of him." Psychologically debilitating guilt over having wished the death of the husband could to be very strong in such cases, however. Another problem is the amount of "unfinished business" (Blauner, 1966) left by the removal of the husband through death. Parkes (1975) concludes that for his young respondents, including widowers as well as widows, "when advance warning was short and death was sudden, it seemed to have a much greater impact and to lead to greater and more lasting disorganization" (p. 313).

Given the severe and persistent emotional, psychological, and psychosomatic aspects of even normal grief, it becomes impossible for a widow to carry out her usual role relationships and to cope with the problems of change in financial and social status that are thrust upon her.

The Widow

Unlike Maggie, Ruth's reaction to Ralph's death, after two years of sickness, was more negative and lasting. Ruth and Ralph had been married for thirty-eight years. Their three girls and two boys were all married and had given them nine grandchildren. Only the oldest son, thirty-seven, had stayed nearby. The others were living as far away as California, South Carolina, and Illinois. Ruth's marriage had been of the traditional type in the most negative sense: a psychologically abusive husband who disregarded her rights and feelings, engaged in many extramarital affairs for the whole duration of the marriage, and had very little to do with the children's upbringing other than providing them with a negative role model. During the two years of Ralph's illness (cancer of the bladder), Ruth was a model of devotion to her husband, disregarding her own feelings and remaining at the beck and call of a very unreasonable and demanding husband/master.

When Ralph finally died, Ruth was the dutiful mourning spouse; however, immediately after the funeral she felt a raw and powerful hatred and rage that she tried to repress because these feelings were so new and so much against her value system. Her unconscious repression turned into conscious suppression, which took the form of alcoholism. Her children reacted with great righteousness to their mother's "misconduct" and became punitive and disrespectful. Their conduct only gave her more reasons to increase her drinking. The situation became so bad that she was hospitalized for detoxification after she was arrested for urinating in a children's playground while inebriated. During her first few days at the hospital Ruth fought every inch of the way, refusing even to answer questions or to eat. She was given a series of electroshock treatments, after which she cooperated with the hospital routine and therapy. At the age of sixty-three, as she told us, she finally realized the marital abuse she had been exposed to during almost four decades of her life. Her therapy had allowed her to accept as valid her fury which she had so well repressed during her marriage and which came up after her husband's death. It had also helped her to change her values and to become a "new woman," as she proudly called herself. She had to travel a long and painful road to arrive at the point where she was now, five years after Ralph's death. His death had caused turmoil in her life and in the lives of her children, but Ruth now realized that was the high price she had to pay to become the new woman she was now. One of the accomplishments she was very pleased with was that she had cultivated a new relationship with each of her daughters. She had visited each of them and prepared her visit by telling them that she wanted to have plenty of time to talk privately. The three visits were successful and a new, mature, and adult relationship was started with each daughter. The two sons offered a great amount of resistance to her new image, and Ruth resigned herself to less intimate relationships with them.

Ruth told us that she still had feelings of love for her former husband, that she had been able to forgive him "because he didn't know better," and that she didn't know any better in terms of not accepting his sexist treatment of her. She said that she attained a state of inner peace by selectively remembering good and pleasant events of those thirty-eight years. Ruth seemed a very wise, calm, and happy person, indeed.

The subsequent life changes and problems faced by widows indicate that widowhood is a role for which there is no comparable role among males. Glick, Weiss, and Parkes (1974) summarize the difference between their samples of widows and widowers: "Insofar as the men reacted simply to the loss of a loved other, their responses were similar to those of widows, but insofar as men reacted to the traumatic disruption of their lives, their responses were different" (p. 262). This differential impact is found in the financial impact after death. For the widow it almost always means the loss of the main source of financial support for the family and a consequent lowering of the standard of living. Two to three years after the onset of widowhood, the incomes of the widows' families were down an average of 44 percent from previous levels, and 58 percent had incomes that fell below an amount that would have been necessary to maintain their family's former standard of living.

In addition to financially devastating final expenses that can wipe out savings, widows are entitled to no Social Security benefits at all unless they have dependents or are over sixty. After sixty years of age, they are entitled to only a portion of what would have been their husband's benefits. The final explanation for the high probability of poverty among widows is that because of age, general low levels of skill and education, and lack of experience, they are often unable to obtain employment. In other words, neither the private economy nor the public welfare system is currently structured to provide economic support in late middle age.

Before widowhood, a traditionally married woman defines herself and relates to others mainly in terms of her status as somebody's wife. At widowhood, most of her role relationships will have to adjust and some will terminate. She will have to establish new role relationships if her life is to be a satisfying one. For example, she is unlikely to maintain close ties with friends and relatives who belonged to social circles maintained with her husband. Changes in finances can require changes in other spheres of life, such as movement into the workforce. A change in residence may result in loss of contact with neighbors. Often, in settling her husband's estate, she has to deal with lawyers and insurance agents, taking on the role of a businesswoman (Lopata, 1975, p. 48).

The difficulties an older woman in U.S. society is likely to encounter in establishing such a new set of role relationships are affirmed by Lopata's research. She found that half of the widows in her sample considered loneliness their greatest problem, and another third listed it second. Social isolation was listed by 58 percent, who agreed with the problem, "One problem of being a widow is feeling like a 'fifth wheel'" (Lopata, 1972, p. 346).

Lopata's (1972) work focuses on the widow's role relationships in regard to motherhood, kin relationships, friendship, and community involvement, including employment. Among her findings are that "women who develop satisfactory friendships, who weather the transition period and solve its problems creatively, tend to have a higher education, a considerable income, and the physical and psychic energy needed to initiate change" (Lopata, 1972, p. 216). These women are not the average widow, who is likely to have a high school education or less, low income, depleted physical energy due to advancing age, and depleted psychic energy due to the trauma of bereavement and its associated problems. Thus Lopata (1973) found that although the death of the husband created greater personal disruption in the life of her more educated respondents than was the case for less educated women, and also greater dislocation of the friendship network since it had been based on couple companionship, the better educated women had greater emotional and financial resources. They were able to move about and meet others whom they could choose as friends, and they also had less stressful relationships with their children than did the less educated women. The same advantages may characterize reintegration in friendship networks after separation and divorce.

The importance of maintaining or establishing supportive role relationships with an understanding "other" such as an old friend, neighbor, or supportive professional or paraprofessional has been emphasized in many studies. For example, Maddison and Raphael (1975) emphasize their "conviction that the widow's perception of her social network is an extremely important determinant of the outcome of her bereavement crisis" (p. 29). "Bad outcome" women had no one to whom they could freely express their grief and anger.

At some point, women accept their new status as widow and begin to integrate it into their sense of who they are. In an interview with widows, most women had a fairly clear idea of the image conjured up by the term *widow*. The three most common associations were that widows were "old," "alone," and "on their own." Some women felt calling someone a widow was the same as saying that they were old. Some connotations that came up during the interview were that widows were "staid and exemplary," and "diminished." These connections of widowhood were not necessarily the way the women looked at themselves. They recognized the stigma that was attached to the word *widow*, and therefore many were reluctant to apply the term to themselves because they did not resemble what they felt was the typical widow. Some believed that simply by taking on the label, they were diminished (Van Den Hoonaard, 2001). Lopata (1996) believes that when a woman becomes a widow, she is deserted by some of her friends because people "avoid all connections to death." Some people report that they find interaction with widows so awkward that they limit contact with them particularly if they were used to seeing the widow as one-half of a couple.

Widows sometimes use the term *couples world* to communicate their feeling of not fitting into society in a comfortable way. They become the "other" in a world that is designed for couples. Their identity is affected as well as the way they interact with others. According to Lopata (1996), entrance into the role of a wife requires a reconstruction of reality. The new reality involves becoming one-half of a couple rather than a totally separate individual. Widowed women often felt like they were "half a person" which contributed to feelings of emptiness, that "something was missing." This lack of clear norms made it difficult for women and their friends to renegotiate the obligations involved in their relationships successfully.

The Widower

The impact of widowhood on men has received little systematic attention, and the role of widower is probably even vaguer than that of widow. Because widowers who have not remarried are not very common in the community until after about age seventy-five, they are not as likely to join one another in groups. Like widows, they are expected to preserve the memories of their wives and are expected not to show interest in other women. Indications are that many widowers adhere to the former but ignore the latter, as can be inferred from the remarriage rates cited earlier.

Clearly something other than simple numbers is operating with respect to sex differences in coping with widowhood. Men who have led their entire lives playing instrumental, at the expense of expressive, marital roles are poorly prepared for widowhood. On one level, men who had traditional marriages had been so dependent upon their wives for the performance of the most basic maintenance tasks, such as preparing a meal or running a washing machine, that they often feel totally helpless in tending to daily necessities. Then too there is also a general unwillingness among some of these men to perform "women's work" if there is any way they can avoid it (Rainwater and Yancey, 1967). They have difficulty breaking lifelong attitudes toward sex-role behaviors.

Also, those men who have taken most seriously the traditional cultural position of emotion or sensitivity among males have often not developed genuinely close friendships. One might argue that they have been preoccupied with their image of what it is to be a man at the expense of true same-sex intimacy. Another reason might be that they have been socialized in such a way that they feel uncomfortable risking their feelings or expressing fears and concerns among peers, whereas within a traditional/subordinate type marriage, a wife can be a confidante without the husband fearing loss of face (Balswick and Peek, 1971). For whatever reasons, studies indicate that among middle and lower socioeconomic groups, male friendships resemble play or meet work-oriented goals rather than serve genuine interpersonal needs. Evidence suggests that men, especially in late middle age, experience awareness of the superficiality of their friendships and express regret (Lowenthal and Robinson, 1976).

Perhaps because women have been permitted, indeed have been culturally coerced, to play expressive roles within families and have been socialized to display such attributes as emotionality and sensitivity to others, they show more flexibility in the objects of their close relationships. Women often have intimate same-sex friendships at various life stages. Thus the prevalence of friendships among older widows not only reflects the dearth of available widowers at that age but also their prior experiences and comfort within such relationships. Both in terms of same-sex friendships and in ability to run a household on a day-to-day level, widowed women tend to be better prepared for living alone than their male counterparts.

It appears that women who are widowed do not experience that life event in the same way that men do. For example, in a study of 403 community residents aged 62 and over, 6 major areas of life functioning were assessed: psychosocial needs, household roles, nutrition, health care, transportation, and education (Barrett, 1978). Widowers were found to experience lower morale, to feel lonelier and more dissatisfied with life, to consider community services more inadequate, to need more help with household chores, to have greater difficulty getting medical appointments, to eat more poorly, and to possess stronger negative attitudes about continued learning than widows. Moreover, widowers were more reluctant to talk about widowhood or death than widows were, and many stated that they did not want a confidant.

An elderly widow usually has more friends available to her than an elderly widower, who may discover that he was more dependent on his wife for physical and emotional support than he realized when she was living. Because men are usually not as close to other people as women are, widowers are apparently more lonely and consequently need marriage more than widows do. This is one reason why the great majority of widowers remarry within a year or so after their wife's death.

Although the problems of adjusting to the loss of a spouse are often worse for a woman than for a man, any man who has lost his wife by death or divorce is faced with loneliness and a need for companionship.

Because men traditionally acquire their identities only partly from being husbands, widowers are probably not as apt as widows to face acute identity crises when they lose their wives. Yet because they are likely to have seen their wives as important parts of themselves (Glick, Weiss, and Parkes, 1974), they too can feel lost. Their wives were probably their main confidants and their links to family and friends. Little evidence suggests that widowhood is any less devastating for men than for women.

Glick, Weiss, and Parkes (1974) report that widowers have more difficulty on the job than do widows during the mourning period. Because jobs are primary in men's lives, widowers may be more sensitive to job disruption than are widows.

Widowers do not differ from widows in feeling isolated from kin or friends. Nor are widowed men and women, on the whole, more isolated than are their married peers. In fact, after being widowed those who have friends tend to see them more often (Petrowsky, 1976). When Atchley (1975) controlled for social class, he found that widowhood tends to increase contacts with friends among middle-class widowers and to decrease them among lower-class widowers. It could be that the large surplus of women in senior centers and similar social groups for older people—generally used more by working-class people than by middle-class people—may inhibit working-class widowers from developing new kinds of community activities. Widowers tend to be embarrassed and even feel harassed by the competition among widows for their attentions. Moreover, they are unaccustomed to participating in such preponderantly female gatherings where women dominate discussions and other activities. Petrowsky (1976) found that widowers were less involved in religious activities than were widows, an effect that is probably due to a continuation of religious participation sex differences established earlier in life.

Between the ages of sixty-five and seventy-four, widowers in general tend slightly more than widows to live in group quarters such as hotels or rooming houses rather than in independent households. After age seventy-five, there is little sex difference in type of residence. Widowers who live in their own homes are only slightly more likely to live alone than are widows and are only slightly less likely to be living with their children. When they live in multiperson households, however, widowers are much more likely to be considered heads of such households.

Harry and Odile had been married for forty-two years. Odile died of intestinal complications after several operations that had unfortunately made her more and more disabled. Harry, in spite of his seventy-six years, was a consultant to several big industries, kept giving seminars, traveling, and maintaining a busy schedule. His health was strong, his hobbies were many: boating, car racing, tennis, and acting in a local theater company. After about six months of mourning, during which he hardly saw any friends and did not socialize at all, though he kept himself professionally occupied, he started to accept invitations from friends to parties and get-togethers. He kept many mementos of Odile in the house, such as pictures, objects, books, and the like. His house was near the ocean and he started inviting people over to keep him company. He told many stories of the many wonderful years he and Odile had traveled all over the world, attended important congresses, and lived in many different parts of the country. They never had children and he had little contact with relatives. But he formed a large circle of friends around him. Through his friends, he met several available widows or divorced women and soon he started dating. About two years after Odile's death, he was dating Connie exclusively.

When we interviewed Harry, he explained that he felt "too old to marry Connie" but that they were practically sharing their lives as if they were married. Although Connie kept her own house, she spent much of her time at Harry's. However, she ran her own business and did not want to depend on Harry. He explained that widowhood had been a very painful shock to him: "I had never really thought of death before." But he made an effort to go on with his life and work, grateful for the great life he and Odile had together, rather than allowing her death to depress him or slow him down. Connie knew how important his wife had been and accepted the fact that Harry had so many fond memories and told so many stories of his wife. He mentioned several of his friends whom he described as "losers" because they kept on living in the past. "I remember Odile with fondness and gratitude, but I realize she's now a memory. The person is gone and now I have the great fortune of sharing my life with another wonderful person. I love Connie, I'm fond of her, we enjoy each other's company and I even suspect that when I am eighty years young, I'll decide to get married. I'm too old now, but by eighty, I've heard, one enters his second youth."

Harry had refused to feel helpless. He thought that joining clubs and groups of old people was a sign of helplessness and had decided to form his own network of friends from among the many people he had met in his long career as a business consultant. He had been perseverant and the result was his new love and his continued professional involvement and activity. He told us that he had several models for this stage of his life: Casals, Picasso, Irving Berlin, George Burns, and Bob Hope. He considered them his teachers: "They live or lived fantastic in their senior years. They are my teachers. I try to live exactly the way they do or did."

Widowhood and Children

When individuals become widowed they often have to renegotiate their relationships with their children. Their children see them as more vulnerable and can sometimes react by becoming more protective. Widows certainly want their children to acknowledge their loss and to be available to support them both emotionally and instrumentally, but when the equilibrium becomes skewed toward overprotectiveness, many feel besieged in their struggle to build a new life for themselves. Children often worry about their mothers, but in some cases relationships with sons can become problematic. Daughters and sons tend to become eager to protect their mothers from perceived vulnerability; however, sons are not as willing to back off when their mothers try to tell them that they are being overprotective. Overall though, when asked if their relationships with their children had changed after the death of their husband, many women stated it changed very little and those who did report a changed relationship most often saw it as stronger rather than a more distant relationship (Van Den Hoonaard, 2001).

Ted was seventy-seven years old when his wife, Sylvia, died. It happened suddenly: one day she was fine and the next she was in the hospital attached to tubes. As he stood watching her breathe, he remembered that she had been complaining of a pain in her back for the past week, but neither of them thought it was anything serious. He talked about this in therapy for the next two years, feeling guilty that he could have possibly saved her life if he had acted sooner. But they both thought she had pulled a muscle playing golf. She died two days later, a consequence of the damage done from a massive heart attack. Everyone was shocked when she died because she was such a vivacious woman. On some level Ted and their children thought she would live forever. She rarely was ill and she remained active after she retired from her job as an office manager. In fact, she had continued to help out at the office up until a few weeks before her death.

After the funeral, Ted emptied the house of all her personal belongings. This was painful for him. As he went through her personal belongings, he remembered when she had worn a particular dress last or when they had bought a certain piece of jewelry. He kept feeling that at any moment she would walk into the room and ask him what he wanted for dinner. He missed her.

They had many friends, so he was kept occupied by people who lived in the retirement community stopping over to make sure he was all right. Many women in their community would bring over food and baked goods, trying to help him as much as possible.

In a few months, his friends began to introduce him to other "ladies." At first he felt very guilty and ashamed, but soon he welcomed the company. It helped him not to think about Sylvia. His children were appalled that he was dating other women. They thought he was having a nervous breakdown. One of his daughters even tried to talk him about "safer sex" practices. He was very embarrassed.

Then he met Ester. Ester was a good woman, kind and sensitive. Her own husband had died a year earlier. He liked Ester right away. She had a quiet way about her, helping him feel calm and content. When he was with her, he didn't feel the incredible loneliness and sadness he'd been feeling since Sylvia died. Their relationship escalated quickly and they began spending more and more time together.

When Ted told his children that he was seriously dating Ester, they were outraged. "How could you do this to Mommy?" his oldest daughter screeched. His middle daughter said she would go along with anything he wanted, but Ted knew she was deeply depressed about the situation. They felt he was not being loyal their mother. Ted felt that he didn't know how much time he had left to live, so he didn't want to waste time.

Six months after Sylvia died, Ted and Ester married. They had a small wedding and only the immediate family attended. Her children were delighted at the marriage and treated him very kindly. Although his children were very polite to Ester, he knew they were extremely upset. His oldest daughter, who generally verbalized everything that was on her mind, told him she understood why he wanted to marry Ester but she was having a hard time handling it. She still felt he was being disloyal to their mother. She said their mother wasn't even dead a year.

A few months later, when Ted and Ester were traveling, they stayed for a few nights at this daughter's home. One evening, when Ted and his daughter were alone, his daughter told him that it was making her sick that he was traveling all over the world with Ester when that was what their mother had wanted to do. It also made her sick that they were sleeping in the same bed together. She couldn't believe that he had just "thrown Mommy away." She was so upset. Still grieving for her lost mother, she couldn't understand why he wasn't feeling the same sadness. She didn't understand that his sadness was different from hers and that the fact that he had such a good, rewarding marriage to her mother helped him seek out another marital partner.

As is illustrated in this case history, there are also problems when the widowed individual has adult children living in the area. The death of a husband tends to cause strains in relationships with children, in-laws, and even one's own siblings and other relatives. Thirty-nine percent of the clients of the Widows Consultation Center reported that relationships with family members were a problem at the time they came to the center. Problems with children were reported by more clients (31 percent), compared to in-laws (8 percent) and siblings (6 percent).

The problems with children were twofold: a perceived coldness or neglecting to give the widow as much "love" and support and time as she thought she was entitled to (17 percent), and what the widow considered serious behavioral problems with the children, such as taking drugs or withdrawing from employment and from communication with the mother (15 percent) (Hiltz, 1975).

What is seen as neglect or coldness by the widow may be viewed as an unfair and unpleasant burden by the child, especially sons. For example, Adams (1976) found that grown middle-class sons perceived their obligations to their mother as a "one-way" or unreciprocated pattern of aid and support giving. This typically results in the sons' loss of affection for their mother and their resentment of her dependence on them.

For younger widows with dependent children, difficulties occur in maintaining the maternal role of effectively responding to the child's needs. Silverman and Englander (1975) found that most parents and children avoided talking about the death to each other. Common reactions in the children included fear that they would lose the surviving parent too; the assumption by the children of new family responsibilities; and poor schoolwork related to rebellion and social withdrawal (Silverman and Englander, 1975).

Relationships with in-laws may be cut off entirely if the widow does not find them pleasant and supportive. As Lopata (1996) points out, this is a unique kind of institutional arrangement, since the patriarchal family traditionally had vested rights over the wife and the offspring of a marriage. However,

> American widows are free to move away from their in-laws, if they were living nearby, and even to lose all contact with them. They are free to cut the ties between their children and that side of the family and even to remarry and change the name of the unit. (Lopata, 1976, p. 3)

None of the studies seem to include the impact of such decisions on the role relationship between paternal grandparents and grandchildren, and on the emotional pain that may be caused if the relationship is severed.

In these cases, loyalties may be divided between the dead parent and the new person the remaining parent is dating, possibly creating hostility toward the new partner. Sometimes adult children feel they must protect themselves from the new relationship. In these cases they tend to deny the existence of the relationship and in very patronizing ways laugh at their parents' "childish" behavior. Many adult children also have difficulty in viewing their widowed parents as sexual persons.

THERAPY STRATEGIES

Lopata (1973) concluded that the greatest short range needs of widows are

1. to express emotions and come to terms with widowhood through grief work with the help of family, friends, and therapists;
2. companionship, especially if the widow is living alone for the first time in her life;
3. to be protected from the hordes of people who want to give her advice—Every one around her is full of advice, and the bits she receives are often contradictory and irrelevant or unbeneficial from her point of view;
4. assistance in building self-confidence and competencies, assistance that can consist of not giving too much advice and avoiding actions that might encourage dependency; and
5. help in reengaging, that is, becoming involved in social activities that will be stimulating and meaningful.

Group therapy is an effective method for dealing with these issues. In looking for ways in which groups can be used to facilitate the grief process, Barrett (1978) organized three different kinds of groups of widows. Half of her sample said they had never thought about the death of their husband before it occurred, and two-thirds had never considered what it would be like to be a widow. Their average income, even though half of them worked, was about one-half of what it had been at the time of the husband's death.

The first group was called a self-help group because the leader was a facilitator and not a teacher. She helped members of the group help one another. This type conformed to what is generally referred to as a widow-to-widow group in England and in some cities in the United States. The second group was called the confidante group. The leader used intimate techniques and group activities where individuals were paired and participated as couples. In this group the leader tried to facilitate a "helping relationship" for each pair.

The third group was labeled a women's consciousness-raising group. In discussions, the focus of this group was on ways in which sex roles were viewed by widows in the group. Such topics as Sexuality Among Widows: Are You Still a Wife? characterized the interaction. Each of the groups gathered for two hours a week for eight weeks.

Barrett (1978) assessed three different therapeutic group interventions dealing with consciousness raising for seventy urban widows. The effects of the intervention were evaluated and the women were compared to a waiting-list control group. Treatments were designed to meet the needs of widows of all ages, because research suggests that stresses may be greater for younger widows (Kraus and Lilienfeld, 1959), even though the frequency of widowhood is higher among older women. Eighteen personality, attitude, and behavioral measures were obtained by written report on three occasions—pretest, posttest, and follow-up fourteen weeks later. At posttest and follow-up, higher self-esteem, increased intensity of grief feelings, and increased negative attitudes toward remarriage were reported by all groups. Intervention groups showed improvements in their ratings of their future health and became less other oriented in their attitudes toward women relative to the controls.

One intervention approach, widow to widow, uses lay widows and widowers who have experienced the event. A helper is matched for certain characteristics, such as age, education, and economic status, with the bereaved person. This person assists in the transition period and helps the widow acquire a new role. The approach appears to be generally successful (Silverman, 1977).

Chapter 3

Single-Parent Family Issues

Since 1970 the number of single-parent households has doubled. Of these households, 70 percent are the result of divorce. Fourteen percent are the result of death of a parent, 6 percent are temporary because a parent is away, and 10 percent have not been involved in a marriage (Weiss, 1979). Because of the problems inherent in this type of family system, the single-parent family frequently comes for therapy. The purpose of this chapter is to present systemic/behavioral therapy techniques that the author has found to be very successful. A brief description of systemic/behavioral theory relevant to single-parent family therapy is presented. A single-parent case history is then discussed, from which behavioral/systemic therapy techniques with the single-parent family are illustrated.

Most parents, whether they be in a two-parent or a single-parent family situation, are not aware of the functions of a family. According to Parsons and Bales (1955), the functions of the family are as follows: to socialize the children; to provide models for relationships with others; to establish cultural norms; to provide religious and ethical values and emotional support; to politically indoctrinate the children; to provide financial care; to give guidance; and to educate the young. When these tasks are accomplished, a functional family provides the children with a healthy sense of self (Walsh, 1982). It teaches them how to relate to other people by providing them with the nurturing, support, and security necessary for each member of the family to develop to his or her fullest potential. The single-parent family with a problem is generally not carrying out these tasks satisfactorily and so is assumed stuck in its definition of the situation (Walsh, 1982).

This is no easy task, even when the traditional two adults are present in parenting roles. The situation becomes even more difficult in a single-parent family household, with only one person responsible for providing the young with an adequate foundation for psychological development. In addition, it is necessary to consider many variations exist among single-parent families. The distinction among the various types of single-parent families is important because they differ considerably with respect to their access to economic and social resources. As mentioned in Chapter 2, widows tend to have higher incomes and experience less social disapproval than do other groups; whereas never-married mothers (mainly adolescent women) have the fewest resources of all single mothers and are most likely to become dependent on government welfare assistance, leading to the notion of the feminization of poverty (Kohen, 1981). According to the most recent U.S. Census statistics, almost half of all children living in female-headed households (48.6 percent) live in poverty (DeNavas-Walt et al., 2003).

GENERAL CONCERNS
AMONG SINGLE-PARENT FAMILIES

Hodgson, Dienhart, and Daly (2001) examined single mothers' qualitative experiences of what may be some unique time pressures and how these pressures influenced their decisions about time allocation in their families. Juggling time between parenting responsibilities and employment demands was a dominant theme. These single mothers described the complexity of decision making and the intricate planning that is necessary to meet the time demands of children, home, and community. The mothers placed a high priority on spending time with their children. They identified frustration and regret when other responsibilities and demands interfered. Most often it was the demands of the workplace which restricted these parents from acting on their personal values and being more available to their children. This was the main challenge the mothers reported: synchronizing their work schedules with those of their children's needs. The women desired some understanding on the part of their employer in order to meet all the time demands they faced, although they did not expect special consideration.

Even though no one type of single-parent family system exist (Mendes, 1979), certain generalities about the problems inherent in this system can be made. For example, Weiss (1979) has identified three levels of possible overload for the single parent. First there is responsibility overload. The single parent has to make all decisions regarding family life and the children's behavior. From financial details to daily domestic duties, there is no one else to turn to for direction. The single parent can feel overwhelmed by these demands. Although children often begin to take on some of the responsibilities, they are unable to make some of the bigger decisions regarding their lives, which are left up to the parent. It is in this area of increased responsibility that the single parent may feel the greatest effects of having lost a system of interaction in which many decisions are shared. Although some single parents feel free to make decisions without interference, many single parents may feel tension, pressure, and confusion (Ahrons and Rodgers, 1987).

The second area pinpointed by Weiss (1979) is task overload or, simply put, having too much to do. The parent has to earn money; make meals; clean the house; discipline the children; make doctor and dental appointments; make rental, insurance, care, and other payments; and so on—all alone. Most single parents have little time for friends or a social life, which often leads to social isolation.

Weiss's (1979) third level of adjustment is emotional overload. The single parent has to be available to his or her children emotionally, even when exhausted or drained of all available reserves. Although some single parents do have family, friends, or an ex-spouse to consult with, for many no one else is available to turn to for needed attention and/or with whom to discuss the children's growth and personality development. For many, no other person can step in at times when the parent is feeling so stretched as to be irrational or thoughtless with regard to the children (Isaacs, Montalvo, and Adelsohn, 1986). In some cases, emotionally overburdened parents may lash out, physically as well as verbally, against a child, not because he or she has done anything wrong but simply because he or she is there (Isaacs, Montalvo, and Adelsohn, 1986).

The loss of the other parent is significant in other ways as well. The parent may no longer have an ally to help him or her in disciplinary efforts. The single parent, with new responsibilities, can suffer in ways that are passed on to the children and are detrimental to the functioning of the whole family. If the single parent is depressed, hostile, or aggressive, and if his or her children are acting out some of their own distress, the single parent may be unable to stop them because no other adult is around to help. The point is that the single parent is the focus, especially for younger children, around which all task performance occurs and through which all anxiety and stress must be processed (Beal, 1980).

"The many roles of single mothers require that they continually make decisions about how time will be allocated" (Hodgson, Dienhart, and Daly, 2001, p. 34). Other pressures on the parent in the primary home include the conflicts between parents regarding child-rearing practices and how time and money are spent on children. These pressures encountered by single mothers certainly are the result of being solely responsible for the day-to-day functioning of the family. The absent parent may actively sabotage the other parent's efforts by trying to get the children aligned with him or her against the primary parent. In all situations the absent parent must be included in consideration of the system (Beal, 1980). Grandparents and other relatives may take sides with one of the parents, serving to confuse the children with divided loyalties. Or they may align with the children against the custodial parent, creating a cross-generational coalition that leaves the family system ripe for dysfunction. Thus, whether brought about through necessity or choice, single-parent families share certain basic problems: how to cope single-handedly with day-to-day decisions, how to undertake supervision and discipline of the children, and how to compensate for the absence of the other parent.

Rosenberg and Guttmann (2001) believe that divorce thrusts the family into a turmoil and imbalance, causing changes in the system and subsystem. This, they believe, has led researchers to move away from examining the effects of single demographic variables in favor of studying more complicated family dynamic variables. They believe that the single-parent household family must redefine family boundaries, rules, and regulations.

> A family systems model emphasizes the importance of renegotiating relationship boundaries after a divorce at the dyadic level between former spouses. Former spouses need to establish new rules for parenting together in their new family structure, and at the same time they need to relinquish their roles as marital partners. A family systems model proposes that the failure to establish relationship boundaries that clearly define the former partner as a co-parent, but not as a spouse, is a major source of co-parental conflict. (Madden-Derdich and Leonard, 1999, p. 588)

Systemic family therapy applies general systems theory to family constellations. The systemic approach to family therapy looks at the symptoms or problems presented in a therapy situation in terms of the whole family. Systems theorists assume that behavior is a communication about relationships (Haley, 1977). Behavior can be understood only within the context in which it occurs and is defined by (as well as defines) and influenced by (as well as influences) all other behavior in the context or system in which it occurs.

The basic assumption of the family systems therapist, then, is that all parts are interrelated. Change in any one part of the system can effect change in another part of the system. Each part of the system has a unique role or function, and these parts work together to achieve common family goals (Hoffman, 1981). Families also have boundaries that separate them from the environment. The family boundary is structured by the values, norms, and attitudes derived from the family's cultural heritage (Minuchin, 1974). Boundaries are the rules and regulations that govern interactions between different family members and between the family and the surrounding society. These rules and regulations define how specific family functions get carried out (Minuchin and Fishman, 1981). For a detailed examination of general systems theory, see von Bertalanffy (1968); for a description of its application to family therapy, see Bateson (1979); Bowen (1978); Haley (1973, 1977); Hoffman (1981); Madanes (1981); and Minuchin and Fishman (1981).

Systems therapists believe that to counsel only the identified patient is missing the point; persons exist in environments, and to look at the problem presented from an individual frame of reference is taking the person out of context, seeing the person as existing in a vacuum. According to systems theory (von Bertalanffy, 1968), family systems have the property of self-regulation. Any input to the family (e.g., change on any one member) is acted upon and modified by the system itself through the mechanism of feedback. Family stability or equilibrium is generally maintained through negative feedback mechanisms, while change (learning, growth, or crisis) is maintained and increased through positive feedback (Walsh, 1982).

A typically traditional two-parent nuclear family system might look like the following: There is a mother and a father, representing an executive authority block from which all authority flows. The mother and father are bonded together more strongly than all other bonds. The bonds with the children are relatively weaker. Chronologically, the bond between the mother and the father, who generally have greater wisdom and judgment, comes first and endures longer (Nichols, 1984), thereby establishing the authority hierarchy. The natural division occurs always along generational lines. In any given family system, there are four subsystems: the children represent one such subsystem (the sibling subsystem); another is represented by the husband-wife interactions (the marital subsystem); the parental subsystem is next (parent-child interactions); and last is the nuclear family interactions with external systems and individuals (extra-familial subsystem) (see Figure 3.1).

In a healthy, functioning system, the boundaries are clarified. There are relationships between the mother-father subsystem, the mother-children subsystem, and the father-children subsystem. In a single-parent family system, the husband-wife subsystem no longer exists; however, the mother-father subsystem does (Ahrons, 1980). In this single-parent family system, the father of the children is an important part of the children's lives and he is available to the mother as a resource person in terms of caretaking and decision making concerning the children (see Figure 3.2). It is helpful to stress this point when working with single-parent families: that while the couple relationship is dissolved, the parental relationship will remain forever; the two persons will become grandparents at exactly the same time. Stressing the parental relationship assists the parents in focusing on the best interests of the child and helps to defocus on the problems they were experiencing in the marital relationship. Also important is

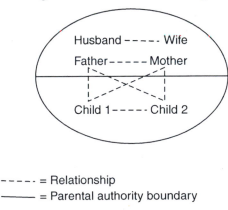

- - - - - = Relationship

———— = Parental authority boundary

FIGURE 3.1. Structural diagram of the two-parent family.

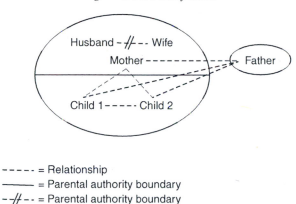

----- = Relationship
——— = Parental authority boundary
--#-- = Parental authority boundary

FIGURE 3.2. Structural diagram of the one-parent family.

the idea put forth by feminist family therapists that when there is a male in the family, as is generally the case in the two-parent family, the family is based on hierarchy; when there is a female running the family, the hierarchical structure generally gives way to a more collaborative structure, based on affection and emotional support (Ahrons, 1980).

The single-parent family system has one parent absent from the household or there is a single-parent ghost (e.g., the influence of a dead husband on a family that is kept alive by the wife) in the case of death or birth out of wedlock. A parent ghost could also exist for either the children or the parent in a single-parent home where there is no contact with the absent parent. In any case, a gap is present in this type of family system and it typically becomes filled by one of the children. This child is called the "parental child." Usually the parental child is the oldest child, but not always (Ahrons, 1980).

The presence of a parental child could lead to a cross-generational coalition; it almost always leads to the formation of a pseudo-adult, who can be overwhelmed and burdened by adult responsibilities (Weiss, 1979). As mental health professionals, it is important to recognize the presence of parental children and to encourage the return of the child to the sibling subsystem, reinforcing the sibling coalition (see Figure 3.3).

From this discussion, we can see that the systemic approach enables us to conceptualize the apparent family structure. In addition,

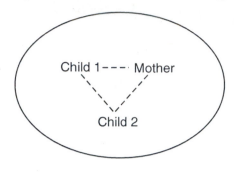

- - - - - = Relationship

FIGURE 3.3. Structural diagram of the one-parent family with a parental child.

we can assess the hierarchy within the system, examine the boundaries of the family members, explore the nature of the subsystems, and look for coalitions.

COGNITIVE-BEHAVIORAL PRINCIPLES

In addition to assessing the family from a systemic level of analysis, cognitive-behavioral psychological principles may be useful adjunctives for the therapist for providing additional information about the system and further in utilizing behavioral therapeutic interventions in order to induce systemic change. Cognitive-behavioral approaches have been shown to be an effective strategy for treating marital distress (e.g., Jacobson and Margolin, 1979; Weiss, 1980). Until recently, little attention has been paid to the potential success of applying it to family therapy. The behavioral approach contributes the specific, step-by-step intervention strategies through which the underlying goals of the family are accomplished via the use of positive and negative reinforcers and punishers (Jacobson and Margolin, 1979). Since one of the basic assumptions of cognitive-behavioral therapy is that emotional disturbance is caused by the persistence of beliefs which are irrational or untrue, cognitive-behavioral interventions may be used to help produce perceptual shifts in thinking, feeling, or acting (Jacobson and Margolin, 1979). Thus the family is assessed at the systemic level and the specific therapeutic interventions used are cognitive-behavioral. The level of analysis is systemic; the interventive strategies used to accomplish structural change are behavioral.

Following is a case history that depicts a "typical" white, middle-class single-parent family system, a systemic analysis of the family structure, and a description of the behavioral goals utilized to accomplish change in the structure.

Nancy, a thirty-nine-year-old assistant banking manager, was referred for therapy by her family physician. She had been divorced for about three years and was having a hard time coping with her two sons, Tyler (age twelve) and Craig (age ten). Prior to the present therapy, she was in group therapy for a drinking problem.

In the present therapy situation, although Nancy stated that her marriage was not good before the divorce, she often expressed both "negative and positive feelings in abrupt alternation" about Roger, her ex-husband. The main reason Nancy gave for her divorce was infidelity on the part of Roger. He was having an affair with his secretary. At the beginning of therapy, the relationship between Nancy and her former husband was antagonistic, often culminating in very unpleasant arguments. They constantly argued about financial arrangements, visiting arrangements, or any other topic. Because of this, the two children began to suffer, each in his own way. Tyler, for example, started to do poorly in school. He did not listen to his mother, frequently called her names, told her he hated her, and had frequent temper tantrums. Craig, the younger child, also had temper tantrums, except his tantrums resulted in him hiding in his closet in his room for many hours.

Most of the time, Nancy aligned herself with Craig. He was behaviorally a better child who achieved more in school and had more friends at home. The other son, Tyler, looked like his father. This carried over into Nancy's interactions with Tyler and was the basis for a somewhat distant relationship between the two. Tyler was a loner and, although there was no learning disability involved, schoolwork was difficult for him. Complicating the matter even further, both Nancy and her ex-husband argued incessantly about whose fault Tyler's low school grades were. Tyler frequently heard these arguments.

Nancy was from an upper-middle-class family background and all her needs were basically taken care of while growing up. At the time of the divorce, Nancy had not psychologically separated from her mother, who fostered attachment and dependency. She invited Nancy and the boys to live with her. She told Nancy that she would take care of her, something which at times was quite appealing to Nancy even though their relationship was generally conflict ridden. As Weiss (1975) points out,

> For the separated woman the parental invitation is not without attractions. Going back home can offer a brief moratorium from responsibility, a breathing space during which the woman can pull herself together without feeling guilty for neglecting her children. But the cost would be reduced autonomy. (p. 141)

For Nancy, this would be psychologically costly. In certain European cultures where there is an accepted extrafamilial subsystem, the psychological cost of moving back home would be much less. In U.S.culture, the move might further widen the power gap between Nancy and her children.

Nancy, originally having little job training, was quite unprepared psychologically and technically for the workforce and began working at a lowpaying clerical position. While she was growing up, and throughout the entire marriage, she had very few extrafamilial responsibilities. Upon her divorce, it became necessary for her to return to work to financially help support the children. For Nancy, this was the first time in her life that she was totally responsible for her own needs and the needs of her children. She appeared fragile, overwhelmed by the slightest thing. When she first came for therapy, she was unsure of her role, sometimes using a rationale, "It's okay not to cook dinner for the children because I'm exhausted. I've had a hard day and I need to relax. It would not kill them to eat bread and butter for one night." This, unfortunately, stretched into more than a few nights and, in the therapist's opinion, was becoming problematic for the children.

The basic pattern of the family was chaotic. All fended for themselves. Things would go along smoothly for a while, but then a crisis would occur and problems would arise. Nancy seemed to suffer from each and every one of the specific problems as presented by Bloom, White, and Asher (1979), "difficulties with children, the need to work, sexual problems, problems with reestablishing social relationships, financial difficulties, and the feelings associated with failure and shame" (p. 193). The communication issues involved either Nancy pleading for the boys to behave or giving in to their whims to prevent them from annoying her. Very little positive reinforcement was given to the boys. Nancy tried to keep their behavior under control through the use of punishment. Thus their positive behavior went unnoticed; their negative behavior was punished, sometimes. Most of the attention that they received from Nancy was in a negative form. This very quickly resulted in an increase in their bad behavior, for it was the only time they would receive attention from their mother. Transactions occurred mainly surrounding functional issues, such as, "Did you do your homework?" or "Put your toys away!"

Although Nancy's approach to the children was mainly chaotic, there was some consistency within the chaotic mess of family interactions. For the most part, Nancy tolerated the children's misbehavior, becoming upset but disciplining them in an inconsistent fashion. When their behavior became very disruptive, she would call Roger and argue with him about his lack of responsibility for the children.

It was hypothesized that Nancy's report of her seeming inability to consistently reward and punish the children was ensuring Roger's participation in their lives. The children contributed their misbehavior to ensure that Nancy would become upset enough to call Roger. Roger would then come to the rescue but make only slight attempts to resolve the problems with children, managing usually to blame Nancy. This ensured that the children would continue to misbehave and thereby make certain that Roger would be called again by Nancy in the near future.

This is an example of how dynamics, as viewed from a behavioral approach, act to mold the family system in such a way that is problematic for the members. This also illustrates the sequence of events that leads to family problems. It is called "tracking the symptom." Once we understand the cycle of interaction, we can find alternate healthier ways of being.

In a "typical" single-parent family with a problem, such as the one just described, the husband-wife bond is usually dissolved; there is generally conflict and hostility between the two parents and the siblings. Sometimes, one of the children has entered the executive subsystem as the parental child, creating a cross-generational coalition, replacing the absent father and taking on adult responsibilities.

THERAPY STRATEGIES

As was stated earlier, there are many types of single-parent households. The case history just presented represents one type—a typical, white, middle-class single-parent family system with young children. It is not typical of other types of single-parent family systems and therefore the principles stated in this chapter are not generalizable to other single-parent family systems (see Richards and Schmiege, 1993). Even among white, middle-class single-parent family systems many variations exist (Mendes, 1979), but similarities do too, and therefore certain principles can be used by mental health professionals to effectively deal with such family systems. Richards and Schmiege (1993) go beyond the negative, pathological view of single-parent families and begin to identify and build on their strengths. They believe that the problems of these families have been the focus of researchers to the exclusion of their strengths. This is perhaps due to the societal emphasis of the two-parent family as the ideal. If this is the case, then variant family forms may be viewed as flawed and thus the potential strengths of such families are ignored or trivialized.

The focus in this type of therapy is always on the family. The goals are to change the structure of the family and the behavioral sequence that has led to the problems and to teach more effective coping skills necessary to accomplish the functions of the family as listed previously (see Minuchin and Fishman, 1981). This goal is accomplished through the use of planned behavioral therapy techniques, based upon a systemic analysis of the family's hierarchy, boundaries, and subsystems. In Nancy's case, the goal was to find ways of addressing her dependency needs and lack of power which would not put her sons' development in jeopardy.

Following are some specific cognitive-behavioral interventions that were used in this family to create systemic change. Although these interventions are discussed in relation to the presented case history, certain structural similarities exist among single-parent systems (Minuchin and Fish- man, 1981). These therapy techniques are therefore generalizable.

Reinforce the Parental Role

As stated earlier, most parents are unaware of the functions of the family. It is therefore most useful in a therapy situation for the mental health therapist to teach and educate. In single-parent families, a child may take on one of two roles in order to maintain the postdivorced family's equilibrium (Ahrons, 1980). A child may become a parental child who relinquishes childhood play and takes over many adult responsibilities. A child may also take on a spousal role, becoming an emotional confidant to the single parent. Both of these situations indicate cross-generational problems in the custodial parent-child subsystem and are indications for therapy (Ahrons, 1980).

Another problem in the custodial-parent subsystem may occur if the parent does not have the coping skills necessary to care for the children. Referring to the previous case description, it was important to reinforce the caretaking role (Berman and Turk, 1981). This basically became a long-term goal of the therapy. Nancy, initially, was still dependent on her own mother and had not been dependent on her husband. She could not become independent without first learning basic caretaking skills. This was accomplished by using short-term behavioral goals (Jacobson and Margolin, 1979). For example, the therapist worked with her on setting up a schedule so that she could utilize her time much more efficiently than she was presently doing. This was reinforcing for her because she was able to spend more time with the children, helping her to feel less guilty about what she called her "mothering" capabilities.

She was helped to set up a behavior modification chart with the boys. Some of the topics on the chart included brushing teeth, making beds, putting toys away, clearing off the dinner table, doing homework, studying, and getting good grades. Each one of the topics was fully explained to the boys. For example, after school from 3 to 4 p.m., the boys were to do their homework and study. If they accomplished this, they would get a gold star for the day. For every six gold stars (they did not have to study on Sundays), they received a prize. The prizes were reasonable ones, such as a trip to Friendly's for ice cream. The purpose of the chart was to create some structure, some order in the children's lives.

Not only did the chart serve to create some sort of structure for the boys, it also taught them to be independent and take care of some of their own needs, something which Nancy originally was not modeling for them. This had the secondary result of freeing up some of Nancy's time. It was no longer necessary for her to come home from work tired only to begin yelling at the boys to do their homework. Her interactions with them started to become more positive, and she began to enjoy spending more time with them.

Help the Parent Become a Nurturing, Supportive Figure in the Children's Lives

The divorce crisis creates systemic disequilibrium. Although this is often a period of increased strain on the family members, it can also be a time of growth and development (Beal, 1980; Isaacs, Montalvo, and Adelsohn, 1986). When a system is in flux, it is most conducive to change. Much can be accomplished during this crisis time when roles are ambiguous, when boundaries are permeable, and when rules are temporarily suspended (McPhee, 1985).

Nancy needed to establish a nurturing, supportive relationship with the boys. Once again short-term behavioral goals were utilized to accomplish this. The therapist worked with the client, attempting to help her maximize the time she spent with the boys so that it was beneficial to all and did not turn into an argument. It was suggested that she make a list of places she was interested in visiting. Nancy was very interested in gardening. Thus, it was suggested that she plan weekly day trips to places that she was interested in seeing. In this manner, she would not feel resentful about "not having any time to do the things I want to do," and the boys would also have the chance to spend enjoyable times with their mother.

In therapy Nancy learned how to make small amounts of time very valuable for both mother and children. For example, it was necessary for Nancy to drive the children to their various after-school activities, so it could be a fun time for all. She learned to create very special quality moments for the children in the car. It was a time when they had her attention. She realized that she did not need to spend large blocks of time with the boys to have a meaningful time with them. This also helped to alleviate some of the guilt she was feeling about her mothering abilities.

Another behavioral goal was to help her to efficiently cook for the boys. Interestingly enough, Nancy loved to cook but was feeling overwhelmed by it on the nights when she came home from work. She decided that it would be more enjoyable for her to cook the meals all at once. It was suggested that she do the cooking on Sunday mornings when the boys generally were with their father. In this way, she could focus completely on the cooking, which she loved, without interruptions from the boys.

After a few weeks, Nancy cooked all the meals for the entire week, packaged them, and froze them. During the week, she would then take them out one at a time, thaw them, and place them into the microwave oven to heat up. Again, because she was cooking decent meals for the children, all family members benefited. Nancy felt positive about her capabilities as a cook and the boys were finally eating nutritious meals. Because Nancy did not have to shop and cook during the week, she also had more time for herself and boys.

Help the Client with Separation/Individuation Issues from His or Her Own Family of Origin

The issue of separation/individuation from the family of origin can be an important one in therapy with single parents. It is therefore important that clear boundaries exist around the single-parent family system—that the single-parent family system is not confused with the extended family system (Isaacs, Montalvo, and Adelsohn, 1986). Nancy was responsible for a great many things and the overwhelming feelings that she was experiencing were perfectly normal. In therapy, she realized that even though sometimes things seemed overwhelming, they could be broken down into small parts and be accomplished quite easily. In so doing, she also learned that she did not have to depend on her mother for help with everyday types of activities and chores.

Nancy's mother represented a problem in that she wanted her to move back home with her. Nancy's father had died about five years before Nancy's divorce and her mother was lonely. This is the typical trap into which single parents often fall. On one hand, Nancy felt it would be easier to move in with her mother. Since Nancy's mother was financially well-off, she would not have to worry about paying the mortgage. Single-parent families are often economically disadvantaged, so the single-parent's family of origin may represent an oasis from financial ruin. In most cases, though, the psychological price is high.

For Nancy, moving back to her family of origin meant that food shopping, cleaning, chores, and babysitter also be taken care of by her mother. On the other hand, Nancy's mother was very controlling, demanding to know Nancy's whereabouts at all times. According to her, there was only one right way to do things; no other way was acceptable. Nancy's mother was very critical of her and wished to change her. If Nancy moved in with her mother, she would set herself up for constant failure.

The other problem involved with moving in with her mother was that of authority. When Nancy's mother was visiting, she became the person in charge and Nancy's authority with her children was often undermined. This created a triangle which produced conflicting feeling in the children. It was no longer clear whom they were supposed to obey, since mother and daughter had different ways of doing things. The potentiality for all sorts of alliances was created, with Nancy never being quite sure whether she was the child or the mother. This probably was a pattern that was repeated in relationship with her ex-husband. So even though the offer to move in with her mother initially seemed quite appealing, upon closer investigation it would have been a psychological disaster for Nancy. In future therapy sessions, Nancy learned to assert herself with her mother and to remain in the authority position when her mother came to visit. During one of the sessions, Nancy verbalized that she finally felt grown up.

As is seen from this case, in single-parent family systems the power hierarchy becomes blurred at times. It is important for mental health therapists to ask, "Where is the power base? Are the children 'mothering' the mother? What is the role of the mother's mother? The mother's father? Other family members?"

Help Dispel the Parent's Feeling of Abandonment and Help the Parent to Dispel the Children's Feelings of Abandonment

Nancy's own feelings of abandonment were crucial and were discussed throughout the sessions. This problem is also discussed by Weiss (1979), who believes the dissolution of attachment bonds can be a source of psychological problems following a separation. When Nancy would feel overwhelmed or abandoned, she wrote her feelings in a journal, which she then brought to therapy session to discuss. A connection was pointed out between unrealistic expectations and unnecessary painful feelings.

Nancy's children were also experiencing fears in the area as exemplified by their not wanting to stay with a sitter. Often they would ask their mother, "Are you sure you're coming back? Tell me exactly what time you'll be home." In therapy, Nancy learned to supportively help her children get through these feelings. She would often reassure them of her love. She also involved them in planning future activities in which they would all participate. In this way the children were able to project themselves into the future situations reassured that their mother would be there with them.

Help the Mother Involve the Children in Her Goals

At the beginning of therapy, Nancy and her children were alienated from each other. It seemed as though they were simply living in the same residence, with very little positive communication and/or affection flowing between them. During the adjustment period after a separation or a divorce, this is often typical. One way to help increase the positive aspects of the parent-child relationship is to help the mother involve her children in her goals. This was accomplished quite nicely with Nancy when the boys joined with her on every other Sunday and helped her to prepare the meals for the week. They were given choices for their meals and were encouraged to cooperate in the food preparation. Soon after this process was begun, preparing the meals became a fun-filled family activity. It was through behavioral activities such as these that the roles of the family members became defined, the responsibilities of each member became known, and the family system began to function more effectively (Ahrons, 1980).

Help the Mother Develop a Support Structure Outside the Home and Help the Mother Help the Children Develop Outside Social Interests

It is important for mental health therapists to help the client make contact with and attach to another system. A single-parent system can be quite successful if the client can look to other strong systems for support (Morawetz and Walker, 1984). These outside systems could be women or men friends, a group of single parents that meets on a regular basis, a sports activity, or even going back to school to take courses. This network can provide resources in the form of people as well as material resources, helping the single parent reach out and form new relationships with supportive people (Warren and Amara, 1985). Initially, Nancy was so overwhelmed with basic survival that she had little time left for anything else. Her entire world consisted of working, cleaning, cooking, and shouting at the boys to behave. Her life was devoid of fun and/or relaxing activities. She felt she had little to look forward to and was in a state of depression. What she missed most was not having anyone with whom to discuss her day. Her life was filled with either professional conversations with people with whom she worked or in conversations with her children about things which were important to them. There was no one in her life with whom she could have an adult conversation—no one with whom she could share an intimate relationship. In short, there were no reinforcers in her life and, according to cognitive-behavioral psychology (Beck, 1970), depression is defined as a lack of reinforcers in one's environment.

During therapy, Nancy was encouraged to seek out other single parents in her neighborhood so that she could begin to develop friends. In this way she was able to share her career dreams, her life's trials and tribulations, and the fun moments that also began to occur more frequently. In other words, she was beginning to develop a support structure of women—a network of comrades who helped make her life more pleasant. In so doing, her children were now free to play with their friends and engage in the extracurricular activities that young boys enjoy—and the sibling subsystem was reinforced. They no longer had to feel guilty about leaving their sad and depressed mother.

Research seems to indicate that the factors which appear to be associated with the perceived psychological response to divorce more as a strength than as a trauma appear to be perception of divorce as normal, certain personality characteristics (self-assurance, ego strength, dominance), age (being relatively young rather than older), sex (being female), having the perception that one is coming from an abusive rather than an ordinary marriage, having had a marriage of shorter duration, having a relatively long period from decision to actual divorce, being the initiator of the divorce, having a low level of attachment to the ex-partner, having a satisfactory relationship with the ex-mate rather than an unsatisfactory one, having adequate income and material resources, having higher levels of education rather than lower (for females only), having nontraditional ideas about gender and/or marital roles, having access to supportive social networks, being geographically mobile, having access to professionally organized support group of peers, and having a dating relationship and or a love affair with a significant other rather than not.

If Possible, Help the Client Develop a Reasonable Relationship with the Ex-Partner

Wallerstein and Kelly (1980) found that a supportive and cooperative divorced coparenting relationship is an essential ingredient for continued growth and development of the children involved in single-parent homes. Many problems arise, however, in the coparental subsystem. Some of the more common ones are concerned with raising children: one of the parents using the child as a go-between; competition with the other parent; the other parent spoiling the children; and lack of support and caring by the other parent (Morawetz and Walker, 1984). Along with these problems, often in a single-parent family system exists quite a bit of unresolved anger and hostility between the two parents. Unfortunately, too often the children become involved in this anger and hostility (Isaacs, Montalvo, and Adelsohn, 1986). Typically the children feel that they cannot express anger to the noncustodial parent out of fear of losing that parent forever. This results in the children expressing anger and complaints to the parent with whom they are living. This could in turn cause resentment toward the children on the part of the parent (Wallerstein and Kelly, 1980). In therapy sessions with single parents, it is important to discuss these issues, helping the client to work through feelings of resentment and anger and to further understand the necessity of not conveying that anger and resentment of the children (Jacobson, 1978).

In some cases, clients present a different reaction to the ex-spouse. These individuals deny the impact of their divorce and report no strong feeling associated with the loss of their marriage or partner. It is as if the marriage or the divorce never happened. This has been likened to Bowen's (1978) concept of emotional cutoff. Here the individual cuts off the ex-spouse either by physical distancing, by keeping contacts with him or her very brief and infrequent, or by total withdrawal and avoidance. Bowen's solution to emotional cutoffs is to have the client recontact the family member involved. Sometimes divorced spouses may need to reestablish contact in order to truly divorce. This, however, could be a very complicated process.

Working through her relationship with her ex-husband, Roger, was another goal in therapy with Nancy. This was discussed in session and Nancy attempted to speak with her ex-husband about taking on some of the extra responsibility with the boys and the possibility of coming for some joint therapy sessions. Involving the absent parent is an important consideration when working with single-parent families. Seeing the primary parent alone, in this case, the mother, reinforces the notion that the problem is hers alone. Thus another goal of the therapy is to help increase the involvement of the noncustodial parent. Roger did seem to want to be involved with the boys. The therapist suggested that one of the ways he could increase his involvement with them was to drive them to and watch them do their sport activities. In this way, Nancy would not have to leave the bank to drive the boys to their games, thereby alleviating some of her anxiety and pressure. At the same time, the boy's father would become more involved, something which ultimately would have positive consequences for the whole family.

Help the Clients Mourn Unresolved Losses

Help clients deal with issues of unresolved mourning. Often when depression is the presenting problem, issues of relationship loss underlie the sadness. Clients in these situations need then to mourn the loss of the relationship (Walsh, 1982). The process of mourning is discussed more fully in Chapter 5. In the case of divorce, these losses are experienced by all members of the family system. Fulmer (1983) believes that the single-parent family is especially vulnerable to problems resulting from unresolved loss. Hoffman (1981) describes a situation of the children's misbehavior as being "collusive mischief" to offset the mother's depression. Seeing her depression, they become anxious, begin to misbehave, and therefore, "impel [her] to take an active position" (p. 84) by their disobedience. This was typified in Nancy's family. Whenever Tyler sensed his mother's depression, he would act out by not doing his homework or by fighting with his brother. This behavior functioned to mobilize Nancy to action, taking the focus away from her depressed state.

In therapy, Nancy expressed her sadness around the loss of the relationship, the loss of her dreams and expectations around her marriage, and the loss of Roger. In family sessions the boys also expressed their sorrow in no longer having a traditional two-parent family and not seeing their father as often as they used to before their parents separated.

Help the Client Recognize That the Single-Parent Family System Is Very Different from the Two-Parent Family Model

As Mendes (1979) points out,

> One of the most important tasks for therapy with single-parent families, regardless of their lifestyle, is to help liberate families that are tyrannized by the two-parent family model. They need to see that is impossible for one parent to be both father and mother. (p. 195)

In this society, people are socialized to believe that the two-parent family is the norm. While it is true that this family system is the norm in many cases, it is not the norm in just as many cases. Between 1970 and 1978, there was 46 percent increase in female-headed family systems. What matters, though, for the single parent is that the two-parent system is considered to be the ideal. This creates the unfortunate situation whereby the single-parent family member may feel inferior—a product of a less-than-ideal arrangement. During therapy, it is important for the individual to evaluate his or her definitions of what a single-parent family system "should" be like—emotionally and realistically and to challenge unrealistic "shoulds." This is true for the therapist as well as for the client. The therapist can help the client evaluate the cost of doing everything. Help them see that by sharing family tasks, they help reduce the inevitable anger felt by an overburdened parent.

It is true that if this chapter's case history were a two-parent family, some of the existing problems would be alleviated because two people would be sharing the responsibilities of the children, finances, and household chores. The interparental conflict would be much less. There also would be another person to share emotions with, for Nancy to talk with about the frustrations of her day. If this were a two-parent family, the focus of the therapy would be to help Nancy share her feelings of being overwhelmed with her husband and to basically work out a task-sharing situation between the two adults. However, while it is true that some of the problems would be solved simply because there would be another adult person to share responsibilities, still it is crucial to realize that some of the same issues would still exist even if this were a two-parent family. For example, the lack of separation from the family of origin, lack of coping skills on Nancy's part, and detachment and aloofness on Roger's part.

Aside from these issues, in this society there is a two-parent family norm. This norm sets up the definition of what a family "should" be. Unfortunately, the single-parent family system cannot fulfill this norm and therefore is by definition considered a failure (Beal, 1980). These social definitions of "failures" define the psychological condition of being in a failed situation. In the therapy situation, it is important to talk these issues through with clients and help them resolve some of their uncertainty, ambiguity, and loss of self-esteem. For a consideration of other therapeutic issues with the single-parent family system, see Morawetz and Walker (1984).

Since the beginning of therapy, the structure of Nancy's single-parent family system changed. The boundaries were clarified. The boundaries between the generations became more clear. The father became more involved, less alienated from the family situation. The children were existing more in "normal" environment, with a strong sibling subsystem. There was more structure; rules and regulations increased.

The executive boundary was reinforced. Nancy became more nurturing and supportive to her children. She felt less overwhelmed. She became more bonded to her children, causing them to feel more secure and helping her feel more fulfilled, more needed, less isolated, and less guilty. As a result, the children had fewer temper tantrums and the anxiety level in the house seemed to decrease somewhat. Nancy even found time to go to an educational movie with her friends.

Reismann (1990) who interviewed many divorced persons in *Divorce Talk* states that "most of those interviewed had no difficulty identifying divorce's benefits, which they summarized as 'freedom'" (p. 163): "I feel like living again, I feel like I was dying a slow death in that relationship. There's a joy in my life . . . I feel a real emotional release" (p. 165). Reismann (1990) states that "as most women understand, divorce is not only a loss but a gain" (Reismann, 1990, p. 161). She indicates that the positive change is in three general areas: (1) competence in the management of daily life, (2) changing meaning of social relationships, and (3) a fuller sense of a whole identity.

Some of the long-range goals with Nancy were to help her to continue to establish a support network, administer career-oriented tests and help her with career planning (something in which she was very interested), and help her reenter the dating scene (something she also mentioned as desirable). Emotionally, Nancy still sometimes relied on alcohol to relax her, so more help was needed in this area. She also need to continue to work through her anger at Roger for abandoning her. There is still much more work left to do with this single-parent family, but positive changes have started to occur.

Although a single-parent family is a difficult organization to run, it can be done quite well even in the most difficult of cases. For example, it may be easier to make executive decisions when there is one executive. Cashion (1982) found that children from female-headed families are just as likely to have "good emotional adjustment . . . self esteem . . . intellectual development . . . and no higher rates of juvenile delinquency" as other children of comparable socioeconomic status.

Help the Family to Discover Their Potential Strengths and Resources

Richards and Schmiege (1993) believe that children in single-parent families may benefit from the increased responsibility. They feel that independence is a highly valued personal trait in our culture and the increased independence of the single-parent family members may be an important survival skill in a rapidly changing world. Some other positive traits they include in their discussion are parenting skills, managing a family, communicating, personally growing, and providing financial support—traits that are not necessarily fostered in the two-parent household. Parenting skills include being supportive of the children, being patient, helping the children cope, and fostering independence. Family management strengths include being well organized, dependable, and able to coordinate schedules. Good communication includes building a sense of honesty and trust and conveying ideas clearly to family and friends. Personal growth includes feeling successful despite many self-doubts, as well as having a positive attitude. Therapists can assist clients to focus and expand on their developing strengths and resourcefulness.

SUMMARY

Many areas may be investigated when working with a single-parent family system. Some of these areas were explored in the present chapter as discussed in the case history. Assessing the family on a systemic level and using behavioral intervention strategies to realign boundaries and extinguish cross-generational coalitions were the main themes of the chapter. The emphasis on assessing the family as a whole is an obvious one. Also necessary is the role of the therapist as an educator, helping the family to restructure and clarify boundaries and roles. The model for intervention was based on facilitating "good-enough" arrangements between divorced parents and their children (Isaacs, Montalvo, and Adelsohn, 1986). The basis of this approach is to include children's open access to the noncustodial parent and assurance that two parents are raising them. Part of the family therapist's role is to teach the family good child-rearing practices and help them to learn age-appropriate behaviors. The basic theme of single-parent family therapy is to stimulate psychological growth, always a developmental process, and to encourage the future psychological maturation of all family members.

Some single-parent women define divorce as an opportunity for reworking developmental tasks or unfinished business. They see it as a chance to achieve separation from historical parents or a spouse in the parent role and to develop new, more mature relationships. Therapists can assist in this process in the sense that part of the experience of the divorce process may be structured by the expectations of the professionals single parents encounter. Therapists' definitions of marital changes as disappointments balanced by new opportunities, as losses balanced by gains, can create comparable expectations in the minds of clients. It may be useful to view the experiences of those families who have experienced divorce as having experienced stressful transitions for both the children and adults involved, while at the time acknowledging that over time and with appropriate supports such transitions may serve as stimuli for personal growth and improved life circumstances for all involved.

It is here that therapists can change their lens in their approach to divorce and develop a new language—that in which the orientation of divorce as disaster is added to or possibly replaced by that of divorce as developer.

Chapter 4

Resiliency and Competence
in Children Experiencing Divorce

Hetherington (1989) reported that although some are losers in the process of divorce, survivors and winners also emerge. In fact, if anxiety and stress are not continuous, most family members will recover in as little as a two- to three-year time span. Wallerstein (1984) reported a series of negative outcomes in her five-year longitudinal study of California children of divorce, but she also reported that about 34 percent of the children studied were happy and thriving. *Happy* and *thriving* are not the typical words associated with children of divorce, and these results warrant further elaboration. What are the factors involved in good postdivorce adjustment? How can therapists assist the single-parent family in fostering these factors? How can therapists help their clients divorce in a competent manner—one that creates an environment which facilitates growth and happiness. How can therapists assist their clients with a competent divorce?

THE COMPETENT DIVORCE

This chapter discusses the variables that influence the competent divorce. As stated throughout this book, social science literature discussing the single-parent family has traditionally focused on the deficits of such a family system. This is not the focus of this chapter; rather, we propose that therapy models which focus on deficits serve to reinforce the deficits. (For a comparison of these two approaches to therapy, see Chapter 10.) Because of the tremendous social changes that have taken place in the family within the past one hundred years, we believe a competency-based model is more appropriate. It is believed that for therapists to focus on the competencies of single-parent family systems, certain assumptions must be challenged.

This chapter presents the reader with recent methodologically sound research that either found no significant differences between children from one- and two-parent households or pointed to the strengths of the one-parent family. In so doing, the factors that influence good adjustment processes in parents and children, or the competent divorce, are stressed. We recognize that this side of the picture is just as biased as the gloom-and-doom picture which is more typically presented; however, we believe therapists are not typically familiar with the positive outcome research on children of divorce and this presentation is crucial in order for them to assess their own biases.

Weiss (1979) studied the experience of growing up in a single-parent household and found that the absence of the traditional hierarchy which characterizes single-parent homes allows children a greater share in the responsibility for the household, thus allowing them to develop a sense of responsibility, self-esteem, independence, and confidence. Weiss noted that the parents, as well as the children, generally considered the changes produced because of this change in traditional roles to be largely beneficial to the entire family. For many children, both younger and older, the new demands on them for autonomy and responsibility led to personal growth.

Focusing also on the resiliency of children of divorce, Hetherington and Kelly (2002) reported that 6 years after divorce 75 to 80 percent of the children in their sample were developing well within the normal range. The findings also showed that within two years of their parents' divorce, most of the children were functioning reasonably well. They also found that women and girls rated themselves as more competent people than did those who stayed in an unhappy family situation. Their study tracked nearly 1,400 families and more than 2,500 children. They concluded that their data stand as a tribute to the children's resilience and to the support, love, and good sense of the parents. They felt that a "self-righting" process seemed to occur in the children as new relationships and experiences appeared to wash away the harmful effects of old stresses. This, they believed, created a push toward recovery and positive adaptation. They concluded, "Coping with the challenges of life in a single-parent family may enhance the ability of some children to deal with future stresses" (Hetherington and Kelly, 2002, p. 256).

Weiss (1979) also reports that consequences for children in a one-parent household may foster an early maturity. One aspect of family life that reflects this maturity is the child's role in the decision-making process in a one-parent household. In a two-parent family, both parents typically share in the decision making, and children are exposed to abide by this decision. In the absence of a second parent, the single parent is likely to incorporate children into the decision-making process, if only because it is the most expedient way to manage a household (Weiss, 1979). These parent-child partnerships often lead to close ties in the enactment of reciprocal friend/confidant roles (Kurdek, 1981). In a one-parent family the parent does not need to check with a second adult before acceding to the children's wishes. No longer is there a structure in which the parent is unable to make common cause with the children for fear of betraying a prior understanding with the other parent. There is more acceptance of the additional responsibility when the child has a voice in the decision-making process. Children can be asked not only to perform additional chores but also to participate in deciding what is to be done. Children in single-parent households are often encouraged to develop a relationship with the custodial parent that is more like a peer and confidante, elevating the child to a coparent status (Kalter et al., 1984) or cooperative colleague (Ahrons, 1980). This means that the structure of this type of family is different from the two-parent variety in that although a hierarchy is present with the single-parent mother in charge, the rules, roles, and boundaries are more collaboratively based. Weiss (1979) concludes that the single-parent family, insofar as it requires children to behave responsibly, may in this respect be a better setting for growing up than the two-parent family. Hetherington (1991) agrees, adding that the nontraditional organization of the single-parent home can actually enhance responsibility communication and closeness between child and parent.

Hutchinson and Hirsch (in Everett, 1989) suggest that children of divorce tend to be good decision makers and are stronger and more mature as an outgrowth of divorce. Blades et al. (1984) conclude that children who are seen as partners in a single-parent household tend to be more capable and self-reliant. In times of crisis they rise to the occasion, because they believe in their ability to handle things. Emery et al. (1984) noted that divorced families can tap into the experiences of the transitional situation and strengthen a child's ability to cope and be independent. They also believe that adolescents living in single-parent families are characterized by greater maturity, feelings of efficacy, and an internal locus of control (see also Guidubaldi and Perry, 1985; Kalter et al., 1984; Wallerstein and Kelly, 1980; Weiss, 1979).

Schwebel et al. (1990) believe that parental divorce forces children to engage in personal adjustment. First, the children attempt to relate effectively to the environment in which they live by developing skills, traits, and behaviors that will bring success, happiness, and other valued goals. Second, they attempt to master the environment and modify it to their own advantage. This statement implies that children might develop strengths as a result of attempting to adjust to their parental divorce. They may develop skills or abilities to meet new challenges, and they may develop new self-cognitions as a result of these new challenges (Gately and Schwebel, 1991).

Cashion (1982), in a review of other studies, found that children in female-headed families are likely to have good emotional adjustment, good self-esteem (except when they are stigmatized), intellectual development comparable to others in the same socioeconomic status, and rates of juvenile delinquency comparable to others in the same socioeconomic status. Other research (Hutchinson et al., 1989) examined depression, self-concepts, and the ability to handle stress, and found no statistical differences between children from one-parent and two-parent families. See also Warren et al. (1982), who reached the same conclusions.

Some research indicates that children from single-parent homes are more creative than children from two-parent families. Albert (1971) and Roe (1953) studied the gifted and historically important people in history who had experienced loss and found that some of them were children of divorce. Regarding divergent thinking and creative potential, it seems that preschoolers who live in single-parent families are very imaginative (see Cornelius and Yawkey, 1986). Wallerstein and Kelly (1980) explored the relationship between divorce and creativity potential. They found that children of divorce exhibited flexibility, tolerance for change, a delay of gratification, and enhanced creative capacity. Others concurring with the idea that originality is positively related to a positive postdivorce adjustment were Guidubaldi and Chiarella (1985). Explanations for these findings vary: Jenkins et al. (1988) seem to question if intensification of feelings and emotions experienced in the divorce process may account for the heightened creative talent of children of divorce; Albert (1971) cites emotional distancing as causation for creativity; and

Becker (1973) explains it as a result of the father's departure from the home.

With the increased divorce rate and family changes due to divorce come changes in the parental role. Some of these changes can be related to changes in child discipline practices. On a more speculative level, parent roles may change as adults opt for more androgynous lifestyles (Kurdek, 1981). These changes may alter both the nature of the models to which the child is exposed and the types of child behavior which is regarded as desirable.

With divorce comes role reallocation. Children are expected and required to take on new roles. Favorable outcomes occur if *children are assigned new roles appropriate to their abilities*. In so doing, they are more likely to experience success, increased competencies, and greater self-esteem (Gately and Schwebel, 1991). If children are assigned new roles based on their abilities rather than on traditional sex roles, it is more likely to foster androgynous sex-role orientations and increase behavioral flexibility.

MacKinnon, Stoneman, and Brody (1984) examined the impact of maternal employment and family form (married/working, divorced/ working) on children's sex-role stereotypes, and mothers' traditional attitudes. They found that the children from the single-parent homes were less concerned about traditional sex-roles stereotypes. The shedding of restrictive sex-role orientation could be a positive growth factor, opening new doors for the newly single and their children.

According to a study by Kurdek and Siesky (1980), children of one-parent families were significantly more androgynous than children of two-parent families, who tend to be more traditionally sex typed (Demo and Acock, 1988). The tendency of children in single-parent families to display more androgynous behavior may be interpreted as a beneficial effect. Children in female-headed families, because of father absence, are not as strongly pressured as children in two-parent families to conform to gender roles. These children frequently assume a variety of domestic responsibilities to compensate for the absent parent (Weiss, 1979). Because of this they broaden the competencies and skills and their definitions of gender-appropriate behavior (Demo and Acock, 1988).

This positive research promotes a "reframing approach," which focuses on seeing children of divorce as healthy and successful. It is most significant that mental health workers and educators often hold a misleading assumption that children of divorce display negative behavioral changes and perform lower academically (see Chapter 8 for a review of children of divorce and the academic system). Whether or not children of divorce have personal or social problems depends on the resources and supports that they receive. It is more helpful for therapists to view problems that result from divorce as a potentiality rather than an inevitability.

Hetherington (1999) concludes that the vast majority of children from divorced families eventually emerge as reasonably competent individuals (see also Hetherington, 1993).

> Divorce is associated with an increased probability of experiencing a series of risk factors (such as economic declines, stressful life events, conflict, psychological, health, and behavioral problems in parents) that disrupt family process and undermine parenting and the adjustment of the children. Parents and children, although suffering some initial perturbations in adjustment following divorce, can adapt to their new situation if it is harmonious, if additional or increased stress is not encountered, and most important if the custodial parent is able to sustain authoritative parenting and avoid excessive parentification. (Hetherington, 1999, p. 323)

FACTORS ASSOCIATED
WITH THE COMPETENT DIVORCE

Instead of focusing on the problems of children of divorce, it seems at least as appropriate to examine factors influencing good postdivorce adjustment. Wallerstein (1984) noted that perhaps the most crucial factor influencing a good adjustment in children after divorce was a stable, loving relationship with both parents, between whom friction had largely dissipated, and having regular, dependable visiting patterns. She found that grandparents provided some support for both divorced mothers and their children. She also notes that a number of other factors seemed common to the children who dealt most resiliently with divorce. One was having a strong personality to start with.

The microsystem represents interactive processes operative in the pre- and postdivorce family system and has been the focus of much research. For children, the threat of divorce lies in the disruption of the relationship with their parents. According to Wallerstein and

Kelly (1980) positive continuity in relationships with both parents is related to the psychological health of the child during the postdivorce years. Children of higher levels of interpersonal understanding and internal locus of control have also been shown to experience more positive postdivorce outcomes than do their peers.

One common theme that surfaced for children with positive results was the manner in which parents approached divorce and how the children perceived the divorce. Favorable outcomes are more likely in children when people significant to them judge the single-parent home as a viable rather than deviant family form (Gately and Schwebel, 1991). As noted previously by Gately and Schwebel (1991), feelings of well-being can result in an atmosphere of nonstigmatization of the single-parent status and divorce.

Kelly (1988) reviewed research on the impact of divorce on the adjustment of children and suggested that it is the conditions created by the divorce rather than the divorce itself which determines the child's adjustment. This is supported by Stolberg and Garrison (1985) who found that more effective parenting was positively associated with better social skills, more involvement in prosocial activities, and fewer internalized problems in children.

Barry (1979) found that children's positive adjustment to divorce was related to four factors:

1. parents having a good rapport with their children,
2. open communication within the family,
3. a sense of sharing and working together, and
4. the ability to accept and support one another in a loving manner.

Portes, Haas, and Brown (1991) analyzed four general factors related to children's adjustment, including child coping skills, family functioning, stability, and family support systems. This topic has been studied by other researchers who have noted that long-term effects of marital transitions are related more to new stresses encountered by the child, the individual attributes of the child, the qualities of the single-parent or stepfamily home environment, and resources and support systems available to the child than they are to divorce or remarriage.

In 1980, Wallerstein and Kelly identified variables which had a positive effect on the adjustment of children in a divorce situation and concluded that factors which appeared to influence good adjustment in children of divorce after five years were similar to those which make for good adjustment in a two-parent home. Guidubaldi (1983) noted seven similar variables. These combined variables concerned the parental conditions and qualities as well as the qualities and needs of the children in general. Yet the most important variable of all may be the amount of marital conflict or discord and how the parents themselves handles it. Hetherington, Cox, and Cox (1982) concluded that in some cases divorce may reduce parental conflicts so the children become less distressed. It seems that with reduced marital conflicts and warm parent-child relationships in which discipline is stressed, children of divorce can receive adequate support and can therefore be well adjusted.

Brown et al. (1991) and Portes, Haas, and Brown (1991) conducted two separate studies to identify which of a number of interactive processes related to parental divorce as the best predictors of children's adjustment. The results of this study showed that roles, child reaction, insight into the divorce, and postdivorce adjustment (lack of conflict between parents) accounted for nearly half of the variance in the children's adjustment to the divorce. In the second study the authors hypothesized that family processes have a profound effect on the children's ability to adjust to divorce. They found that four factors were important:

1. child coping skills,
2. family functioning and stability,
3. strong support systems, and
4. postdivorce conditions (tendency to agree and get along without turmoil and aggression).

This study confirmed the hypothesis that a child's susceptibility to socioemotional and behavioral problems can be due to faulty predivorce family functioning and that social support systems can help ameliorate the effects of dysfunctional family functioning.

Tschann (1989) cited six predictors that may be most responsible for children's adaptive functioning during divorce. They are

1. family structure and other demographic variables, such as child age, gender, number of siblings, socioeconomic status, and length of separation,

2. difficult baby temperament,
3. preseparation marital conflict,
4. postseparation parental conflict,
5. hours spent with the visiting parent, and
6. parent-child relationship.

The conclusion of this study was that parents who were warm and supportive of their children helped their sons and daughters become better adjusted. Tschann (1989) concurred with findings in the literature that girls demonstrated better postseparation emotional adjustment than boys but that no differences in behavior adjustments were found according to gender in either one-parent or two-parent family models.

Emery (1982), Magrab (1978), and Everett (1989) agree with Tschann's (1989) viewpoint which says that parents who had less marital conflict had better relationships with their children after separation. This in turn was associated with more adaptive child functioning. Further, Tschann (1989) states that children in high conflict two-parent families show less favorable adaptations than do children of divorce in the socioemotional and behavioral areas.

Another aspect of divorce to consider is the circumstances that led up to the divorce. It has become apparent that the consequences of a divorce are far less damaging than a child living in a poor two-parent family system. It has been suggested that unhappy, conflictual families may have more negative effects on children than do voluntarily divorced family units that successfully avoid further prolonged conflict (Kulka and Weingarten, 1979). In fact, Garber (1991) studied 324 college students from two-parent and one-parent homes. The goal of the study was to examine the long-term effects of family structure and conflict at home on the self-esteem of these students. The results indicate that interparental conflict may have long-term effects on general and social self-esteem of young adults, while family structure does not.

These conflict-ridden two-parent families may be more harmful to children because they are unable to successfully resolve the difficulties within them, whereas divorce may do just that. Furthermore, it is reasonable to assume that children of divorce who come to consider their parents' choice to separate as exemplifying successful problem solving will have fewer barriers to overcome if later confronted with irreconcilable conflicts of interest in their own significant relationships (Kulka and Weingarten, 1979). If divorce comes to be construed as a successful strategy rather than as a personal failure, a potential barrier to leaving a similar stressful situation in one's own adult life could thereby be removed and a more flexible set of coping mechanisms and appreciation for the complexity of relationships could be learned.

The support of others outside the family is another factor influencing positive postdivorce outcome. It cannot be underestimated in fostering positive outcomes for single parents and their children. Brown et al. (1991) called this factor the external support system. Portes, Haas, and Brown (1991) cited external support systems as one of the four major factors contributing to children's positive adjustment to divorce. Kurdek (in Everett, 1989) believes that siblings may have an important consoling effect on children of divorce. Hetherington (1989) states that because children in the divorce arena are in a painful situation during which time trust in the adults may be shaky if the situation is unstable, children may rely on their siblings for support. They form an alliance that is sometimes found in a friendship with another child outside the family unit. Interestingly, grandparents, another extension of the unit, were found not as important in buffering roles unless they actually lived with the child. She also found that the age of the siblings had a great deal to do with adjustment. Older siblings fared better than younger ones, perhaps because of their understanding of the divorce process was greater. In terms of gender, female siblings were able to understand conflict resolution better than their male counterparts and so their reactions were more positive. Also, parents rated their older children as less dependent on the adults than were their younger siblings.

Studies identify family functioning and stability as one of the most important factors in determining positive outcomes in children of divorce, as did Thiriot and Buckner (1991) in their study of 204 single custodial parents. Brown et al. (1991) also noted that the family's abilities to maintain family rituals, provide a sense of security to its members, support one another emotionally, and maintain the overall organization of the family system are critical. This finding strongly emphasizes providing resources, nurturance and support, life development skills, and system's management and maintenance. Here healthy families are characterized by adequate fulfillment of all family functions, appropriate allocation of responsibility, and clear accountability. It appears that maintaining important family rituals helps provide emotional support and can help stabilize the family following divorce. In coping with a family transition such as divorce, many of those involved are protected by factors such as positive personality dispositions, a supportive family milieu, and support from external sources.

Legal aspects of the divorcing process also have an effect on postdivorce outcomes. They affect children in terms of the extension or dissolution of conflict associated with the divorce process. Saayman and Saayman (in Everett, 1989) see the court system as detrimental to the adjustment of children. They suggest mediation as a viable alternative. They also note, in the cases they reviewed, that family functioning improved once the divorce process was expedited. Courts are considered adversarial while mediation is supportive. In relation to courts, custody issues (including who gets the child and when) and coparenting arrangements especially exert a positive influence in the child's life following divorce. Neugebauer (Everett, 1989) found that children whose parents were able to arrange successful coparenting were unlikely to suffer distress. They did not experience the loss of either one of the parents and seemed to be well adjusted overall. They also found that nonadversarial postdivorce parental relationships are related to increased self-esteem and more positive adjustments.

Perhaps no other factor in the single-parent family's postdivorce adjustment is as important as the economic situation of the family. Chapter 9 discusses this phenomenon in more detail. Economic considerations are crucially important to the successful adjustment of children of divorce. A study by Guidubaldi (1983) noted that divorce often results in reduced economic status, especially for single-parent families with women as the head of household. If the parent's employment needs are met, often the adjustment of the parent is better, which in turn facilitates better adjustment in the children.

Consistent with research by Guidubaldi and Perry (1985), Tschann (1989) believes that lowered socioeconomic status can manifest in greater behavioral problems. This is further supported by Schnayer and Orr (in Everett,1989) in their discussion of family structures and interactional patterns. These researchers believe that the SES variable must be controlled in studies as it may be a better predictor of children's behavior problems than the sex of the single parent.

When a single parent experiences economic hardships, all aspects of his or her life are effected. As previously mentioned, in families that are financially comfortable, a moderate postdivorce financial decline may foster increased maturity in adolescents, characterized by reasonable adultlike attitudes toward financial matters and a greater appreciation for the value of goods (Wallerstein and Kelly, 1980).

Thus, a major impact of divorce involves economics. The economic situation of a family has a tremendous bearing on the children's postdivorce adjustment. Specific measures designed to improve the economic conditions of single-parent families would have a positive impact on many children's postdivorce adjustment and foster more favorable outcomes (Braver et al., 1989). For a summary of the factors influencing the competent divorce, see Exhibit 4.1.

In terms of successful adjustment in the parent, in a review of the literature Veevers (1990) identified seventeen factors that may contribute to growth, rather than trauma, as an outcome of divorce. Most important, she found that the definition of divorce as a normal event is essential to this belief. She believes that given the current percentages

EXHIBIT 4.1. Summary of Factors Involved in the Competent Divorce

Based on a thorough review of the literature and research on children of divorce, the following summary conclusions may be drawn and used as guidelines to assist social workers and their clients in the competent divorce.

- *Nonstigmatization of the single-parent status and divorce.*

  The manner in which parents approach divorce affects the way they and their children perceive the divorce. If people significant to them judge the single-parent home and the divorce process as a viable rather than a pathological situation, adults and children do better.

- *Reduced parental conflict.*

  Parents who are able to reduce their marital conflicts and friction and who have a tendency to get along with each other without turmoil and aggression create better adjustment environments for their children.

- *Family functioning.*

Families that provide a sense of sharing and emotional support for one another in a loving manner have better adjusted children. Single-parent families who maintain family rituals around birthdays, holidays, etc., provide a sense of security for the children.

- *Stable, loving relationship with both parents.*

Children adjust better if they maintain consistent, predictable, positive relationships with both parents and have regular dependable visiting patterns.

- *Appropriate role allocation.*

Single-parent families who have assigned chores and roles appropriate to their children's abilities have better adjusted children.

- *Effective parenting.*

Effective parenting is defined as parents who have a good rapport with their children, provide for open communication within the family, have warm parent-child relationships in which discipline is stressed, and provide stable, predictable environments with clearly specified rules.

- *Strong support systems.*

Single-parent families do better if they have strong support systems, consisting of regular friendships with relatives, such as grandparents, and peers.

- *Nonadversarial divorce.*

Single-parent families do better if they have a nonadversarial postdivorce adjustment and a friendly coparental relationship.

- *Parent's own sense of well-being.*

One of the most important predictors of children's postdivorce adjustment is the single parent's sense of well-being. If the single-parent mother/father has adjusted in a healthy way to the divorce, the children will also. This process can be facilitated through counseling and support structures.

- *Economics.*

Probably the most important factor involved in the adjustment of the single-parent family, corroborated by recent research, is adequate economics. If single parents have adequate money to support themselves and their families, many of the problems associated with divorce disappear. Given the current laws around child support and the associated problems with the percentage of reneging fathers, it is difficult to ascertain how this problem could be alleviated in the very near future.

of divorce on the United States today, the social stigma and psychological stain associated with divorce as a "deviant" activity of the last generation no longer applies. Veevers (1990) suggests that one factor in considering the extent of psychological distress ranging from extreme trauma to short-lived unpleasantness is each partner's ideological beliefs about marriage and divorce combined with one's personal perceptions of experiences. She also noted, contrary to the prevailing distress theories, some individuals reported divorce as being a positive, strengthening event. Her review of other studies shows that divorced persons may experience divorce as being on a continuum from relatively painful to causing relief.

The factors that appear to be associated with the psychological response to divorce more as a stren than as a trauma are

1. perception of divorce as normal,
2. personality characteristics (self-assurance, ego strength, dominance, etc.),
3. age (being relatively younger than older),
4. sex (being female),
5. having the perception that one is coming from an abusive rather than an ordinary marriage,
6. having had a marriage of shorter duration,
7. having a relatively long period from decision to actual divorce,
8. being the initiator of the divorce,
9. having a low level of attachment to the ex-partner,
10. having a satisfactory relationship with the ex-mate rather than an unsatisfactory one,
11. having adequate income and material resources,
12. having higher levels of education rather than lower (for females only),
13. having nontraditional ideas about gender and/or marital roles,
14. having access to supportive social networks,
15. being geographically mobile,
16. having access to professionally organized support groups of peers, and
17. having a dating relationship and/or a love affair with a significant other rather than not.

Gately and Schwebel (1991) proposed a challenge model for the process of adjusting to divorce that will foster favorable outcomes in adults and children. They believe that the outcomes of parental divorce, whether favorable, neutral, or unfavorable, are shaped by the nature of the challenges that the children face, and by moderating factors, such as the children's characteristics and the level of coping resources, including the social support that they have available.

Certain types of parental behavior foster favorable outcomes in children following divorce. Kaslow and Hyatt (1981) state that parents who cope well model for their children how to deal with strained interpersonal relationships and major life crises, and provide vicarious experiences that may increase children's feelings of self-efficacy. Santrock and Warchak (1979) believe that an authoritative parenting style characterized by warmth, clearly specified rules, and extensive verbal give-and-take between parent and child is associated with social competence and maturity. A high level of parenting skills is also related to a higher level of social competence in children (Gately and Schwebel, 1991). Parenting styles, especially the authoritative approach, were associated with a higher level of social competence, lowered behavioral problems, and overall better adjustment. According to Hetherington (1993), a supportive, structured, predictable parent-child relationship plays a critical protective role.

Thiriot and Buckner (1991) found that the custodial parent's own subjective sense of well-being was the strongest single predictor of divorce adjustment, pointing out that parents who feel good about themselves also feel good about their parenting skills as a single parent.

We can conclude from the previous section and from other research presented in this book that divorce per se does not have a negative effect on children and that certain factors can engender a competent divorce. This idea is supported by the empirical sociological studies of Ganong and Coleman (1984). They hypothesize that divorce is *not* confirmed as having an effect on emotional well-being. They found a failure to confirm large negative effects on different family structures. These researchers believe that divorce does not necessarily result in the deterioration of children's well-being. They raise the question that, in light of the theoretical, clinical, and empirical studies conducted, can we really expect emotional maladaption in divorce? And also, can we objectively measure for the analysis of such nonfactual and dynamic variables as "well-being"?

In conclusion, one could argue that little evidence suggests the existence of any long-term effects of divorce coming from a home that is headed by a single parent. It may be concluded that the early experiences of divorce have at most a modest effect on adult adjustment. Thus, the notion that experiencing parental divorce during childhood is an important contributor to later life adjustment derives little support from these representative samples of the American population.

WHAT CHILDREN CAN LEARN FROM DIVORCE

Children can learn that they do not have to stay in unhealthy relationships. They can know that life offers many choices and it is okay to terminate marriages which are hurtful to the family unit. These children can also learn to become more independent, flexible, and self-reliant. They become familiar with mediation and develop skills along those lines.

Children of divorce can learn to be realistic about adults by accurately assessing their parents' strengths and weaknesses. If they have insight into divorce's effects on the family members, it can lead to a desire to work for changes in their own relationships as adults. Many children of divorce work hard to see that the same histories do not repeat. In living through divorce the children come to find that views of opposition may both be true. Many children of divorce acquire better communication skills as an outgrowth of therapies associated with support groups. Resilience develops along with greater access to feelings within and about themselves. Children of divorce do not necessarily harbor unromantic notions of suffering, and they are often more adaptable to change than their two-parent counterparts. Because many of them are brought up in several family groups, they become more familiar with choices about child rearing and different lifestyles. Appreciating limits and developing a sense of intact self comes from acquiring a wisdom about life, and many of these children are more mature than their peers.

Learning to seek therapy is a new skill for survival which awakens a fuller and more realistic self-concept in many. In naming their reality and their pain, children of divorce begin to take responsibility for themselves. As adults, children of divorce may have a greater concern for future generations. They have learned survival skills and become decision makers. When preparing for marriage many years later, they know that divorce is a viable solution to marital problems especially if provided with a workable model. Their level of self-control is just as developed as the self-control of those peers coming from two-parent families and, because they often had to care for their siblings, they may be better caretakers. As adult children, they are able to have intimacies similar to their two-parent family peers. Academic records are found to be no different when compared to the "traditional" child, nor are differences found in the quality of parent-child relations when divorce is the key moderator.

SUMMARY

Hetherington (1989) concludes that when she first began to study children in divorced families, she followed a pathogenic model of divorce. However, after more than two decades of research on marital transitions, depending on the characteristics of the child, available resources, subsequent life experiences, and especially interpersonal relationships, children in the long run may be survivors, losers, or winners of the parents' divorce or remarriage. This is a more accurate summary than is generally portrayed in the literature.

Divorce is a complex cultural, social, legal, economic, and psychological process (Kurdek, 1981). Hence, children's divorce-related experiences need to be understood in terms of hierarchically embedded psychological, familial, social, and cultural context. Brofenbrenner (1979) has described human development as occurring in an ecological environment composed of such nested contexts. Each system involves a different aspect of the child's environment. The macrosystem involves the cultural beliefs, values, and attitudes surrounding modern family life. The stability of the postdivorce environment and the social support available to the restructured single-parent family make up the ecosystem. The microsystem is the nature of the family interaction during the pre- and postdivorce periods.

According to Fassell (1991), a tendency exists to compare the two-parent family with the one-parent family. She suggests that four forms of one-parent and two-parent families exist, which include both nonproblem and problem subsets in each category, and she further indicates that comparing children from two-parent and one-parent homes results in an oversimplification of a complex reality. Divorce is a process rather than a static event and should be viewed as such. Since, as Baydar (1988) suggests, researchers have failed to confirm large negative effects of divorce on children and concludes that divorce does not necessarily result in the deterioration of children's well-being, this process could be viewed as positive or neutral. In other words, pathological versions of the nuclear family as represented in the literature appear to be unfounded in light of the more methodologically sound research. The literature supports the notion that parental separation, in and of itself, is not a factor in emotional disorder. Rather, myriad variables may account for any children with problems in divorcing families. For example, the changes that children experience as a result of divorce may be the strongest predictive variable—change from a two-parent home to a one-parent home, change in the economic situation (usually a decrease), change in home location (perhaps a move from a house to an apartment), change in school, change in friends, to mention only a few. Conversely, many other variables may assist in creating well-adjusted children without problems, despite or because of the divorce process.

Most of the cases coming to the attention of the professional therapist involving children of divorce and their parents are those which have resulted in problems, and it is not our intention to minimize these problems. For many, adults and children alike, the divorcing process may be traumatic and seriously painful. However, situations in which children of single-parent households are doing well and perhaps thriving are not necessarily brought to light. As stated, in many school settings the child's family status is only discussed after a problem arises. However, as a review of the literature shows, it becomes seemingly more evident that family configuration effects are small and much less pervasive than frequently assumed. As therapists, we need to be aware of the current research findings that will assist us in examining our own biases and in so doing help us empower single-parent families.

Based on a thorough review of the literature and research on children of divorce, the following summary conclusions may be drawn and used as guidelines to assist therapists and their clients in the competent divorce.

1. *Nonstigmatization of the single-parent status and divorce:* The manner in which parents approach divorce affects the way they and children perceive the divorce. If people significant to them judge the single-parent home and the divorce process as a viable rather than a pathological situation, adults and children do better.

2. *Reduced parental conflict:* Parents who are able to reduce their marital conflicts and friction and who have a tendency to get along with each other without turmoil and aggression create better adjustment environments for their children.

3. *Family functioning:* Families that provide a sense of sharing and emotional support for one another in a loving manner have better adjusted children. Single-parent families who maintain family rituals around birthdays, holidays, etc., provide a sense of security for the children.

4. *Stable, loving relationship with both parents:* Children adjust better if they maintain consistent, predictable, positive relationships with both parents and have regular dependable visiting patterns.

5. *Appropriate role allocation:* Single-parent families who have assigned chores and roles appropriate to their children's abilities have better adjusted children.

6. *Effective parenting:* Effective parenting is defined as parents who have a good rapport with their children, provide for open communication within the family, have warm parent-child relationships in which discipline is stressed, and provide stable, predictable environments with clearly specified rules.

7. *Strong support systems:* Single-parent families do better if they have strong support systems, consisting of regular friendships with relatives, such as grandparents and peers.

8. *Nonadversarial divorce:* Single-parent families do better if they have a nonadversarial postdivorce adjustment and a friendly coparental relationship.

9. *Parent's own sense of well-being:* One of the most important predictors of children's postdivorce adjustment is the single parent's sense of well-being. If the single-parent mother/father has adjusted in a healthy way to the divorce, the children will also. This process can be facilitated through therapy and support structures.

10. *Economics:* Probably the most important factor involved in the adjustment of the single-parent family, corroborated by recent research, is adequate economics. If single parents have adequate money to support themselves and their families, many of the problems associated with divorce disappear. Given the current laws around child support and the associated problems with the percentage of reneging fathers, it is difficult to ascertain how this problem could be alleviated in the very near future.

Chapter 5

Redefining Relationships

Several of the most pertinent differences between the experiences of divorced versus widowed single parents were highlighted in Chapters 1 and 2. To work effectively with these clients, the therapist must employ his or her knowledge of these variations in the planning of interventions and strategies. As an extreme example, while the widowed are often counseled to visit the grave site as one means of finishing up business with the spouse, it would seem highly unlikely that the divorced would be directed to return to the courtroom where the divorce was granted.

This chapter's focus is one factor that widowed and divorced single parents share: before single parents can begin to redefine their relationships with family and friends, or to form new adult relationships, they must first come to terms with the loss of the spouse. Even while new roles and functions are assigned to the remaining family members, and even while the family struggles for emotional acceptance of its loss, the memories of what used to be persist.

The external reality of single parents is permanently altered: a one-time partner is absent; economic status generally changes; fewer people are available to complete requisite tasks, etc. Relationships with in-laws, with one's own family, and with coupled and single friends are all made different to the degree that they had previously been predicated upon the presence of the now-absent partner. The successful redefinition of these relationships is of central importance to the well-being of the single parent.

The memory of what used to be can create an alternative, subjectively held reality for some single parents. For these persons maintaining a relationship with the ghost of the absent partner can become a central therapy issue: living with ghosts while ignoring the living is not an adequate adjustment to an altered lifestyle. Redefining relationships with family and friends in the present becomes impossible for those who refuse to acknowledge the differences between then and now.

The maintenance of a past-oriented, subjective reality that is at odds with the external reality is normative to some degree. Every single parent's external definition is changed at a discrete moment in time—at the hour of the death or when the divorce decree is made final. Internal, subjectively held self-definitions take much longer to change, however, than do legal ones. These changes do not happen at a specific point in time, but are better understood in terms of the developmental processes outlined in the previous chapters. Because of this gap between the times when legal and psychological self-definitions change, it is to be expected that in some circumstances single parents will think, feel, and behave as if they are single; at other times their cognitive, affective, and behavioral responses will resemble those of coupled people. In most cases, over time, the two sets of self-definitions become reconciled and external and internal realities become congruent. Memories of what used to be either fade in importance or become fond recollections of an earlier time that is in no way confused with the present.

The clinical picture is different for those persons who, at the level of the unconscious, refuse to give up the ghosts of the past. For these single parents, the ghost makes impossible an adequate adjustment to life's real demands.

The following discussion concerning the redefinition of relationships after loss does not always differentiate between widowhood and divorce. The therapist is advised to apply his or her knowledge of these general principles to specific clients' situations.

The present authors do not agree with the position taken by many theorists (e.g., Pollock, 1975) that one of the reasons for studying loss reactions following death is that such study will inform the understanding of reactions to all forms of loss. Frantz (1984) writes,

> Coping and grieving are things we learn, we are taught, and we develop from the time we are infants. . . . By the time we are adults we've all had a lot of experiences with loss starting with the rattle in our own crib, up on through our baseball gloves, dolls, teddy bears, high school boy friend or girl friend, graduation from high school or college, moving away from friends, and grandparents dying. (p. 21)

The implication seems to be that a loss is a loss is a loss—regardless of whom or what was lost. We believe this to be true in only the most general way: all losses involve the breaking of an attachment bond (Bowlby, 1980). Not all bonds are equally strong; neither are all equally desirable. It seems reasonable, therefore, that loss reactions are moderated by these variables.

THE GHOST VERSUS REALITY:
STRESS REACTIONS

Mourning is the process through which the subjectively held internal reality of the single parent becomes aligned with external reality. The burden of change is upon the mourner. Parkes and Weiss (1983) write,

> Those who recover from bereavement do not return to being the same people they had been before their marriages or before their spouses' deaths. Nor do they forget the past and start a new life. Rather, they recognize that change has taken place, accept it, examine how their basic assumptions about themselves and their world must be changed and go on from there. (p. 81)

Most people do not give up the past as easily as this passage may imply. Perhaps the most thoroughly researched aspect of adult reactions to loss concerns its effects as a stressor.

In his review of the literature, Jacobson (1983) cites studies that report adverse health changes and increased mortality among the separated and divorced. Other works cited in this article independently report findings of increased anxiety, depression, resentfulness, anger, feelings of incompetence, suicidal ideation, death wishes, somatic complaints, weight loss, tiredness, difficulty concentrating, blaming others, increased rate of smoking and drinking, self-neglect, and sleepiness. After reviewing the literature, Parkes and Weiss (1983) conclude that a deterioration in health often follows loss, as does an increase in death rate. They do not speculate about how specifically bereavement influences death but, as a stressor, it seems likely that loss impacts significantly on the immune system.

The review by Hodges (1986) reports that the suicide rate for divorced men is three times greater than that for married men. Other stress-related outcomes include that risk of death by homicide is far greater for the divorced than the married; death rate by disease is much greater for the divorced; the widowed and divorced have higher age-adjusted death rates from all causes than for married people of equivalent age, sex, and race.

Evidence from the works of Wallerstein and Kelly (1980), Jacobson (1983), and Garfield (1982) agrees with the position taken in previous chapters that emotional resolution of the loss—and its concomitant stress reactions—take a number of years to complete. The ghost often does not leave gently.

THE GHOST VERSUS REALITY: RELATIONSHIP ISSUES

Some of the most powerful influences over behavior are covert rules that people cocreate to choreograph their interactions. Consider a fictional relationship between two adult couples with children. The tacit rule may be that when all four adults are together, it is allowable to complain about the behavior of children but not that of the spouses. When the two wives or the two husbands are alone, however, the rule may be changed to include talk of dissatisfaction within the marriage. While covert, the effects of rules such as these are enormous.

The process of renegotiating relationship rules following death or divorce can be a difficult one. Changes in rules about the relationships between the newly single parent and his or her family and friends must reflect the change in the marital relationship. At times it is the single parent and at other times it is the family or friends, but often it is both parties who refuse to renegotiate relationships based on a new reality.

Stacy's status changed from that of a young, happily married mother to that of a widow without warning. She and her husband, Bob, had been trying to conceive and deliver a child for several years. It had not been easy. As each was less than maximally fertile, the couple had become involved with a lengthy and trying medical regime in order to fulfill their dream of becoming parents. Two conceptions resulted in miscarriages. Although the losses of these unborn children stressed their marriage, the bond between Stacy and Bob remained strong. A third pregnancy resulted in the birth of the couple's son, Zach.

Stacy and Bob, both in their thirties, were very healthy and health-conscious people. With the exception of their fertility problems, the only real medical problem either had ever faced was Bob's childhood bout with asthma. He had been symptom free for decades.

One Sunday morning, when Zach was three months old, Bob complained of feeling run down. When his complaints continued through Wednesday, Stacy, a nurse, insisted that he see a physician. The couple visited the doctor together, and Bob was diagnosed as having a recurrence of his childhood ailment.

Returning home, Bob went to bed and asked that Stacy bring him some soup. While she was preparing the meal, she heard Bob call for her. As Zach and the soup both required her attention at that moment, she did not respond immediately to Bob's call. When she arrived at the bedroom, Bob was unconscious. She began CPR. He was dead in minutes. The doctor had missed the diagnosis—Bob's heart had been invaded by a virus.

Stacy entered therapy four months after Bob's death. She was angry and depressed and knew her reactions had to do with her loss. While her symptoms and the pain they caused were real, they were in no sense pathological. Stacy's relationship with Bob had been good. She could review it realistically. She neither idealized nor bastardized him. She had no psychological need to stay married to the ghost. She was progressing through the mourning process well, but oh, how it hurt!

RELATIONSHIP RULES

Anger is a common reaction shortly after loss, and Stacy's anger had a favorite target. Two of her married friends, in an effort to help, had made comments to the effect that they "knew what she was going through" as their husbands were so unhelpful in maintaining the household that they, also, "might as well be widowed." At times, Stacy hated these women.

"I used to think that Bob did nothing, too," Stacy stated, "until I had to do all the things I didn't realize he was doing."

One of the things Bob had done was enforce the rules governing the relationship between the couple and Zach's paternal grandparents. Even before the boy's birth, Bob's parents tended to intrude upon the couple's life. Their efforts to become more involved redoubled after the birth of their grandson.

In therapy, Stacy realized that one of the rules she and Bob had cocreated was that he would, when necessary, be as blunt and forceful as required to keep his parents at an appropriate psychological distance. This allowed Stacy to play the "nice guy" role with her in-laws while Bob became the target of his parents' anger over the ongoing situation.

After Bob's death, the rules had to be changed. Bob's parents would call daily and offer unsolicited advice to Stacy. If she chose to ignore their advice, they would become punitive. She arranged her incredibly busy schedule so that they could see Zach three or four times a week. The grandparents wanted more of the boy and would often drop in unannounced at inopportune times. Clearly, the "nice guy" role and the rules around the relationship between Stacy and her in-laws were not working. The status quo was causing her to become angry, agitated, and depressed.

Stacy was able to assume the role of adult with her in-laws and to assertively insist that they respect her boundaries. The changes were not easily accomplished, but they were put into effect. In adopting a new role and insisting on changes in the relationship rules, Stacy had essentially eliminated a significant source of stress from her life.

The success Stacy enjoyed in renegotiating with her in-laws derived from the fact that she dealt realistically with the demands of her current situation rather than behaving as if Bob were still alive. To be sure, her fantasy was to have her husband back. The unconscious wish for reunion is completely normal shortly after a loss. Stacy, however, was able to separate from the fantasy. This separation allowed her to function adaptively, with a new set of rules, in the present. Had she instead relied on the old rules and behaved as though Bob's ghost would continue to protect her from her in-laws, Stacy's growth would have been thwarted.

After several weeks of treatment, Stacy expressed one of her core beliefs: her husband did not have to die. Her widowhood and the burdens of single parenthood could and should have been avoided. She spoke with absolute conviction and with an intense anger that was directed at the attending physician. In her view, the doctor had misdiagnosed the condition. He had done an inadequate assessment of her husband's health status. He had been overfocussed on the history of asthma. He had ignored the subtle manifestations of viral infection. He had based treatment on the faulty diagnosis. He had been the proximal cause of the husband's death, her widowhood, and her son's loss of a father.

Stacy's words impacted her therapist at several levels. They had both diagnostic and prognostic meanings. Her anger was a predictable and biologically based response to her loss (Bowlby, 1980). The therapist would reassure her of this and, in so doing, help normalize her feelings. The realistic way in which she described the husband and the marital relationship indicated that Stacy's bereavement was not complicated by feelings of extreme ambivalence. The therapist would not, without much more inquiry, jump to the reductionistic conclusion that the anger directed at the physician was "really" meant for the husband. The unexpected and untimely nature of the loss suggested the possibility that Stacy may have been suffering from a post-traumatic stress reaction (Rynearson, 1987). The therapist would factor this into any assessment and intervention decisions. The creation of a story that "explained" her loss served to inoculate her against unrealistic fear of future losses and was indicative of her progress with the work of mourning. The therapist would make no effort, at this time at least, to have Stacy examine the validity of her version of the role played by the doctor. The therapist would, however, vigorously assist her in disputing any belief system that suggested the death of her husband had rendered her unable to cope with the demands of single parenthood (Beck et al., 1979; Meichenbaum, 1977; Mince, 1992; Rynearson, 1987).

At another level, meta to Stacy's individual story, her words reminded the therapist that an accurate and thorough assessment is as important for therapy clients as it is for medical patients. Thorough assessment is an ongoing and difficult process. The sorts of problems that therapists are asked to help clients deal with often have multiple and interacting causes (Krupp, Genovese, and Krupp, 1986).

Not all single parents are as successful as Stacy in redefining relationships. The case of Teresa and Fred illustrates a rather common therapy situation: the perpetual divorce.

PERPETUAL DIVORCE AND AMBIGUOUS LOSS

Although divorced for several years, Teresa and Fred managed to keep their dysfunctional relationship alive. Their refusal to give up their anger was manifested through endless unnecessary legal squabbles. Moreover, each was involved in overt attempts to convince their children that the other parent was "to blame."

The paradox is as common as it is interesting: the despised ex-spouse continues to be the person who has greatest control over the other's thoughts, feelings, and actions. The children of parents who are perpetually divorcing often manifest a problem. Typically, the children are brought to the therapist's office by the custodial parent who requests help with some behavioral or academic problem. Careful assessment in these cases often leads to the conclusion that the problem does not reside within the children, but rather within the unrenegotiated relationship between the ex-spouses.

In most cases of perpetual divorce, the ex-spouse is physically absent from the family but psychologically very much alive within it. Boss (1991) refers to the situation as ambiguous loss. When the ex-spouse is simultaneously both in and out of the family, confusion and conflict ensue. Boss labels this phenomenon boundary ambiguity and points out that its purpose is often the denial of loss. Anger and hostility can serve to keep the dysfunctional marital relationship intact to some degree: the relationship with the ghost renders adaptation in the present unattainable.

While boundary ambiguity often allows for the denial of permanent change in a former relationship, it is much more than an intrapsychic event. Very frequently, the ambiguity is maintained by a complex pattern of interactions among the former spouses, their children, families, and friends. The plot of this play impacts enormously on the thinking, behavior and feelings of all the actors involved.

Prior to the decision to divorce and during the divorce process, Fred could be described as emotionally distant from his children, acting out his sexual and angry impulses without regard to consequences, hostile, other-blaming, and without insight to his role in the disintegration of the marriage. Teresa, at this time, gave free rein to her hostility by openly attacking Fred in conversations with the children and limiting his access to them. When any of the children would manifest a caring or concerned attitude toward their father, Teresa would respond in a punitive fashion. She was as unaware of her contribution to the problem as Fred was.

After the divorce, and when each former spouse was temporarily removed from battling ghosts, both made remarkable strides. The details of their growth patterns were different. Fred chose to return to school and changed from an underpaid, underachieving, and unhappy worker to a competent and successful accountant. He was able to form stable, intimate relationships with his family and friends. His new relationships with women showed none of the sexual and angry acting-out behaviors that had characterized his relationship with Teresa. He became a caring father. Teresa, for her part, became highly responsive to her children's needs and was able to separate those needs from her own. Her professional life blossomed. Where before she was rather lax in her approach to her work, she now was a highly focused and successful attorney. Her relationships, too, were more mutually satisfying.

Common to the growth of both Teresa and Fred was a change in focus from blaming the former spouse to a realization that each was responsible for his or her own life.

As is often the case, however, the ghost has many reincarnations. Fred or Teresa would, it seems, take turns resurrecting the patterns of their problem-based relationship. They would, at these times, become consumed with "righteous" anger at the former spouse and would fire off a salvo, usually in the form of some legal maneuver. The salvo would initiate anger in the other, and soon the old relationship would be alive again: Fred angry and acting out; Teresa, enmeshed with the children, punitive and blaming.

Some instances of boundary ambiguity are characterized and complicated by not only the psychological presence of the former spouse but also by his or her physical presence as well. These cases are not to be confused with those successful divorces in which both adults have been able to separate their spousal and parental roles well and are available to each other in the task of raising the children. Rather the boundary ambiguities in question serve to maintain nonadaptive relationships that are emotionally alive but legally dead.

Katlin and Rob provide a most stark example of how some people refuse to live in the present. Their boundary ambiguity not only makes the establishment of new relationships difficult for them, as adults, but it also has made adjustment for their children impossible.

After fifteen years of marriage, the relationship between Rob and Katlin was dead, and each was aware of it. No longer friends and no longer lovers, neither found satisfaction in the other. For a number of years, however, they had tacitly decided to remain married in order to preserve a "normal" lifestyle for the children. The relationship rule was simple: each was expected and allowed to find personal and sexual intimacy with lovers; these affairs, however, were not to interfere with each partner's functioning as a parent.

For some time the rule seemed to work, although the children showed some relatively minor academic and behavioral problems. Dinner was a nightly family gathering; both parents attended PTA meetings, the girls' swim meets, and the boys' soccer games. Birthdays and holidays were celebrated. The extended family was unaware of the condition of the marriage.

When one of Katlin's affairs turned into a romance, the relationship rule was broken and, predictably, chaos ensued. Typical of the romantic love phase of a relationship, both Katlin and her lover idealized each other and conspired to be together as much as possible. As a result, Rob had to assume essentially all of the parental duties. He felt furious and cheated: it was not that Katlin had an affair. As a matter of fact, he continued his own affairs. It was that the facade of a happy, two-parent, functional family unit was exposed for what it truly was. The divorce settlement called for Rob to have sole physical custody of the children. A substantial cash settlement was awarded to Katlin, but there was no spousal support payments. Rob and the children were to reside in the marital home until the youngest completed college.

By the time the divorce was final, Katlin's romance had faded. Her financial need and Rob's need for someone to care for the children combined to allow the former spouses to exponentially compound the boundary ambiguity: Rob hired Katlin to babysit for the children. Once again, the children had two parents in the home. Once again, each adult led separate lives. And once again, the fact that each of the parents had "significant others" was kept hidden from the children.

It was almost predictable that the reestablishment of old relationship rules would eventually lead to a similar outcome. When next Katlin fell in love, she left the children and Rob without warning. The rule had been broken once more, and once more Katlin was cast as villain. The children were devastated: the mourning work was greatly complicated by having lost the same mother twice.

The case of Bill and Diane further illustrates boundary ambiguity:

In addition to whatever intrapsychic and interpersonal issues were at work, the boundary ambiguity around Bill and Diane's relationship was compounded by Diane's poverty. She entered treatment as a single parent who was having difficulty with her three children, aged nineteen, seventeen, and fifteen. The situation at home improved dramatically when Diane and her children began to allow each other the psychological space necessary for them to become mutually weaned from each other, which is the central developmental task for families with adolescents. When Bill reentered the family, however, the old patterns reemerged.

Bill and Diane had a twenty-two-year common-law marriage. After the birth of the children, Diane became financially dependent upon Bill. She used her welfare benefits to provide her family with a marginal existence, but she needed Bill's contribution to provide the children with a first-class private education. It was her goal that each of the three would be given the opportunity to graduate from college at her expense.

This dream was at odds with the reality of her life. Diane found Bill to be simultaneously withdrawing and overwhelming. When her dissatisfaction and anxiety concerning the relationship became unbearable, she would become overly focused and involved with the children. As the children grew older, they would rebel at Diane's overinvolvement. The anxiety decreased when Diane would throw Bill out of the house. The separations would last from a few weeks to half a year. Diane would at first reject Bill's pleas to come home. Over time, however, she would feel guilty about taking money from Bill and allow him to return. The process would begin anew. No true gains were made in therapy until the goal of eliminating the boundary ambiguity was attained.

As students of the intricate interplay and mutually influencing behavior among family members, systemic therapists and theorists have created a literature that abounds in examples of how some families endeavor to keep the ghost alive.

LOSS AND THE FAMILY

For example, it is to be expected that, at times, some single parents will become withdrawn and depressed as they go through the developmental process of renegotiating past relationships. Garfield (1982) describes the process as a complex set of biological and psychological reactions that often involve a withdrawal from life's normal activities. Theorists such as Bowlby (1980), Freud (1917), Parkes and Weiss (1983), Rando (1984), and Sanders (1989) include descriptions of developmentally appropriate withdrawal and depressive stages.

What may be developmentally appropriate for a single parent's individual growth may, however, spark abandonment fears in the children. In most cases, father is already gone, and a depressed and withdrawn mother may appear to be unavailable as well. Hoffman (1981) suggests that behavioral problems on the part of children may serve to "bring back" the attention of a depressed mother. Another example is provided by Fulmer (1983), who describes the enmeshment between a single mother and her adolescent son, as well as the mother's depression, in terms of the mother's inability to mourn the death of her parents and the loss of her marriage. It is clear from the literature that renegotiation of the relationship with the former spouse often impacts the ongoing and evolving relationships between the single parent and other significant persons.

As most relationships are best understood in terms of the dyadic, and at times triadic, interactions between and among people (Hoffman, 1981), an understanding of systemic factors is invaluable to the therapist in helping single parents renegotiate relationship rules with the important people in their lives. At times, however, a thorough knowledge of the individual's intrapsychic processes is required (Bowlby, 1980; Freud, 1917; Genovese, 1992; Krupp, Genovese, and Krupp, 1986; Rando, 1984). This is especially true of those single parents for whom the loss of the marital relationship recalls thoughts of those unresolved relationships that predate the marriage.

Many theoreticians (Bowen, 1978; Kaslow, 1981) have suggested that powerful, unconscious motives may underlie mate selection. Often a partner is selected based upon the unconscious wish for the reparation of old relationship wounds, or in an attempt to make the self whole through union with the other. Rynearson (1987) suggests that the marital relationship can have a large positive impact upon the self-concept of certain individuals. For these persons, distress during the early stages of the separation-individuation process (Mahler, Pine, and Bergman, 1975) has translated into a self-concept characterized by feelings of incompetence, dependency, and self-loathing.

The establishment and development of the attachment bond (Bowlby, 1980) forged between the couple serves to change the self-concept into a "we concept." The we concept can be in stark contrast to the self-concept: "I am incapable; we can do it." These individuals become dependent upon the marital relationship to ward off the ghosts of problem relationships from the family of origin.

Thus, the loss of the marital bond through death or divorce is a compounded one. Not only is the partner gone, but the positive we concept is also replaced by the negative self-image. In a sense, these individuals must learn first how to deal with, and then how to bury, two generations of ghosts.

Twenty-five-year-old Lynne adored her father, and he doted upon his little girl. She felt that her mother was distant and uncaring, but that her father could always make things right. She felt intensely jealous of her sister and competed with her for her father's love. The father, a gangster of sorts, was murdered when Lynne was five years old. She has been searching for him ever since.

During her early and middle adolescence, Lynne's depression, lack of self-esteem, and need for her father took a most self-destructive turn. She became sexually involved with a number of much older men, all of whom operated at the fringes of society. They introduced her to drugs and alcohol, and she became an abuser of these substances. One of these relationships resulted in an unplanned pregnancy. Lynne married her son's father but the marriage lasted only a short while. She divorced the man to be with Jack.

Five years ago, when she was twenty, Lynne fell in love with Jack. Her search for her father seemed completed. Jack, a mobster like her father, was also in his forties. Through the machinations of projective identification (Krupp, Genovese, and Krupp, 1986) and family projective process (Bowen, 1978), Lynne and Jack re-created her childhood. The relationship was "ideal" so long as Lynne played the incompetent, all-loving little girl and Jack the paternal hero.

As is often the case in relationships, what is desired in fantasy is unbearable in reality. Over time, Lynne began to feel stifled by her relationship with Jack. Her increasing need for autonomy from him resulted in relationship strain. Their frequent arguments were an angry negotiation for autonomy within the context of the relationship.

This battle in the here and now is complicated by the ghost of Lynne's father. When the psychological distance from Jack becomes too great, threatening the continuance of the bond, Lynne becomes panic stricken. She loses control, throws temper tantrums (as well as pots and pans), becomes insanely jealous, and loses interest in her children. She, in fact, becomes a child who needs her daddy's guidance. The patterns are reestablished.

ROLE OF THE PROFESSIONAL THERAPIST

Whatever the therapist's particular theoretical orientation may be, the establishment of an open, honest, caring, accepting, and empathetic relationship (Rogers, 1951; Minuchin, 1974) with the single parent is prerequisite if treatment is expected to result in growth.

To be empathic, however, is not to completely accept the client's view of his or her own reality. Much of society and many single parents themselves relate to single parenthood as if it were a diagnostic entity—a pathological state—which explains behavior, emotions, and cognitions. Teachers often attribute a child's poor academic performance to the fact that he or she is "from a broken home." Single parents often attribute their depression, anxiety, and anger to their single-parent status.

One important role of the professional therapist is to help the single parent dispute the validity of the assertion that single parenthood "causes" anything. To be sure, the loss of a marital partner is a pivotal event in one's life. To be sure, pivotal events are anxiety producing in that they demand changes must be made. However, the role of the therapist is to help the client reframe single parenthood from that of a toxic state which dictates the direction of one's life to that of a development phase in the individual's and the family's life cycle. As in all developmental phases, there are clear tasks to be accomplished.

Walsh and McGoldrick (1991) posit that the three primary tasks to be accomplished are the reorganization of the roles of the remaining members of the family in order to accomplish necessary tasks, the shared acknowledgment of the loss, and the reinvestment of energy into new relationships and activities. The therapist must help the client focus on the necessary family structural changes and to create an atmosphere where the single parent and children are free to openly express any and all feelings of loss, and are open to the possibility of new satisfactions.

The therapist must be aware that many of the most powerful behavior-directing relationship rules are covert and below the level of the client's consciousness. The therapist must help the client to make the covert overt.

The therapist serves an educational function when he or she is able to take what is known from theory (Bowlby, 1980; Parkes and Weiss, 1983) and apply it to the client's experience. In so doing, the therapist not only normalizes the single parent's experience but also provides a unifying theme for the many disparate and distressing manifestations of loss.

In adopting a developmental stance with regard to single parenthood, the therapist helps the client become aware of the possibility of new and satisfying relationships in the present and in the future.

In helping the client renegotiate old relationships and establish new ones, the therapist is aware of the dyadic nature of relationships. In taking this position, the therapist helps the client explore the renegotiation from a systemic as well as from an individual perspective. The therapist thus remains open to the possibility and desirability of joint sessions with the single parent and the children, or extended family members and friends.

The therapist is aware that the impact of the dissolution of the marital bond in the present may be exacerbated by whatever family-of-origin legacies the single parent brings to his or her own situation. Is divorce shameful? Does it represent failure? Is it an act of selfishness? Does the death of a spouse rekindle previous unresolved loss? The therapist helps the client understand these historical issues not only through insight-oriented therapy but also through sessions with the client's family of origin (Framo, 1992).

The therapist is aware that one very important effect of single parenthood often is a greatly reduced income (McLanahan, Garfinkel, and Ooms, 1987). He or she must be knowledgeable of the workings of social service agencies, school systems, etc., and must help the client negotiate any dealings with such organizations.

THERAPY STRATEGIES

While not all single parents who enter therapy need help adjusting to the loss of the marital partner, nearly all need to effect significant changes in the way their families work. The number of tasks that needs to be completed does not diminish after the family is transformed from a two-parent to a one-parent system. There are simply fewer hands available to accomplish what must be done. Remember Stacy:

> Working a full-time job, nurturing and tending to young Zach's needs, reestablishing and redefining her relationship with her in-laws, as well as gardening, painting the garage, taking out the trash, and doing the myriad other things that Bob used to do, Stacy's usual condition was one of near exhaustion.

What has to be done and who is responsible varies over the course of a family's life cycle (Carter and McGoldrick, 1988). The degree of family restructuring required following death or divorce is also a function of when it occurs in the family's history: the divorce of a married couple both sixty-five years of age with grown children requires less restructuring than the divorce of two forty-three-year-olds with adolescent children.

Very commonly in single-parent families, children must take on new roles and responsibilities at a younger age than do their peers who live in two-parent families. Their status is reflected in the nature and direction of flow of communication between the children and the single parent. These children are often consulted and have input into many decisions from when the dinner hour should be to where the family should vacation. To a greater degree than others their age, these children are more important to the family's functioning and have a greater amount of power in negotiating family decisions.

In and of itself, this is not a pathological situation. Rather, it represents an insightful and artful solution to a difficult problem. Taken to an extreme, however, this particular family structure can engender more anxiety and nonadaptive behavior than it solves.

The works of Minuchin (1974) and Minuchin and Fishman (1981) state that to function effectively, the boundaries between the generations and the structure of the power hierarchy must be clear to all family members.

The use of family maps (Minuchin and Fishman, 1981), a schematic which depicts the boundaries between the family's subsystems, its coalitions and alliances, and its power hierarchy, is a useful therapy tool. It not only provides an assessment of the family's structure but also suggests in-session maneuvers and between-session tasks designed to clarify boundaries and hierarchies.

Among the many structural moves described by Minuchin and Fishman are seating the family in groups based on age and having the children solve problems alone. For example, the therapist might suggest to the single parent that the children may be able to solve some problem—getting ready for school in the morning perhaps—as they may have insights not available to the adults. The adults observe as the children wrestle with the problem. Then, the single parent takes what is valuable from the children's solution and modifies it from the adult perspective. This strategy strengthens generational boundaries and reinforces the single parent's position at the apex of the power hierarchy. The therapist may also employ Madanes'(1991) technique of blocking any parent-talk or children-talk that implies that the children have either parity or superiority in making family decisions.

Sherman and Fredman (1986) list many structural moves designed to reinforce generational boundaries. Important for the single parent are those aimed at ensuring the privacy of the parent and the children, and those enabling the parent to enjoy activities unrelated to the children.

Herz Brown (1988) makes an observation that can be of great value to the therapist. Adolescents in single-parent families are often more closely tied to the family than are their age peers. Again, this is a function of the increased responsibility these young people have for the functioning of the family. The primary developmental task at this point in the life cycle—the mutual weaning of parent and children—can be made more difficult because of the structure of single-parent families. It is as if the adolescent's developmental needs are in conflict with the family's need for cohesion. Often, the usual rebellion and extrafamilial focus employed to effect adolescent-parent weaning are unavailable. The therapist must strive to make these processes overt.

Restructuring techniques can also be useful in the renegotiation of relationships between the single parent and various members of the extended family and friends. The therapist must be open to the use of joint sessions, however, if the restructuring is to be most effective.

The therapy goal is the formation of clear boundaries and power parity among adult peers. Renegotiation to peerhood with the single parent's own parents may be met with resistance: often the relationship rules between parents and adult children disallow peerhood. The use of tracking, a sort of multiperson functional analysis of repetitive behavioral sequences described in detail by Sherman and Fredman (1986), is a highly effective technique of making overt the covert relationship rules which govern interactions and define relationships. Tracking can be used in any joint sessions regardless of whom is in attendance.

Delving into the family legacies with regard to death and divorce can be accomplished in joint sessions with the single parent and his or her own parents. Such inquiry is made easier if the genogram—an extended family tree—is employed. The use of the genogram is explained fully by Carter and McGoldrick (1988).

One of the primary goals in working individually with single parents is to change their stance from passive pawns to active problem solvers. The adoption by the therapist of a developmental view of single parenthood aids in this conceptual shift. The cognitive restructuring techniques of Ellis's (1962) rational emotive therapy are well suited to attack irrationally held beliefs about powerlessness in changing nonadaptive behavior patterns. These same techniques are useful in undermining any beliefs which suggest that the single parent, children, former spouse, former spouse's ghost, members of the extended family, friends, co-workers, or new partners must, should, or have to behave in some specified way for the single parent to feel well and happy.

The cognitive techniques of Beck and colleagues (1979) can be employed in dealing with any depression brought about by the loss of the marital partner, as can inquiry into the nature of the ambivalence in the relationship with the former spouse (Krupp, Genovese, and Krupp, 1986). Normalizing the negative aspect of the ambivalence can bring relief to inappropriate guilt feelings around the relationship with the former spouse.

The goal of having the single parent reinvest in new relationships and activities can be made difficult by the stress produced in meeting new people. In instances such as these, Meichenbaum's (1977) stress inoculation procedure can be employed. The first phase of this treatment is to convince the single parent that much anxiety is generated not by the situation per se but by the client's interpretation of the situation and the nature of the internal dialogue generated by that interpretation. In the second step, the single parent practices stress-reducing dialogue in the therapist's office. Anxiety generated by an imagined social situation is labeled as a result of nonadaptive internal dialogue and is used to signal more adaptive self-talk. In the final phase, the single parent creates situations that allow for practice in vivo.

To address the problem of boundary ambiguity Sherman, Oresky, and Rountree (1992) offer the empty-chair technique, which they refer to as a real "ghostbuster." In this procedure, family members would speak to an empty chair as if the missing spouse were there. They take turns role-playing responses likely to have come from the person represented by the chair. The technique serves to diminish the incongruity between psychological presence and physical absence. It serves further to externalize the problem. Once externalized, each family member can be helped to explore his or her relationship with the "problem" (White and Epston, 1990; Epston and White, 1990).

For those single-parent families who need help dealing with the ghost of past relationships, McGoldrick (1992) places great emphasis on the open flow of information among family members. In the relationship review technique, each member tells the story of his or her own relationship with the former spouse. The review begins with each individual's first memory of the relationship. Ghost-related issues are often highlighted by an unrealistic view of the person—the former spouse is often seen either as an angel or a demon. The open expression of these misrepresentations allows other family members to serve as reality checks for each other and to dispute irrational beliefs. The authors also suggest that asking the family very specific questions concerning the details surrounding the loss will serve to open up the system. In the case of the death of a parent, visits to the cemetery, writing letters to the deceased, making picture albums, and keeping a journal of memories and feelings are also suggested.

Rynearson's (1987) work suggests that the choice of intervention employed with single parents should be predicated upon the type of loss involved. In cases of untimely or unexpected loss, he suggests the use of posttraumatic shock techniques. Weiss (1975), Wallerstein and Kelly (1980), and Peck and Manocherian (1988) all refer to the differences between the reactions of the spouse who makes the decision to divorce and those of the one who has been left. Perhaps, in working with single parents who were left, therapists might also at times employ posttraumatic shock procedures. In cases where the single parent had a highly dependent relationship with the former spouse, Rynearson (1987) suggests the use of cognitive restructuring techniques to attack any self-images characterized by feelings of weakness and incompetence. Rynearson believes insight-oriented psychodynamic therapy to be the treatment of choice in dealing with single parents whose previous relationship was highly conflicted. The therapist should strive to ensure that the client gain insight into his or her own contribution to the dysfunctional relationship.

Parkes and Weiss (1983) separate the process of recovery from loss into three phases. The goal of the first is intellectual recognition. During this phase, the therapist helps the single parent to formulate a story that settles the question of why the loss occurred. Without such an account, the ability to reinvest in new relationships is diminished. If people do not know why they have suffered a painful loss they will be loath to form new attachment bonds which may again, for no reason, be taken from them.

The goal of the second phase is emotional acceptance. Operationally, emotional acceptance implies a diminished fear of being overwhelmed by grief, pain, or remorse. Part of the recovery process involves working through what Parkes and Weiss (1983) refer to as the obsessive review: the painful and time-consuming task of dealing with each and every trace memory of the former relationship, grieving over it, and ultimately neutralizing it. No change in the content of the review is contraindicative of growth.

In the third phase, identity transformation, the single parent creates new self-definitions that are not predicated on the previous relationship. While a single parent may sound wistful when he or she reports, "I don't feel married anymore," the therapist sees the meaning behind the words: the ghost has been put to rest.

PART II:
SEXUAL EXPERIENCES OF THOSE
WHO ARE SINGLE AGAIN

Chapter 6

Relational and Sexual Considerations After Divorce

ISSUES IN SEXUALITY

Few human activities have as many facets as sex. Sex can be the height of sharing and the extreme of selfishness. It can be animalistic and a spiritual experience. Honorable and despicable, tender and brutal—the attributes of human sexualities go on and on. But, most of all, sex can be many things at once.

Sex is one of the human activities that has kept moralists, philosophers, politicians, and poets busy for centuries. The opinions about sex waver, the meanings change, the values shift, but sex remains. It is as if the gods have imposed this burden on humans: the puzzle of something so familiar, so much part of themselves. "We may think it merely the crowning of bodily urges," wrote Jan Morris (1989), "but it is also an intimation of the divine." We still struggle with the puzzle: sex is at the cutting edge of flesh and spirit. The puzzle will never be resolved because, as Morris also explains, "If evolution decreed that sex must be a pleasure to ensure the continuity of the species, a higher will conceived it more sacramentally, and its ultimate delight is nothing else that a glimpse of that final unity, the infinite."

The puzzle of sex is especially troublesome to the growing number in our society who become "sexually single again" through divorce and widowhood. Perhaps it was always so for the widowed. But in a culture that gives lip service at least to the goodness of sex, it becomes now doubly difficult to deal with it, given the presence of the HIV/AIDS. Mary is a case in point.

She had just turned fifty when the separation shock took place. Her husband had left her for a younger woman—again! They had been separated two times before for the same reason. So this was the end and they obtained a divorce a year after the separation. At first Mary's rage consumed her. From morning to night she was angry, furious. "What's a woman at my age going to do? Where will I find a partner? Not that I want one now. But I don't want to be alone either." Her two children were teenagers on the way to adulthood. They had adjusted, and their father was providing for their financial needs. Mary, however, could not survive on the court-mandated money he sent her every other week. So, she went back to teaching, the career she had left eighteen years earlier. It was tough to get up before dawn every day, to fight traffic for a whole hour, to face the unmotivated and undisciplined students, to come back home again in the middle of heavy traffic, exhausted, only to take care of the house chores, watch some television, and go to bed early, just to start the same routine all over again the next day. And it was lonely. Her life had changed. Her neighbors, friends—the ones that were left after the divorce—even relatives treated her differently. It was very lonely. But all this happened more than two years ago.

Now Joe had started to show an interest in her. Mary liked him too, but she felt so insecure, so full of doubts. She couldn't believe it. The fear of being hurt was very real and the whole sexual side of the situation scared her silly. That was the real problem—sex. Nothing had happened yet, but Mary felt so uncomfortable and self-conscious. She felt inadequate, full of questions, childish. Yes, that was it—she felt like a young teenager! She had never been sexually involved with any other person besides her husband. Now the mere thought of sex with Joe reopened areas of sensitivity from her marriage. In spite of all of this, she knew that she wanted physical closeness with Joe. But how would he react if she agreed to it? All the old prejudices were still there. And she had thought she was grown up, finally! The thoughts kept coming. *All a man wants is sex. Once he gets it, forget it.* Would he then lose interest in her? Will he think less of her? And what about infection? The word infuriated her, but it kept sticking to her brain. Joe had been widowed for more than six years and had no children. He was religious and had traditional and rather conservative values; she knew that. But who knows for sure? Infection! If he had been sexually involved, maybe even with a prostitute . . . She felt ashamed of her own thoughts. She was getting angry at herself. This whole thing was becoming so complicated and stressful.

For months Mary felt like a fool every time physical closeness was a possibility. She and Joe got along very well, enjoyed each other's company, and had similar tastes and interests. He was attentive to her, considerate, and cheerful, while also secure in himself without having to impress her in any way. Joe also got along well with Mary's children. All in all, she really liked him, but she started to dread the moments of intimacy. In five months they had not yet been completely naked in each other's presence, let alone had sexual intercourse. One day, on a weekend when they had planned to stay in his house while her children were both out of town visiting friends, they had come home from a wonderful evening: theater, dinner, a relaxed stroll on a glorious autumn night in Manhattan. Neither was really tired when they finally got home. Mary was happy and grateful for the evening. She hugged him tenderly and he responded in kind. The sexual stirring was instantaneous. Their caresses became more intimate. She followed the flow of passion while he undressed her, and she undressed him on the way to his bedroom. But all of a sudden, with the same unexpected speed that her sexuality had been kindled a few moments before, she panicked. She just froze and started to cry, begging him to stop. The next day, after a rather quiet breakfast, she returned home, as they had planned. But he changed toward her from that day on. He was friendly and polite but never invited her out again and the relationship came to a gradual and uneventful end.

Mary's case is not unique. She was not more "abnormal" or pathological than any other woman in her circumstances. In other chapters we discuss men also, since what happened to Mary happens to many men too. To be sexually single again brings about many real problems in adults who otherwise handle their lives very adequately. In the area of intimacy, those who are sexually single again often are surprised to experience a form of emotional regression, as Mary did: a conflict of feelings they have not had since adolescence.

The sexually single again, like Mary, need a great deal of information, reassurance, and guidance. They have to be clear about their own sexuality; they need to know concrete facts about this new and unexpected chapter in their lives. They need especially clear knowledge about HIV/AIDS from the very practical point of view of sexual conduct. Because of this, this chapter is mainly informational. We cannot afford not to know about sexuality in the age of AIDS. Whether we like it or not, ignorance can literally kill us.

However, human sexuality cannot be dealt with in the abstract or as a set of rules to follow, as the story of Mary and Joe shows. We write of human beings with their questions and doubts, with their suffering, hopes, and dreams, with their fears, joys, disappointments, pettiness, and heroisms. We write about life being threatened as never before by a mysterious virus, besides the threat to life and happiness that humans are wont to impose on themselves by their prejudices and by the mental tricks they play on themselves, as we suggest later in this chapter.

Sex in itself—the act—is interesting acrobatics: a smooth fitting of parts marvelously engineered for each other. But sex, beyond the pleasures of the flesh, involves emotions, meaning systems, and the spirituality. Most humans, at least in Western culture, do not just copulate. They make love. We express feelings through our bodily interaction. Our attraction for each other, our need, desire, emotion, love, and passion are all expressed through our fingers, lips, tongue, skin, mucosa, orifices, and genitalia. Communion of the flesh reflects communion of the spirit. This mingling of flesh and spirit is what makes sex so complicated. Our own culture has been obsessed with sex for a long time. The obsession appears in the form of the multimillion-dollar pornography industry and of the moral/religious watchdogs. It is either sex without spirit or sex without playfulness and fun: the rootless, dehumanized, pornographer caught up in the mechanics of sex, or the joyless, dehumanized, fanatic concerned with the "sinfulness" of sex. Both miss the true complexity of human sexuality and both are equally deficient.

We are keenly aware of the delicate balance of sex between flesh and spirit. Neither beasts nor angels, we humans have to strike a unique compromise, oppositional to the pornographer and to the watchdog alike. Because sex is neither beneath nor above human nature, it is a constant challenge. The issue is not "to sex or not to sex." The issue is not to miss the joy and enrichment of human sexuality. In this respect, we subscribe to what can be called the principle of autonomy: *Anything sexual is acceptable among consenting adults which is not harmful to them or to third parties either physically or emotionally.*

A consequence of the autonomy principle at this point in history is that sexual activities that before were considered normal, such as copulation, might be harmful if one party is infected with the AIDS virus. Similarly, other sexual activities that in previous times might have been considered "less than normal," for example, sexual arousal without copulation, might now be acceptable due to the AIDS epidemic.

One issue we have not dealt with specifically is that of voluntary sexual abstention. "For myself," said Jan Morris (1989) in her colorful way, "I find [sex] more moving, on the whole, without the bodily functions at all—for the gods have so arranged things that the symbolism of sex can be exerted without the practicalities." This sentence touches on the mystery of sexual beings who renounce the sexual function. From time immemorial, sexual abstinence, at least temporary, has been valued for its spiritual enrichment, especially in religious contexts. This is the "symbolism of sex," just mentioned: the feeling of closeness and intimacy, of union, love, self-giving, without the bodily functions. It is what Andre Guidon (1977) calls "celibate fecundity." The concept of fecundity implies that to be fully human, people do not necessarily have to exercise their biological sexuality but always *must* be loving beings. Because, as Guidon states, "the radical meaning of human sexuality is to create loving bonds," as opposed to nonhuman sexuality, whose basic meaning is procreative. That celibacy, like fasting, can be salubrious is not difficult to see if it is a temporary condition. Buddhist and Christian monks, among the best-known cases, have recognized its advantages. The difficulty—practical, philosophical, and physiological—comes when this state of sexual abstention is made permanent. In our research for writing this chapter we found many people in the sexually single again category who had welcomed celibacy as a period of self-reevaluation and reflection which actually strengthened their sexual nature. Their solitude became an experience of being alone, at peace with themselves, in touch with the mystery of their existence in the world. "[One] who fears to be alone," said the American Trappist monk Thomas Merton, "will never be anything but lonely, no matter how much he may surround himself with people." He added that it is in solitude, "that the deepest activities begin. It is here that you discover act without motion, labor that is profound repose, vision in obscurity, and, beyond all desire, a fulfillment whose limits extend to infinity" (p. 40). Or as Dag Hammarskjold (1966) put it, "your loneliness may spur you into finding something to live for, great enough to die for." Rollo May (1975) adds that without solitude modern persons, constantly bombard by television, radio and internet activities, are deprived in finding those insightful breakthroughs that come from the depths of the unconscious.

Les, whose wife fell in love with a woman friend and left him with the children in order to live with her, confirms these sentiments. He told one of us, "Her lesbianism came as a total surprise to me. After twelve years of marriage and three children, with all that we had gone through together, I was convinced that I knew Ellen. Her decision crushed me. I thought I was less of a man because . . . I don't know why. Fortunately, my sister was able to help me out with the children. She had always been a second mother to them, especially since her only child died of leukemia. She lives only one block away. The kids love her and do not mind spending more time at her house. She also spends much time at our house with them.

"During the first three or four months after Ellen left me, I was in a state of shock, as I said before. Work was my only medicine. I'd put seventy to ninety hours in a week. Then I 'retaliated': went out with, went to bed with, sought out any available woman for about six or seven months. But after that, the futility of the sexual conquests hit me. I stopped dating altogether. For about a year I became celibate. Didn't even think about sex much. I reflected a lot, I read, I listened to music, I visited museums, I took long walks in the woods. I enjoyed doing all this alone. I looked forward to my moments of solitude.

That year without women—without sex—is one of the most enriching experiences I've ever had. By the end of 1986—two years and three months after Ellen took off—we divorced and I felt that I had been reborn. I attribute this sense of freedom to my year of solitude and celibacy. I was ready to start again and was very lucky to meet Sally, my present wife of almost two years. One thing I want to emphasize is that I found myself gravitating toward this solitude and lack of sex. I hadn't planned on, it but it started to feel right when I got into it. And really, it was very good for me. I would recommend it."

Many people who become sexually single again report experiences similar to Les's. Two points are interesting to note. The first is that their choice of celibacy is always voluntary, out of the felt need to be in touch with themselves and reach a higher level of honesty and genuineness. The second point to remark is that all these people evaluate their period of sexual abstention very positively: it helped them settle down and make a satisfying commitment to another person. Only one of the subjects, married two years and without children, whose wife had died of cancer, moved on to prolonged celibacy by becoming a Roman Catholic priest.

It is beyond the scope of this book to deal with permanent celibacy. Guidon (1977) offers one of the best modern treatments of this complicated topic, and to him we refer our readers. However, one area of sexuality needs to be mentioned in this chapter. This is the cognitive component of human sex (Araoz, 1982).

Thought and imagination—cognitive processes—make human actions different from those of other animals on this planet. Thought and imagination make art possible, one of the activities which distinguishes us and makes us unique among all other living things. Art is the creative expression of human imagination: it transforms nature, either in what's called artistic expression or through technology, another type of artistic expression. The transformation of nature is especially true of sex. In humans the predictable stages of animals leading to copulation become highly sophisticated. Thought and imagination transform sex, and sex becomes art. The evidence is overwhelming, from the few erotic engravings of the Stone Age (see Tannahill, 1980) to the delicate sexual portrayals on Egyptian and Greek plates, vases, and murals. Sex is depicted as varied, playful, and far from predictable and monotonous. From the explicit sexual scenes preserved on artifacts from pre-Columbian South and Central America or the Middle East, India, China, and Japan to our twenty-first century erotic art in paintings, much more than mere instinct, makes human sex always new.

Studying those who became sexually single again, we realized the important role of cognitive factors in sexual behavior. What we think about sex either enhances or damages our sexuality. What people think and believe about their bodies, their physical needs, pleasure, sensuality, their own attractiveness, and their self-esteem makes a significant difference in how they act sexually. In therapy with these people, we found ourselves often helping them question their cognitions in these areas. By this process of self-questioning, people come to realize that many of their beliefs about sex are purely cultural and have changed in different societies at different points in history. This realization frequently helps people to become more tolerant and more understanding of differences. The sociocultural beliefs people accept serve to establish a common meaning system from which structure and behavioral scripts flow. Since all human beings are culture bound, these injunctions serve a positive function not to be dismissed lightly. However, they may also restrict and inhibit freedom of action and choice and often confuse what is "natural" with what is cultural. For example, in our own lifetime, homosexuality has been considered right and wrong sexually, not based on nature but on culture. For example, time has seen the conventional meanings surrounding homosexuality shift from medical illness to social deviance to psychological disorder. Clinically, a review of the past revisions of the *Diagnostic and Statistical Manual of Mental Disorders,* presents a telling time line. A full inclusion of homosexuality appeared in DSM-II (APA, 1968), to partial inclusion as ego-dystonic homosexuality in DSM-III (APA, 1980), to full expulsion in DSM-III-R (APA, 1987), DSM IV (APA, 1994), DSM IV-TR (APA, 2000) to recent biological explanations, possibly producing efforts to reincorporate homosexuality into future DSMs (Kirk and Kutchins, 1992). In the past two decades, many in the United States have come to recognize the diversity in sexual orientation. Media outlets no longer shy away from homosexuality, they embrace it. Paradoxically, full adaptation of this belief (diversity) to social, political, legal, and economic policy (e.g., the ongoing legal debate surrounding gay marriage) lags considerably behind.

Prostitution is another area of much confusion. Is it against the nature of humans, or is it a cultural taboo? Historically, prostitution has existed quite universally since time immemorial, which leads us to believe that it fulfills some important role for humans. However, we in the United States officially refuse to accept prostitution, except for a few notable exceptions, depriving it from the controls which would give protection to children and other nonconsenting adults from exploitation. By ignoring prostitution we neglect the rights of innocent persons. We also allow the continued spread of venereal disease at a crucial epidemiological time, endangering the health of the general population. Finally, by not accepting it, we miss out on the government revenues that regulating this sexual activity would bring. Society embarks on a negative course of action in proclaiming prostitution to be wrong. Our attitudes about prostitution are socially created. Is it wrong in itself or do our beliefs about it make it wrong? This is another example of one of the many sexual activities which becomes what our cognitions make it to be. Other sexual behaviors that are given ethical value by social and psychological meaning systems are, for instance, oral sex, anal sex, polygamy, and active forms of sex education for adolescents, to name just a few.

Moving away from sociosexual issues, we stress the positive side of cognitions in individual sexual behavior. When people start questioning and challenging their own belief systems and convictions, they find a new freedom—not necessarily to act differently but to accept and respect other forms of sexual behavior. Prejudice is difficult to change. When it comes to sex, it is usually a "prejudgement" that comes from childhood and has been accepted without examination or criticism. For instance, more than a few of the sexually single again have self-conflicts about masturbation. In therapy, we never encourage people to act one way or another. We do help them examine the benefits and harm they experience in their activity. We found that most people who have difficulty about masturbation allow the old unexamined injunction of childhood against it to continue to be operative. When they explore it in therapy and evaluate masturbation as adults, they begin to question the prejudice that they took for granted as being the truth. People can be forced to change their behavior by forceful means and violence, but when they change themselves willingly, a cognitive restructuring has always preceded the external—behavioral—change. However, this cognitive change may not be conscious or necessarily based on objective truth. For example, the recovering drug addict who "believes" that he or she cannot live without the drug and gives into again has made a behavioral change stemming from a false belief. The cognitive change leads him or her to discontinue the recovery program and return to the drug. Consciously the individual believes that he or she cannot do otherwise. What the person does not know is that he or she is being self-deceiving and giving up the opportunity to recover and lead a more fulfilling life (Araoz, 1982).

One of our clients, Olaf, experienced that cognitive-behavioral change regarding masturbation.

As a child, Olaf had been severely punished for "touching himself." This behavior had so effectively inhibited him that he never masturbated during adolescence. Then he got married. Sexual intercourse was frequent during the marriage and so he did not masturbate in sixteen years of marriage either. After his divorce, not being able to establish a steady sexual relationship with a woman and tired of the complications of "touch-and-go sex," as he called it, as well as the health dangers of paid sex, he "found (himself) using morning erections to masturbate in a half-sleep state," as he put it, feeling very guilty and ashamed of himself. However, Olaf had the courage to question and examine his beliefs about masturbation and to change his cognitions. From then on he was able to enjoy this activity without giving it undue importance. Eventually he found a steady partner. He told us, about a year later, that he still enjoyed, without any guilt, occasional "self-pleasuring," as he now called masturbation.

In sexual behavior the cognitive elements are always at work. W. I. Thomas (1993) said that if we believe something is real, it is real in its consequences. What we believe becomes real for us. Because this is so, we encourage people who have difficulties with their new sexual status after having become single again to

1. become aware of their hidden sexual beliefs,
2. question and examine them (since they might be creating the problem),
3. change perceptions and beliefs accordingly, and
4. change their behavior, if change is in accordance with their adult self-interest.

The general principal is that positive thoughts stop negative ones while negative thoughts, on the other hand, crowd out positive ones (Araoz, 1982). This, when specifically applied to sex, improves the situation greatly. For those who have become sexually single again, learning to use their thoughts for their own benefit, not against themselves, gives them a new sense of inner liberation and of being in control of their lives. The cognitive elements in human sexuality can never be ignored and especially should not be ignored when a person has become sexually single again.

Sex is a complicated aspect of human existence because it is right there on the very thin border between body and soul. It, like a Greek tragedy, is an eternal puzzle that keeps humans humble in the recognition of their lack of satisfying answers in such a basic area of living. But we humans have been given the marvelous gift of imagination. We use it as a tool to enjoy sex more and thus to live richer and happier lives, whether we are sexually single again or not.

SEXUALLY SINGLE AGAIN

Interestingly enough, our thorough review of the literature with regard to sexual practices of the single parent (or sexual practices of the American people in general) failed to show current methodologically sound studies. Several current studies on human sexuality exist; however, they suffer from severe methodological difficulties, such as restricted geographic location or population, poor response rate, or nonrandom or nonrepresentative sampling. Further investigation proved interesting in that researchers of sexual conduct found the same problem when they looked to current research on sexuality in order to predict the spread of HIV in the American public. Not knowing the sexual practices of the American people presented an inability to predict how quickly the disease would spread or into which population. To date, the Kinsey et al. (1948, 1953) studies are the best that are available. For a description of the methodological flaws in the available studies on human sexuality or the problems with sex research in general, see Atwood (1981).

In any case, making the transition from constructed marital definitions of oneself as a sexual person to postmarital constructions about sexual relationships often presents challenges to divorced individuals. Along with these challenges, the newly divorced person may also experience considerable ambivalence about sexuality in general, as well as fears of intimacy. Feelings of anger, rejection, or fear remaining from the problems of the divorcing process may inhibit the sexual desire of some persons, preventing them initially from reentering intimate relationships. Some individuals, to protect themselves from emotional vulnerability, may withdraw completely from potential sexual relationships. Others may react by seeking numerous superficial sexual encounters. The next section examines available sexual outlets and the reported sexual behavior of those individuals who are sexually single again.

SEXUAL OUTLETS

For separated and divorced men and women, four main outlets of sexual behavior appear to be most employed. These outlets are not mutually exclusive and at any given time any individual may choose one or more of them.

Sexual Interaction with the Ex-Spouse

It is not unusual for separated or divorced couples to engage in sexual relations with their former partners. Individuals may be reluctant to discuss or report this behavior in therapy because in many states it is legally defined as "contamination" and may hinder or deem null and void the legal process of the divorce. However, individuals in clinical settings often report engaging in intercourse with their divorcing or former spouse. Usually it occurs while they are in the midst of the divorcing process and typically discontinues once one of the individuals begins dating. However, when it does occur, many individuals report feeling confused as to what it means. Some people may feel that it must mean that there is "hope" for the marriage. In other words, it may rekindle feelings of care or attraction for the former spouse. For others, it may reinforce feelings of having made the right decision to separate. Having sex with an ex-spouse typically serves to complicate the divorcing process and is frequently a cause of concern for the participating individuals. Mia typifies this situation.

Mia was a thirty-four-year-old bakery manager. She had been a single parent for about three years and was having a hard time coping with her children and her single life in general. The main reason Mia gave for the divorce was infidelity on the part of her husband, Roy, who was having an affair with his co-worker. After the divorce, Mia, feeling lonely on several occasions, had sex with Roy. While she enjoyed the sexual release and the emotional comfort, afterward she often felt guilty. It always made her think about the good times in their marriage and she would then spend weeks questioning her decision to divorce. Though Mia stated that at other times, under the best of circumstances, the marriage was unfulfilling to her. After these sexual encounters with Roy, she usually felt ambiguous about her decision.

Mia was an attractive woman and began dating shortly after the divorce. This also created many problems for her because, on one hand, she enjoyed sex and often wanted to sleep with the man she was seeing. On the other hand, she felt that it would serve only to confuse her children. At times she would allow a boyfriend to sleep over, but only if he promised to leave by four o'clock in the morning. She believed the children would not know the person had slept over. In these cases, she would then worry about whether the neighbors had seen the man leaving the house. If she slept at a boyfriend's house, she felt she had to be home by four in the morning so that her boys and the babysitter would not know she had been out all night.

Aside from trying to arrange the logistics of sex, Mia also had many mixed feelings about it. Raised in an upper-middle-class home where she was taught that "nice" women had sex only with their husbands, she often said she felt torn between her intellectual self and her emotional self. Although her intellectual self felt that standards of sexual behavior had changed since she was a girl, her emotional self felt guilty every time she had sex with anyone other than her ex-husband. Aside from these emotions, Mia also did not know how to respond to the men she was dating. She often asked questions regarding what was appropriate sexual behavior for a woman in her status. She was unsure of the part sexuality played in her new role as a single parent. It was at this point that Mia came for therapy.

Masturbation

Masturbation is another outlet of sexual behavior used by separated and divorced individuals. While masturbation is more commonly reported by men, women also report engaging in it (Kinsey et al., 1948, 1953; Atwood and Gagnon, 1987). Divorced women also report having erotic dreams that result in orgasm (Kinsey et al., 1953). It is probably true that no other sexual behavior elicits as much guilt as masturbation; yet we know from Kinsey et al. that the majority of people do engage in masturbatory activity at some point during their lives. If individuals feel guilty about masturbating, it is important for them to obtain accurate information regarding the widespread use of the activity as a sexual outlet and to explore some of the underlying motivational reasons for their guilt. Most therapists believe that masturbation is a legitimate form of sexual expression but for those who have emotional reactions around this behavior, a motivational self-exploration would also be useful. It is helpful for some people to prioritize their sexual outlets and options. For some, developing autoerotic patterns of sexual expression can help them to define themselves as being sexually independent. For others, it can be avoidance behavior surrounding a fear of intimacy.

Dorothy, a very attractive blonde accountant, entered therapy because she felt she was obsessing on depressing thoughts. Recently divorced, she lived alone with her thirteen-year-old son. She was preoccupied with his life, at times being intrusive (as defined by him). For example, she would clean out his bedroom drawers once a week, allowing him little privacy. She increasingly became more and more focused on his diet, worrying that everything he ate had some kind of unhealthy chemical in it. She had many friends and was quite outgoing and gregarious. Yet she seemed to have ambivalent feelings about dating. On one hand, she spoke of her desire to date, reporting that she felt sexually deprived. She had many opportunities to date because she worked in a large corporation where many men were available. On the other hand, every time she was approached, she rejected the person.

After exploring the nature of her fears in therapy, she stated that while she seemed to want to date she was really afraid of men. She reported that every time she came in contact with a man, she felt nervous, shaky, and afraid. Her father had been a stern, controlling force in her life, leaving her with the impression that all men were dominant and controlling.

As far as her sexual needs, she masturbated frequently, stating she had no reason to go out on a date or to become sexually active because she had her "trusty vibrator."

In this case, Dorothy was avoiding sexual contact out of a fear of men, which then became the focus of therapy.

Short-Term Partners

For many divorced men and women, dating several partners is crucial because it affirms their sense of attractiveness to the opposite sex. In these cases, individuals typically engage in short-term, uncommitted sexual encounters and relationships. Ultimately, most individuals report that they would prefer to be in a long-term relationship and that sex with many partners feels shallow. This type of sexuality is more frequently practiced by men than by women. Women tend to prefer sexuality within the context of a relationship, having the ultimate goal of establishing a new long-term intimate union. Generally, individuals report that they feel guilty when they engage in what they define as meaningless sexual activity. In such cases, it would be useful for them to deal with their feelings, attempt to set boundaries around their behavior, and mobilize their willpower. In other words, they can begin to make personal choices concerning sexual issues and then take responsibility for their choices. This type of sexual activity, short-term partnering, is recently reported by divorced individuals as being a less attractive option than it once was, due to the fear of contracting HIV.

Ongoing Monogamous Partners

Some men and women are involved in a long-term monogamous relationship that began prior to the divorce. In these cases the divorcing individual's sexual needs are typically met within the context of this relationship. In other situations individuals satisfy their sexual needs in a long-term monogamous relationship that began subsequent to the divorce. The great majority of men and women report that finding an ongoing relationship is their goal.

INCIDENCE OF SEXUAL INTERCOURSE

With regard to the actual incidence of sexual intercourse among the divorced, Kinsey et al. (1948, 1953) found that divorced males and females engaged in less sexual activity than did married men and women of comparable ages. However, Hunt (1974) found a very different picture twenty-five years later. He found that 100 percent of the men under age fifty-five and 90 percent of the women in his divorced sample had engaged in sexual intercourse in the year prior to the survey. In a later study involving a national questionnaire given to 984 separated and divorced persons and 113 widowed persons, Hunt and Hunt (1977) reported that a great majority of the formerly married became sexually active within one year after their divorce. Only one man in twenty and one woman in fourteen reported that they had not engaged in intercourse. In an even later study, Zeiss and Zeiss (1979) found that 50 percent of the divorced persons they studied began having intercourse within one month after their marital separation and 81 percent had done so within one year. From these findings, it appears that sexual activity among the divorced is quite a bit higher than previous measures had shown.

FREQUENCY OF SEXUAL INTERCOURSE

With regard to the frequency of intercourse, Hunt (1974) found that the typical frequency of intercourse for divorced individuals was twice per week. Zeiss and Zeiss (1979) found that their divorced respondents averaged intercourse once every other date. In Cargan's (1981) research, 36 percent of the divorced reported that they engaged in intercourse three or more times per week. Even among divorced singles, however, this level of coital activity is characteristic of a minority. Divorced individuals report the greatest frequency of sexual activity among all the singles, but they still report that they would prefer to have even more frequent sex than they actually have (Zeiss and Zeiss, 1979), indicating on some level a dissatisfaction with their sexual lives. This finding cannot be taken to mean that divorced singles are frantically hopping from one bed to another in the search for sexual ecstasy. Despite the possibility of an initial flurry of postdivorce sexual activity, divorced individuals tended to have sex less often on the average than most married people. These researchers also found that at any one time, divorced people in their sample were dating only one person and sexual selectivity was the rule rather than the exception. Many singles in fact find that sexual and dating exclusivity sometimes is a problem because, even though the opportunities and attractions may be available, many single people do not feel comfortable about being sexually active with more than one person (Stein, 1976). American society is a traditionally monogamous society, more so now in light of the AIDS epidemic.

NUMBER OF PARTNERS

With regard to the number of partners, a definite increase occurred from the time of Kinsey's surveys to the 1970s. In the Kinsey et al. studies (1948, 1953), the typical man reported four partners in a year, and the average woman reported two partners. In a later study, divorced men had a median of eight partners annually prior to the survey and women reported a median of four partners (Hunt, 1974). More recently about one-third of divorced individuals reported more than ten sexual partners in a year (Cargan and Melko, 1982). It is difficult to assess the actual incidence and frequencies of sexual behavior in the general population, let alone in the divorced population. No national sample of human sexuality has been conducted since the Kinsey studies in 1948 and 1953. (The data for these studies were gathered in the late 1930s and early 1940s.) The studies since then have suffered from serious methodological problems and have been subject to much criticism from academic researchers. That there is still so much hesitation about researching human sexuality in the United Sates does not go unnoticed in terms of attitudes and values toward sexuality; however, even more important, our ignorance has profound implications for the society in terms of the spread of HIV. Not only do we know very little about the sexual behavior of the American people but we cannot predict the path of the AIDS virus. Although most of the studies reported in this chapter are old, the data confirm our clinical experience of those individuals who are sexually single again.

A count of the sexual partners of divorced people may not accurately reflect their sexual activity. Many divorced people go through a variety of sexual partners during the first year after their divorce. This stage of sexual experimentation may be motivated by the feeling of having escaped from a sexually restrictive marriage, by a search for intimacy with someone new, by a wish to avoid commitment in another intimate relationship, or by an attempt to ascertain their attractiveness to the opposite sex. The divorced person's sense of new freedom may quickly wane, however, because before long most men are looking for "meaningful relationships" and most women are complaining that casual sex lowers their self-esteem and leads to feelings of depression and even desperation (Hetherington, Cox, and Cox, 1976).

INITIATING SEX

Not all sex appears to be initiated by men. Approximately two-thirds of men and one-fifth of women reported that sometimes sex is initiated by the woman (Hunt and Hunt, 1977). With regard to how quickly sex occurs after it is attempted, only one in five women stated that they accepted sex the first time, whereas four-fifths of the men claimed that women accept their advances on the first attempt. It is difficult to ascertain what the disparity in male and female reports means. It is possible that gender stereotypes which exist regarding male and female sexuality caused men in the sample to inflate their sexual desirability, while women in the sample were hesitant to express their sexual aggressiveness.

QUALITY OF SEX

The divorced group in Hunt's (1974) study indicated that some of the qualitative dimensions of their sexual lives were better than their marital sexual experiences. Divorced men and women both reported greater variety of sexual arousal techniques and sexual positions, and the women reported higher orgasm rates. While orgasm is not necessarily an indicator of the quality of sex, women often reported more orgasms in postmarital relationships than in their former marriages, and they also reported higher orgasm rates than married women of the same age (Gebhard, 1970). Almost all divorced persons rated their current sex lives as very pleasurable or mostly pleasurable. Although they rated their current sexual pleasure as higher than their experiences in marriage, it should be remembered that they were probably comparing their present sexual situation with disintegrating marriages in which they were perhaps experiencing numerous sexual and related problems. It is possible that the feelings of inadequacy, communication problems, and financial stress which some had experienced in their disintegrating marriages inhibited their ability to experience satisfying sexual responses and enjoyment within the context of the new postmarital relationship. Getting a divorce may resolve some of these issues and thereby allow the person to engage in a more fulfilling sex life. Of course, the opposite can also occur. In these cases, the trauma of the divorce leads to feelings of sexual inadequacy, doubt, and dysfunction (Gebhard, 1968). In a later study, Cargan and Melko (1982) found that the divorced individuals in their sample reported they were more dissatisfied with their sex lives than the married, the never married, or the remarried. They found married individuals were the most satisfied with their sex lives, followed by divorced persons, followed by the never married. In their study this same pattern was somewhat evident when individuals who were divorced compared their present sexual life with that of the period when they were married. Marital sex still held a slight edge. Thus, the findings are somewhat inconclusive. It is probably reasonable to conclude, though, that the data support the notion that there is much variation and a great deal of ambiguity on the part of those who are sexually single again.

While divorced women have been falsely depicted as lonely and sexually deprived, divorced men have been incorrectly portrayed as having full sex lives with scores of partners. Hunt and Hunt (1977) feel that the formerly married are much more open and liberal about sex with new partners than their counterparts were a generation ago. Years ago, sneaking around, particularly if there were children involved, was the norm. But in contemporary society, at least some divorced individuals appear to be more eager and spontaneous about sexual encounters, and fewer report that they hide their activities from their children (Hunt and Hunt, 1977).

Lisa's postseparation experience portrayed the ambivalent feelings women often experience at this time. Initially, when she first began dating, she was unsure of herself. She didn't know if men would find her attractive; she thought she was too fat; she felt she didn't know how to behave. She had never had sex with anyone but her husband and felt strange about the prospect of being with another man. She felt so unsure that after her first date, she asked her therapist if perhaps she "should" have slept with him because he had bought her dinner. She was insecure in her role as newly single person. She had entered marriage at a young age and now, many years later, she felt cast out into the singles scene unprepared.

It appears that immediately following a divorce some divorced men and women engage in a short period of increased sexual experimentation, but in most cases they soon settle down to a more stable sexual life-style within the context of a longer-term relationship. In some situations, this increased sexual activity enables persons to construct a reality that includes far less emotional attachment and commitment to their sexual relationships. The interviewees reported confusion about and difficulty with suddenly finding themselves required to date and engage in various types of courtship behaviors after years of being in a monogamous situation. They reported that they often did not know the current appropriate behavior in dating situations, frequently felt insecure with members of the opposite sex, and were often unsure of themselves, feeling value conflicts about their actions. It was not unusual for men to experience occasions of erectile dysfunction as they tried to have intercourse with new partners whom they perceived as being sexually more demanding and aggressive than their former wives. For some men and women, these anxieties and insecurities led to long-term postmarital sexual problems.

After divorce it appears that many individuals are wary of another involvement. They may feel lonely, rejected, and sexually unsatisfied. A typical reaction, although occurring less frequently in the era of the AIDS epidemic, is to have casual and friendly sexual relationships with little commitment. These new relationships can serve an important psychological function, for they can heal a sensitive ego and encourage people to involve themselves in an intimate relationship again. For some, they can even result in more satisfying sexual expression.

SEX AND SINGLE PARENTS

Many of these divorced individuals are single parents. If children are involved, even if an individual is not the primary caretaker of the children after a divorce, at times the noncustodial parent may become the primary caretaker for a period of time. Census experts estimate that about 45 percent of children born in 1978 will live in a single-parent household for at least a while before they are eighteen. In 1980, 20 percent of children under the age of eighteen lived with only one parent. About 17 percent of all living arrangements including a child under eighteen are with the mother only, with about 1.6 percent living with the father (Glick and Norton, 1979). Approximately 90 percent of single-parent mothers are custodians of their children. So for the most part, when we speak about single parents, we are speaking about women as heads of households.

The Single Mother

Since mothers are more likely to be given custody of their children in cases of separation and divorce, and since they are more likely to be widowed, it is not surprising that most children in single-parent homes live with their mothers. Over 8 million children in this country live with their mothers, while 800,000 live with their fathers.

Money is an especially critical problem for single parents. One-parent families in general have considerably lower income than two-parent families, and their problems are often tied to economics.

Single working mothers make less than half of what single fathers make, and since child care must often be arranged and paid for, single mothers are usually fraught with financial worries. It is no wonder that some writers speak of the "feminization of poverty." Because of these very real economic pressures, the single mother may find it difficult to go out to social events to meet potential new partners. She may be unable to buy new attractive clothing or she may not be able to afford a babysitter. These factors may restrict the likelihood of her entering dating situations. She may feel uncomfortable about bringing new men to her home to meet her children.

When she first started dating, Lisa felt compelled to meet her dates at shopping malls or parking lots. She didn't want her children to see her dating different men. She thought they would lose respect for her, and she didn't want her children to see her with "one man after another."

The Single Father

Relatively few (less than 10 percent) one-parent families are headed by men (U.S. Bureau of the Census, 2000). When they do exist, they usually arise because the mother has died. In these cases, the widower experiences many of the same psychological and emotional problems faced by widowed mothers, including loneliness, sorrow, bitterness, and a sense of being overwhelmed by the full responsibility of child care. Most motherless families have fewer economic problems than do fatherless families. However, if many single mothers are at least initially unprepared for the breadwinning role, many single fathers are unprepared for child care responsibilities and home management tasks, such as shopping, cooking, doing laundry, and cleaning house —tasks formerly done by their wives. Some men do these chores themselves; others rely on relatives or friends for help or they hire outside workers. In spite of the additional responsibilities a single-parent father takes on, it is often less difficult for him than for a single-parent mother for the following reasons: finances are often more stable for the single-parent father, and generally many women are available to him for caretaking services. Many women will fuss over a single-parent father and generally ignore the single-parent mother.

Larry's wife left him after twelve years of marriage. He became the custodian of their two sons, David, age eleven, and Christian, age nine. The women in the neighborhood, believing that Larry could not possibly handle all the responsibilities of a job and the children, would take turns cooking supper for David and his sons and doing their laundry. They would also introduce David to available women.

Barbara's husband, Clint, left her with two young children, ages four and five, for a younger woman. Barbara, devastated by her feelings of abandonment, was forced back into the labor force to provide for herself and the children. The women in the neighborhood were threatened by Barbara's attractiveness, and even her close friends would be hesitant to allow their husbands to help Barbara out if her car broke down. Occasionally they would babysit for the children if Barbara had a date, but they were reluctant to interact with her. As time passed, she saw less and less of her once good friends. Eventually she moved out of the neighborhood and bought a condominium where many singles lived.

The single-parent father often invokes idealization by other women in that they fuss over his abilities to caretake; conversely, the single-parent mother is often devalued. Sisterhood is not very powerful in these cases.

As stated in an earlier chapter, teenage daughters are sometimes put in the role of "little mothers" or the "parental child" and given considerable responsibility for the house and the younger siblings (George and Wilding, 1972). In these cases, this child is often resentful that she is unable to enjoy childhood activities and often feels overburdened by feelings of responsibility for the emotional well-being of the parent. Other children in the family system may also feel resentment toward the parental child for they believe that she holds a special favored position in the parent's eyes. The father may come to rely on the company of this child, and in some cases, this may prevent him from seeking appropriate social partners of the opposite sex. This is typified by the case of Ron, a forty-seven-year-old construction worker.

Ron's wife left him with two children, a boy and a girl, ages thirteen and ten. Initially, he was lost, unfamiliar with their physical and emotional needs. Gradually, though, with the aid of a cleaning person, he learned how to manage the children and the household tasks. All his extra time was spent with the children. He planned weekend activities with them, took them on vacations, and monitored their lives. When he visited relatives, he spoke only about his involvement with them. Gradually, his friends dwindled, and his adult activities virtually ceased. Two years later, he came to therapy for depression.

On the other hand, meeting sexual and intimacy needs while taking care of children without a partner is sometimes fraught with problems of privacy, energy, and time. In an interview study with thirty-eight single parents, Greenberg (1979) reported that most of her sample believed that their sexual activity should not be known to their children. The double standard was evident, since more men than women accepted sex among single parents, even if it was apparent to their children. In a study of 127 separated or divorced fathers with full or joint custody of their children, Rosenthal and Keshet (1978a) found that when the father dated a new woman and stayed overnight, it was more typically at her home than at his. The women involved in the sample reported that they felt more comfortable and more romantic in their own homes or apartments. They reported that they did not have to worry about their date's children in their own homes. If a serious relationship eventually developed, the sense of being a new couple would emerge. Eventually, 75 percent of the single fathers asked their new partners to sleep over (Rosenthal and Keshet, 1979b), although they reported that this was initially very difficult for them to do. Single fathers also reported that they were generally uncomfortable about having a female sleep over when the children were home. They reported that they worried their children might feel sex should be totally uncommitted and free. This idea was uncomfortable for them (Rosenthal and Keshet, 1979b) and is typified by the situation in the movie *Kramer vs. Kramer* in which Dustin Hoffman's naked female friend encountered his four-year-old son in the hall.

It may be especially important to the single father that his new partner get along with his children. If the relationship leads to a traditional marriage, the woman might be expected to assume much of the responsibility for managing the household and caring for the children. Single mothers, on the other hand, may consider financial security more important in their mate selection. Women who are not working and who rely solely on their former partners for support might consider the possibility that the children's biological father would renege on support payments, thereby making the stepparent more responsible for the child's welfare. In this sense, these single mothers' assessment of the financial security of the future mate is an important variable, while for single fathers the person's ability to assume responsibility for child care and household maintenance might be more important considerations. In more modern arrangements based on convenience and partnership, these considerations become minimal as more and more androgynous roles are the norm, with child care and household chore allocation beginning to approach equality.

THERAPY STRATEGIES

In general, then, the single parent must confront several issues regarding dating and sexuality. First, there are time considerations. The decision to begin dating may lead to guilt feelings concerning the children. If the single parent works and his or her children are in child care all day or in school, he or she is faced with the decision of either going out on a date or spending time with the children. Second, there is a potential parent consideration. The single parent generally also looks at the men or women he or she meets not only as potential marital partners but also as potential parents as well. A new criterion then enters the process by which the single parent evaluates the parental capabilities of the person. Although an individual may be fun to be with, he or she may not be interested in assuming parental responsibilities. This type of relationship is probably time limited. In another situation, an individual may be willing to assume parental responsibilities but the children may be so threatened by his or her presence that they sabotage the relationship, attempting to maintain the status quo. One parent reported that as her boyfriend was leaving the house after a date, he walked over to her darling five-year-old to say goodbye and shake hands. Her gracious son smiled devilishly and, looking up with big blue eyes, shouted, "Penis breath!"

Third, there are also financial and fatigue considerations. Aside from all of the dilemmas mentioned, all the practicalities of dating must be considered, including the costs in time, energy, and money. If the children are young, dating requires finding and paying a babysitter. Both men and women need attractive clothes. If finances are limited, competition between these needs and the needs of the children may occur. Going out also imposes a cost in fatigue. It means less time to get other things done and less time to sleep and rest. It also means less time for the children. Single parents who work may feel that they spend too little time with their children as it is. Dating means that the children will be left once again with a babysitter. This may create a great deal of guilt in the parent who opts to leave the children with a babysitter and may also create much conflict when he or she tries to decide whether to date in the first place.

Fourth, there are reputational considerations. Some individuals, especially those from very traditional families who live in traditional neighborhoods, may worry about their reputations. In family neighborhoods many worry about what the neighbors think and the consequential repercussions on the children. It is also possible that the single parent fears the former spouse would use the parent's dating to malign the parent to the children or to argue in court for renegotiation of support or custody. Most single parents also worry about their children's reactions as they begin to date. They are likely to be aware that their children will now see them as having sexual needs. They may be concerned about their children's reactions to the people they date. The children may actively discourage parents who are already uncertain about entering into dating. Children may cause immediate problems, either by being negative to anyone they see as possibly taking their mother's or father's place or by being excessively positive and frightening others off immediately by asking, "Are you going to be my new daddy?" Although parents may feel it a relinquishing of their rights as independent adults to permit their children to control their personal lives, their children's objections may in fact affect their dating behavior.

Fifth, there are personal considerations. Single parents further recognize that society has changed, and they have as well. They are older. They may feel less attractive. They may worry about the condition of their bodies. Women may be concerned about sagging breasts and stretch marks. Men may worry about pot bellies, thinning hair, and impotence. And as parents, they come as a package deal: adult with children. The person with children is likely to feel himself or herself less "marriageable," for many prospective partners are hesitant to take on the added responsibility of parenthood with someone else's children.

Sixth, there are often also considerations of a sociosexual nature. Meeting eligible mates can be difficult. Many single parents do not know where to go to meet available persons. Many detest the bar scene and are leery of placing personal ads. Often single parents will despair of meeting the right person and feel that no one is out there. Furthermore, when they do meet someone, they must decide whether to permit a date or a lover to spend the night when the children are present. To allow someone to spend the night who is not the children's mother or father is often an important symbolic act for the parent. For one thing, it generally involves the children in the relationship with the person. If no commitment to the person has been made, the parent may fear that the children will become emotionally involved with the person and, if the relationship then ends, the parent will have to deal not only with his or her own feelings about the breakup but with the children's feelings as well. Allowing a date or a lover to sleep over also reveals to the children that their parent is a sexual person. This, in many cases, may make the parent feel somewhat uncomfortable for he or she may feel that the children are passing moral judgment—and they very well might be.

Finally, there are "right person" considerations. Single parents, both men and women, can easily despair of finding the right person. Single fathers may have an easier time meeting someone. But they may complain that those they meet are too young or, if older and never married, are too involved with their careers or too "prudish." If they are divorced, men report that many feel bitter toward men. If the woman is a widow, she may idealize her former husband, creating an unrealistic ideal person for her date to compete with. Single mothers who are themselves in their thirties or forties espouse similar complaints. There may be men around, they report, but not the right type. If the men have never been married, then it is probably because something is wrong with them and no one else wants them. Maybe they are unwilling to settle down, or perhaps they are still tied to their mothers, or they may be homosexual. If the men have been married, then they likely still have responsibilities to their former families, still have wives to whom they must furnish child support and children whom they must see. There is also the phenomenon called the "mating gradient," which refers to men's tendency to marry younger women who are generally less educated, so there remains two pools of eligibles: a group of very educated successful women who remain at the top of the gradient and a group of socially unfortunate men who remain at the bottom. Many single parents, male or female, feel themselves drawn to the conclusion, "Why bother?"

All single parents experience at times the difficulties of providing for the physical, social, and emotional needs of themselves and their children. Problems of fatigue and role overload occur irrespective of the family's financial situation, though surely those with financial difficulties are more likely to experience such problems. The pressures of family responsibilities can prevent the single parent from spending long periods of time with members of the opposite sex in order to get to know them better. Child care problems make the chance of going away for an evening, weekend, or vacation with someone of the opposite sex very slim. There is lesser movement into marriage from the world of single parents than from some of the other unmarried populations. Some of these structural impediments add to and account for a lack of desire for remarriage in many of these single parents. However, many single parents feel good about their newfound freedom and look forward to dating and meeting new people with positive anticipation.

So although there may be emotional, physical, and social needs pressing the single parent toward finding a new partner, very real reasons for hesitancy exist, including the financial costs of dating and concerns about dignity and self-respect. This adds to the notion that not one model of single parenting can account for the concept of the single parent. Just as many types of two-parent households exist and have many different value systems, economic levels, and educational achievements, so too are these differences found among single-parent families, and these differences manifest in the sexual arena as well.

Chapter 7

Relational and Sexual Considerations After Widowhood

SEXUAL CONSIDERATIONS OF WIDOWHOOD

Where do widowed persons seek companionship and how do they live if they are unwilling to search for a husband or wife or unable to find one? It is helpful for therapists to explore the sexual concerns of widows and widowers.

People who are widowed may have very different responses from the divorced or separated. Their marriages ended through death rather than choice, and many widowed people feel a deep loss. They are likely to fear or resent experiences that might devalue memories of the deceased partner. Others retain a sense that the dead partner is still present—almost like a conscience—inhibiting them from sexual involvement; they may view a new marriage or relationship as cheating their dead spouse. This also occurs in the divorced group but to a lesser degree. Consequently, the research indicates that widowed persons have fewer postmarital experiences than their divorced peers of any age group.

As stated earlier, most widowed people are women. Since widowed persons have a median age of 67.8, they are profoundly affected by age and sex stereotypes concerning sexuality. Widows in particular are affected by age and sex stereotypes. The double standard of aging makes it more difficult for aged women to find partners. Not only are they considered less attractive and erotic than younger women, the pool of older men is considerably smaller, since men die at a younger age than women. Virtually all widowed men return to an active sex life, while substantially fewer widowed women engage in postmarital sex (Gebhard, 1968).

Since widowed persons tend to be elderly, the death of a partner often means an end to their sexuality. The availability of a marriage partner and good health are the primary determinants of an active sex life in old age. Yet what older people generally miss most is the companionship and comfort of their mate.

When we examine the factors related to sexual activity in older persons, we find a very important difference between males and females. For males, the variable most strongly related to sexual activity is age. Among females, the most important variable is marital status.

The reason for this difference between males and females is a socially constructed one: Marital status, especially for women, still means the presence or absence of a socially approved sexual partner. For women, if there is a socially approved sexual partner (a husband), sexual activity is likely to continue. If the woman does not have a socially approved sexual partner, her sexual activity is most likely to cease. For males, the existence of a socially approved sexual partner (wife) is much less important for the continuation of sexual activity (Persson, 1980; Pfeiffer, Verwoerdt, and Davis, 1972).

These socially constructed definitions of appropriate sexuality for older men and women are especially important when we note that a married woman in the United States today can expect her husband to die approximately thirteen years before she does. Consequently, it is possible that she will spend a considerable portion of her life as a non–sexually active person if she follows the traditional sexual script.

Most widows are aware of unmet sexual needs after the death of their husbands (Barrett, 1978). The social construction of female sexuality in American society tends, especially for older women, to make it very difficult for most widows to come in contact with a socially approved sexual partner. Women learn via social definitions to strongly connect sex and interpersonal relationships, so a person who has been married for forty years may find it difficult to see herself with anyone else. Most widows are therefore unlikely to seek out another socially approved sexual partner. Bornstein et al. (1973) studied a sample of widows with an average age of sixty. They found that thirteen months after the death of the husband, only 7 percent had dated and only 2 percent had engaged in intercourse. Gebhard (1970) found that only about half as many widows had engaged in intercourse as had divorced women. Of those widows who had had sex, the frequency was low. As Gebhard points out, in-laws and married friends of the widow are comforting but also stifling in terms of her maintaining the same patterns of behavior as when her husband was alive. A lack of sexual activity is further supported by the romantic ideal of "being loyal to the memory" of her husband (Gebhard, 1970). For males, the widower status has much less impact on one's sexual activity (Persson, 1980).

Even before her husband's death, the older woman is faced with a lack of sexual opportunity not of her own choosing. Research repeatedly finds that when sexual activity in marriage ceases in the later years, the cessation is due to the husband, not the wife. Pfeiffer, Verwoerdt, and Davis (1972) found that of elderly married men and women who no longer engaged in intercourse, 86 percent of the women and only 42 percent of the men attributed the cessation of sex to their spouse. In another study (Pfeiffer, Verwoerdt, and Davis, 1972), 6 percent of the men said they no longer engaged in coitus because of their wife, while 40 percent said the cessation was due to their own lack of ability.

One piece of research (Pfeiffer and Davis, 1972) notes that sexual interest on the part of older married women declines quite rapidly. The researchers argue that this is a protective mechanism. It is adaptive for a woman to lose interest in sex as she ages since the odds are that she will be without a socially approved sexual partner for a considerable period of her life. If her husband does live as long as she does, it is highly probable that their sexual activity level will drastically decline or stop altogether through no fault of hers.

The United States is on the brink of a longevity revolution. By 2030, the number of older Americans will have more than doubled to 70 million, or one in every five Americans. As our population ages, it also will become more predominantly female. Today, there are 68 men for every 100 women over the age of sixty-five. With age, the ratio of men to women decreases steadily. There are 83 men for every 100 women between the ages of sixty-five and sixty-nine, and only 40 men for every 100 women among those eighty-five and older. This trend is expected to grow into the next century. This disparity in numbers of men versus women result in significant numbers of older women living alone (U.S. Bureau of the Census, 2000; CDC, 1994-2000).

According to the Duke studies (Pfeiffer, Verwoerdt, and Davis, 1972), the sex lives of women born sixty to eighty years ago depend heavily upon the availability of a partner who is socially approved and sexually capable—that is, a husband who is still alive and sexually interested. Since women tend to marry men several years older and then outlive them by ten or more years, many older women are widows. Because they have no husbands, they are sexually inactive. The starkness of this issue can be shown by the unequal sex ratio of persons over sixty-five—146 women for every 100 men. A recent survey of married men and women showed that 87 percent of married men and 89 percent of married women in the sixty to sixty-four age range are sexually active. Those numbers drop with advancing years, but 29 percent of men and 25 percent of women over the age of eighty are still sexually active. Research found that 50 percent of the women surveyed who were between the ages of sixty and seventy-four, and four out of five women age seventy-five and over, were widowed. This was contrasted with one out of five men age seventy-five and older who were widowed. (National Council on the Aging, 1998). If socially constructed notions about the acceptability of singles and extrarelationship sex were to change, women who wished to do so could realize much more of their sexual potential.

Sexual needs are similar for the divorced and the widowed, who have been conditioned by years of marriage to expect and desire both physical release and emotional closeness of a continuing sexual relationship. Although their needs may be similar, some important differences exist between the widowed and the divorced with respect to their social situation.

During the last months or years of a marriage that ends in divorce, sexual relations usually deteriorate or are terminated. The recently divorced person has therefore often gone through a period of relative sexual deprivation (Waller, 1967). Also, although changing, many people are left after a divorce with a sense of having failed in an interpersonal relationship. Divorced people may compensate for both their recent sexual deprivation and their sensitive ego by seeking sexual encounters.

Recently widowed people are in somewhat of a different situation. Unless their spouse was ill for a long time, they typically have not experienced a deterioration of their marital relationship just prior to their spouse's death, and consequently they do not have a sense of having failed in their most important sexual relationship.

Another factor that may affect the sexual adjustment of the widowed and the divorced differently is the quality of the emotional tie to the absent mate. Widowed people seldom feel hostile toward their deceased mate and in fact may retain strong emotional ties with his or her memory. Over time, the survivor may exaggerate the good qualities of the deceased and selectively forget all the shortcomings. This filtered memory can be a deterrent to the establishment of new relationships, sexual or otherwise, because no living person can possibly equal the exalted image of the deceased.

Friends and family of the widowed often exert a subtle pressure on them to remain faithful to the deceased, because many feel that a new love would be disloyal and for some even sexually immoral. The widowed person more often than the divorced one will have a supportive group of in-laws and married friends who encourage maintenance of previous patterns of behavior. Although possibly not intending to do so, well-meaning friends and relatives, through their moral support, lower the chances that a widow or widower will soon seek new relationships.

Men are already largely free from narrow ideas about acceptable sex partners. Whereas 90 percent of the women in the Duke studies (Center for Health Communication, 2004) cited spouse-oriented reasons for stopping sexual activity (death of a spouse, divorce from spouse, illness of spouse, spouse unable to engage in sex, spouse lost interest), only 29 percent of the men noted spouse-oriented reasons for stopping. Instead, they emphasized three things about their own incapacity for sex: 14 percent cited personal loss of interest, 17 percent cited their own illness, and 40 percent thought they were unable to perform sexually (Pfeiffer, Verwoerdt, and Davis, 1972).

Nevertheless, people's close ties to someone now dead can be transcended—either personally or socially. Reaching out, especially sexually, to a new person can evoke guilty feelings of cheating on the deceased lover. This reaction prompts reticence and perhaps impotence, and makes reentry into social life with others difficult. As the years pass, people may feel increasingly awkward about sex, as if they have forgotten how to do it (Kohn and Kohn, 1978).

In addition to their own hesitations about getting sexually involved again, widowed people may be treated as outcasts if their social world consists of paired couples only . Some widowed people report feeling awkward because they are always thought of as the "widowed person"—part of a couple, not as a single person. In addition, widows may remind "friends" too vividly of the nearness of their own spouse's death and their own possible singlehood—so they may be politely shunned.

Most of the research discussed so far in the literature has been based on the study of married older couples. Marital status has emerged as one of the most important factors determining the level of sexual activity of older men and women. Obviously, sexual intercourse is much more frequent among married elderly couples because married life provides continued opportunity for sexual stimulation. Widows and widowers, on the other hand, faced with the need to find an available sexual partner, have much more difficulty satisfying their sexual needs.

Aging widows, widowers, and single elderly people make up an increasingly large segment of our population. They are particularly prone to isolation and depression. Their sexual contacts are very limited. In a study reported by Newman and Nichols (1960), only 7 of the 101 single, divorced, or widowed men over age 60 reported any sexual activity.

The loss of a spouse by death invariably produces trauma or conflicting emotions. Questions about the meaning of life and the significance of the passage of time can lead the surviving spouse to shut off from sexual activities, sometimes temporarily, sometimes forever. During widowhood many elderly men and women are inclined to adhere to the customs of their youth—no sex outside of marriage—and are therefore forced into celibacy regardless of personal inclination.

Many authors who write about widowhood must assume that most widows and widowers have relinquished all sexual interests because many books on the subject never discuss sex. A notable exception are Kreis and Pattie (1969), two widows who worked as a team collecting data on sexual problems during widowhood. They noted that once the initial shock, grief, and suffering are over, the sexual appetite of healthy men and women rekindled. The authors give many examples showing how widows and widowers handle their feelings about sex during and after bereavement. Some are plagued with feelings of guilt when attempting to separate sex from marriage, whereas others, particularly widowers, can work out their problem without entering into another permanent relationship. Women who establish a new sexual relationship after a period of mourning are likely to either remarry or form a new stable partnership with a man they consider a boyfriend (Bornstein et al., 1973).

The double standard of aging is also apparent in the different options available to widowed men and women. Socially constructed definitions clearly depict remarriage or a continued sex life in some other type of arrangement more favorably for widowers than widows. The widowed man, although not without problems, still appears to have distinct advantages. Because widows outnumber widowers considerably, the widower is, in effect, in a buyer's market. While the chances of remarriage for older widows are slim, the widower has a choice of possible partners. Socially, the widower is an asset; the widowed woman is a liability. As widows become older, the pool of available men shrinks continuously. The sex differential in mortality rates may create a real shortage of partners for women in their sixties or older. Perhaps polygamy could be legalized in old age as a way of resolving the dilemma.

Even the Social Security system used to favor widowers over widows because it was the widow who was forced to give up her husband's benefits when she remarried. Economically, the widow had a greater incentive to live with her partner rather than marry him. The practice of the elderly widowed people living together has been described as the "Social Security sin," in which widows and widowers live together but do not marry in order to preserve their pensions. Fortunately, the problem was recently recognized by Congress and legislation was passed allowing a widow to retain her previous pension or choose her new husband's benefits, whichever sum is greater.

In addition to greater opportunities to remarry, the widower can choose nonmarital affairs, sexual fantasies, or masturbation. Most of these expressions of sexual interests are socially disapproved of for widows, who are expected to devote themselves to their children or grandchildren, volunteer services in the community, and the memories of their husbands. While many assume that the elderly widowed man needs a woman to look after him, this assumption is no longer valid in the case of the elderly widow.

Both widows and widowers complain that society does not provide suitable outlets for them to express sexual needs relevant to old age and widowhood. For senior citizens without available partners, masturbation has become a major alternative to gain release from sexual tension. Still, many men and women feel that it is wrong for people of their age to engage in this practice.

Although widows and widowers are faced with many problems in their attempt to find sexual happiness in their later years, many remain vigorous people who are not willing to surrender a meaningful relationship with someone of the opposite sex.

Current data on the sexual life of the widowed are scarce. One study of divorced and widowed women interviewed between 1939 and 1956 found that widowed women were slower than divorced women of the same age to resume an active sex life after losing their spouse. Eighty-two percent of divorced women had postmarital coitus, and 43 percent of widowed women did. As stated previously, the lower incidence of postmarital sex among widows is due in part to the fact that widows are, on average, older than divorced women. But even when matched for age, widows are still less likely to engage in postmarital sex. There are probably several reasons for this. Widows are more likely to be financially secure than divorced women and therefore have less motivation for engaging in sex as a prelude to remarriage; they have the continuing social support system of in-laws and friends, and so they are less motivated to seek new friendships. There is also a belief that a widow should be loyal to her dead husband, and having a sexual relationship with another man is viewed as disloyalty. Many widows believe this or tell themselves that they will never find another one like him.

Most widowed women who have postmarital sex begin such relationships about a year after the spouse's death. Gebhard (1968) found that 16 percent of the widowed had postmarital sex with more than one partner. More widowed than divorced women in all age ranges remained celibate. When widowed women did resume coitus, their frequency of intercourse was lower than that of divorced women of the same age. Widows, however, were equally as likely as divorced women to reach orgasm in their postmarital sexual intercourse (Gebhard, 1970).

Comparable data for divorced and widowed men are not available, but we would assume that the percentage who have postmarital coitus, the frequency of postmarital coitus, and the speed with which postmarital coitus is begun after the end of the marriage are all higher than the comparable figures for widowed men. This assumption is based on three facts: First, sexual aggressiveness in our society is more acceptable in men than in women; hence a widower is less likely to be criticized for pursuing new partners than a widow. Second, the higher male death rate means more women than men are available in the middle and later years. A widow might have more difficulty than a widower in finding a new partner because of the scarcity of men in her age range.

For some older women and men, masturbation can become or continue to be a form of sexual release and expression. A study of more than 800 people between the ages of sixty and ninety-one years of age reports that older women are becoming more accepting of masturbation as a means of sexual expression (Starr and Weiner, 1981). In 1998, 79 percent of men ages sixty-five to seventy-four were married, compared with 55 percent of women in the same age group. Among persons age eighty-five or older, about 50 percent of men were married, compared with only 13 percent of women. Women are much more likely to be widowed than are older men due to a combination of social and biological factors, including sex differences in life expectancy, the tendency for women to marry men who are slightly older, and higher remarriage rates for older widowed men than widowed women. In 1998, about 77 percent of women age 85 or older were widowed, compared with 42 percent of men.

Older people may redefine their sexual and affectional relationships. Nonsexual friendships with either sex can offer affectionate physical contact, emotional closeness, intellectual stimulation, and opportunities for socializing. People of two or more generations may live together or an unmarried couple may share a household. Although probably rare because of traditionally negative social definitions, sexual relationships with same-sex partners may be explored. Remarriage may also be an option; each year more than 35,000 marriages take place in the United States in which one of the partners is 65 or older (Vinick, 1978).

Third, it is socially acceptable for a man to date a younger woman, but still less acceptable for an older woman to date a younger man. This means that the widow of middle age or older is less likely than the widower to find an acceptable mate, because the few men in her age range may seek younger women. Often the choices of the single woman in the middle or later years are limited to men who are much older than she is. A widow may feel reluctant to become involved with an older man who is likely to become senile and ill and to die much before she does. Once widowed, a woman may hesitate to risk being widowed again. For a number of reasons—one being the reduction in Social Security benefits that formerly occurred when retired people married—the elderly have sometimes engaged in what geriatric therapists refer to as "unmarriages of convenience." These are companionable sexual relationships not formalized by license or ceremony. The Social Security law was changed in 1977 so that newlyweds who are sixty or over now lose none of their benefits. Certain older people, especially men, still confess to enjoying the secretive "swinging singles" experience of living together without the benefit of a legal marriage. But most elderly couples are not swingers and elect to marry rather than face the censure of conventional society and their own consciences.

The proliferation of retirement communities may be one answer to the segregation of single older women. In these communities single women may find some wholesome associations with men (even though married) in educational classes, volunteer work, social activities, recreational activities, and neighboring. An occasional swim, dance, or card game with a married man is not the equivalent of living with him, but it does provide contact and companionship. In many of these communities such men are perfectly willing to act as a handyman and take on household tasks for their widowed female neighbors. This kind of friendship is not sexual, but it does provide the basis for emotional support. In cases where a married couple has had a long history of a stormy relationship, the husband may find comfort in the arms of another woman. A few have tried communal living; some like it, and some do not.

No direct studies have been made of the postmarital sexual adjustment of widows and widowers. This does not mean that they do not have sexual problems. In fact, the problems for such people may be far more complex than they are for younger people. It does, however, reflect our socially constructed view that older people should be nonsexual and that any sexual interest among the older population is unnatural. Researchers of sexuality also appear to have accepted this view, at least as evidenced by their historical lack of attention to this group. With the increased awareness that sexual interest and activity can continue indefinitely, perhaps greater concern about and interest in the special problems of widowed individuals as they face postmarital sexual adjustment will develop.

A large percentage of the singles population is composed of the divorced and widowed of both sexes. Singlehood is often thrust upon them by circumstances and may not be a chosen lifestyle. These people have often been involved in exclusive relationships for many years. Suddenly they find themselves in the arena of dating and courtship. This can be a particularly difficult transition because socially constructed values have changed so radically since they were a part of the dating scene. The inability to cope with the demands of dating today often leaves the older divorced or widowed person in a state of confusion. Some retreat into a celibate single life, unable to cope with the pressures of dating in present-day society.

In many cases, the social, psychological, and sexual lifestyle adjustments and the grieving process described in our discussion of divorce are experienced, often to a greater degree, by widowers and widows.

Regarding sex, Harry, whom we met in Chapter 2, told us that with his first wife, sex was a very important part of their lives, but that, after her death, for the whole six or so months that he was mourning her, he had lost all sexual interest. "Toward the end of those six months I started to get a bit concerned," he said with a smile, "because I had even lost my normal sensations in the sexual area. It was as if my sexuality was dead. I didn't think of sex, I didn't feel anything sexual, I didn't even think of the great sexual moments Odile and I had for so many years."

Then, slowly, as he started to meet old friends and new people, he realized that his sexuality was far from dead. His general energy and vitality extended to his sexuality. Before he settled down with Connie and accepted her as his new companion and lover, he had dated other women and had gone to bed with a few of them. Initially he was surprised that he had responded so well in these encounters after the lack of sexual feeling of the previous period of mourning. Then, when Connie became his new love, sex became again an essential part of their relationship. When we interviewed Connie, who was twenty-four years younger than Harry's seventy-six, she talked very positively of their sex life. They made love regularly, up to five times a week, and they spent a long time "playing with each other sexually," as she described it. We inquired whether Harry had difficulties functioning sexually at his age. Her response was a spontaneous laugh while saying, "Are you kidding me? He is more vital than other men I have been with who were twenty years younger. He's a gourmet of sex. He really makes love like a musician makes music or an artist paints a picture. I am more satisfied sexually now than I've ever been in my life before. He doesn't look his age. He doesn't act it either."

When we asked Harry about AIDS and whether he was or had been concerned about it, his quick reply was, "Oh, sure I was concerned," and went on to explain that he had taken all the precautions he knew how, latex condoms, spermicide, even in one case, double condoms. This was with the women he dated before he met Connie. But what about with Connie herself? He had spent several hours talking about it with her before they had "regular sex," as he called it, that is, without a condom. He assured us that he had been monogamous and faithful to his wife for the forty-two years of their marriage. Then, the women he dated starting about six months after his wife's death had all accepted his "condom condition," in his words. "At my age, I didn't want to end up with AIDS for being careless and stupid." One woman refused his condition and he walked out on her. Connie, on the other hand, had also been faithful sexually to her husband of twenty-eight years. She also had been very firm with the men she had dated about "safe sex." She had also refused to get sexually involved on a couple of occasions when the man had not taken her seriously and wanted to have sex without protection. In conclusion, Harry felt that Connie and he were "safe" and did not have to be concerned about AIDS anymore.

Harry introduced us to his friend Sam, whom he described with great affection and even admiration. Sam was now a retired dentist and they had been friends for more than twenty-five years, even though Sam was twelve years younger than Harry. Sam had been married for thirty-eight years, had four daughters, all independent and three married. Sam had had a very successful dental practice in an affluent part of town. His wife died of cancer. Four years later, when we interviewed Sam, he told us how much his wife's death had affected him. He had even thought of suicide and had lost almost thirty pounds in less than seven months. Then a male friend of his, whom he had known for many years when they were both married, helped pull him out of his severe depression and they became inseparable. His friend had been asexual since his own wife's death a few years earlier. Then "something happened," and they entered a homosexual relationship, Sam at the age of sixty-one and his friend at the age of sixty-three. Sam confessed that both were initially embarrassed and even shocked but that they were unable to deny the happiness and goodness that this relationship was affording them. His friend had no children, but Sam's daughters were never told directly of their father's new committed relationship and, as Sam said, "I'm sure they suspect, but they haven't asked. I have a good relationship with all of them and I guess my fear is that this thing might damage our relationship. What the heck, my daughter Bobby is gay and lives with another woman and her sisters have accepted her gayness without any problem. But I don't have the guts to tell them. Maybe some day in the future. Who knows?"

Both Harry and Sam accepted their sexuality after their wives' deaths—each differently, to be sure, but ultimately with a sense of inner resolution and peace. Sam still fears condemnation by his daughters, which is unfortunately quite common in our rather homophobic society. But he is happy and at peace in his relationship with his male lover.

THERAPY STRATEGIES

Grief, as painful as it is, heals. Theoreticians such as Bowlby (1980), Parkes and Weiss (1983), and Sanders (1989) believe that the process is a developmental one. As such, these authors have described specific stages through which grievers must pass if the process is to change their relationship with the deceased and allow them to emotionally invest in new, potential satisfactions. For the widowed, one potential source of satisfaction may be a sexually intimate relationship.

These developmental theorists hasten to warn their readers that the actual experiences of the bereaved are much more complex than the neat and precise charts which depict the developmental stages might suggest. Therapists ought not be confused, for example, if clients seem to overlap the stages or to regress from time to time.

The previous sections have described the social, psychological, and sexual issues that are commonly experienced by single parents. Whether they are single through divorce or the death of a spouse, the common factor involved is that they have experienced intimacy dissolution. Specific guidelines and therapy strategies were presented that addressed common issues presented in therapy by these populations. The following section summarizes some of the main points in the prior sections and presents additional guidelines for the therapist.

Sufficient similarities among the grief reactions of these populations will guide, not lead, the therapists' work. Table 7.1 presents a guide to the process of intimacy dissolution which we have found helpful in clinical practice. It broadly outlines the steps involved in the process and suggests issues likely to be found in each. Therapy techniques are also included. In the clinical use of Table 7.1, therapists are reminded that it is only an outline, not a road map, of the process. Sanders's (1989) caveat is repeated here: No two griefs are alike.

The decision to dissolve an intimate relationship is rarely reached quickly or without difficulty and pain, even in unhappy marriages. Therapy during this time frame may help to reconstitute individuals' sense of stability and help them to focus on future aspects of their new lifestyle. The general goal of therapy during this time is to help the client optimize personal development as he or she pursues a new life. It is crucial for the therapist to examine his or her own assumptions

TABLE 7.1. The psychological issues and therapy techniques utilized during specific stages of the intimacy dissolution process

Stages	Issues	Therapy Techniques
Stage I (Denial)	Loneliness Sexual deprivation Lack of sexual interest	Help client develop outside support networks. Aid client in dealing with emotionality associated with separation shock.
Stage II (Conflict)	Possible sexual acting out Emotional instability	Help clients clarify values about dating relationships and sexuality. Help the clients "own" their ambivalent feelings.
Stage III (Ambivalence)	Identity problems (social, psychological, sexual)	Help the clients make the identity transition of defining themselves within a "married" script to defining themselves within the context of a single script.
Stage IV (Acceptance)	Stability maintenance	Help the clients internalize their new sociopsychological identity.

about this particular lifestyle to help the client identify a social role and attitudes toward it. The therapist's attitude should reflect that the singles lifestyle is a legitimate one and a viable alternative way of living. Therapists need to help the client explore personal and interpersonal needs and attitudes, aiding the client to develop and maintain his or her socially constructed identity in a realistic way. In some cases, the therapy process may include educating the client with regard to single life. During the stages of divorce adjustment, it becomes apparent that clients frequently present several common problems. Although these problems may not appear to be initially overtly sexual, the task of the therapist is to be tuned in to the possible sexual implications, to understand the underlying sexual dynamics, and to be comfortable and competently trained enough to give the client permission to deal with the problem and instill confidence that it can be solved. However, therapists helping clients deal with sexuality or sexual issues after divorce must be keenly aware of the basic emotional process and stages that individuals experience during the divorcing process. It is impossible to separate out the sexual issues a divorcing person experiences without also considering the individual's other strong concurrent emotions.

It is crucial for therapists to recognize the emotional stages of intimacy dissolution and the sexual aspects within each stage. It is crucial for therapists to be aware of these stages in order to help their clients with the sexual issues inherent in this time frame. For example, as was stated earlier, during Stage I, clients experience denial. It is also possible that during this time, clients may not be interested in sex at all, let alone sex with a person other than the lost spouse. Along with the denial of their basic emotional state, they also may deny the existence of their feelings of sexuality or their fears about sexuality. This is manifested in a therapy session by a repeated, "I don't have to worry about sex. I'm simply not interested in it. It just isn't important anymore." Or "I certainly won't have any problems dealing with sex." Most clients still feel married at this point and to encourage them to engage in dating would be detrimental to their healing process. Any sort of denial, repression, fear, and ignorance imperils any type of eventual healthy sexual expression. Clients during this stage usually experience sexual deprivation. Even if the marriage was disintegrating, some individuals still engage in sexual intercourse with their ex-spouse. For many, ending a marriage means that they are deprived sexually. Therapists dealing with clients in Stage I of the divorcing process should help their clients acknowledge their sexual needs and help them decide how they could comfortably deal with their sexuality.

Also important in Stage I is the client's reactions to loneliness. During this stage, therapists should help the client explore and deal with feelings of loneliness. Loneliness has many components. First, there is a feeling of emotional insufficiency. The person may feel empty and sorrowful. This may be a healthy sign, for it may signal that the person is ready to seek out a new emotional partnership. Another component is anxiety. In this case, the person may feel as though the world is without comfort. He or she will never meet anyone satisfactory. This may be accompanied by a feeling of impending doom. The person may feel restless, may feel a need to keep busy, may be involved in random activities. The single person must, at times, deal with feelings of loneliness and isolation. A degree of comfort with solitude and with oneself is essential.

Epstein (1974) has suggested that loneliness appears to be a greater problem for divorced men while autonomy is a greater problem for women. This is especially true for women who have young children still at home. The presence of children may prevent much of the potential loneliness women can experience in this situation because they give some organizational structure to everyday life and also provide emotional satisfactions. At the same time, however, they come with numerous responsibilities and may further restrict the mother's ability to fully utilize her newfound freedom. Sometimes single parents can find solace in their children's presence, but reliance only on the children for amusement and company is unhealthy for the parent; it can prevent them from seeking more appropriate alternatives and it further may place too much of a burden on the children. Some parents blame the children for their loneliness: "If I didn't have the children, I would be able to go out more and meet people."

Loneliness, then, is one of the most painful feelings that accompanies divorce and widowhood. The individual often experiences hopelessness at facing the prospect of making new friends as a single person. Clients complain that they do not know where and how to meet people. The loneliness can turn to depression when they have tried the singles bars or experienced the Michelletic search to pair up that is common in certain self-help divorce adjustment groups. For some individuals, loneliness may become a chronic condition—a way of life. They feel they will be lonely forever. Certain times of day may be more difficult than others. For example, after dinner may be particularly lonely for the individual who, prior to the divorce or the death of the spouse, socialized until bedtime. For others, the holidays may represent a problem. The therapist, in these cases, must help the person get in touch with his or her own motives and needs, explore the extent to which sexual needs are part of the loneliness, understand the extent to which fantasy of a new ideal partner or of the former spouse dominates the effort to make new friends, and evaluate options for dealing with the problem in terms of where the person is in the divorce adjustment process.

As therapists it is important to help clients openly face feelings about loneliness and come to understand their own responsibility in its making. Denial of these feelings and the resulting displacement of anger and blame will only increase the problem. Often during this time individuals feel doubtful about their own capacities to love or to maintain stable relationships. The therapist should help the clients understand the feelings of loneliness and aid them in gaining self-acceptance.

During Stage II of the intimacy dissolution process, the conflict stage, it is possible that individuals might feel curious about dating, interested in dating, or even compelled to date. At this point, they may in fact enter the social world yet are still unsure of themselves. They may push themselves to date and have sex, only to feel ashamed and depressed afterward. Some individuals in this stage may use their sexuality as a weapon—to rebel against a sexually restrictive former spouse or a sexually restrictive upbringing. Some individuals in this stage use sexuality as self-punishment much in the same way that some allow themselves to be used sexually to prove to themselves that they are indeed worthless. In these cases, sex is used for manipulation, rebellion, and punishment. Areas for exploration in therapy are self-worth and self-esteem. Sexual needs are legitimate ones and, in these cases, the therapist could help the client understand the basic purposes of sexuality: enjoyment, communication, playfulness, and to build deeper relationships. At this time also, it is not unusual for men to report impotence or women to report orgasmic dysfunction or sexual disinterest.

During this stage it is also important to help the client clarify values about dating, relationships, and sexuality. Clarifying their values means they become aware of the beliefs and behaviors that they feel are important to them and are comfortable with. It also helps them to consistently act on their values and beliefs. Basically, therapists help clients sort through their sexual values and why they hold these particular values. It is useful for therapists to help clients set up realistic values for themselves so that they are not constantly failing to adjust their behavior to their values. After a sexual value has been clarified with the client, planning must be done to optimize the clients' chances of carrying the plan into action. Anxiety about newly achieved sexual freedom and the changes that have taken place in sexual codes and behavior is another common problem clients report in the therapy situation. Some persons appear to enjoy the freedom to have many sexual partners without commitment; others find the expectation that they must have sex with every new friend or date oppressive. Somewhere between these two extremes, others explore by trial and error their new sexual self-concept. With the individual who feels that sexuality should be free and easy, it would be useful for therapists to help the person fit sexuality into his or her own life. In other words, while sexuality may be very important to some clients, it is not their whole life. In this sense, the therapist helps the client put sexuality into a perspective. As clients cope with the dating and sex game, they often find they have to confront additional feelings of anger at having been used sexually, guilt over sexually exploiting others, or depression when intimacy needs are not met. In addition, both male and female clients often express concerns about the new emphasis on female orgasm and other changes in sexual mores. For these kinds of sex-related anxieties, the therapist could help the client recognize specific fears and anxieties; bring to consciousness personal needs, expectations, and values about sexuality; and hasten the reintegration of the sexual self so that the person can deal openly and honestly with potential sexual partners and choose whether and when to engage in sex and on what terms. Therapists can help the client deal with prioritizing and setting limits and boundaries on their sexuality. Boundaries are the dividing lines between constructive and destructive sexual expression. Persons who are in these situations at some point will have to practice willpower. Once they have set up their values and established a plan of action, ultimately they will have to mobilize their willpower in order to incorporate the values into their lifestyle. It is only with this kind of self-knowledge and comfort with one's own needs and values that a person can communicate honestly about sex and take responsibility for his or her own sexuality, thus gaining protection from the hazards of trial-and-error sexual encounters. After clients have accomplished this and are well on the road to consistency between values and behavior, it is important for them to evaluate and assess their sexual value system. If they feel comfortable with their actions, then they have affirmed their value system; if not, more value clarification work is needed.

Therapists should help the client approach new roles and responsibilities from a positive perspective. The individual may feel a sense of pride in his or her newfound competencies. For example, help the client find emotional support in friendships and family relations. It is crucial for the single parent to establish a support network outside of his or her family system. In this way, the person can achieve a new level of adult communication whose uncritical acceptance can greatly aid in reducing the person's feelings of guilt and shame.

In Stage III of the intimacy dissolution process, ambivalence, the person may sexually experiment. They may date and have sex with several individuals in an attempt to learn about their new sexual identities. One client reported having sex three times in one weekend with three different partners. Feeling youthful and free, they may enter into a relationship with a much younger person and engage in youthful activities. Some clients will seem to be picking up where they left off as a socially and sexually involved individual before they were married. Usually, these relationships are time limited and eventually the individual typically begins dating someone closer to his or her own age, emotionally and biologically. During this time also a person may feel, "My body is not getting any younger. I'd better have sex with this person now." In such situations, persons feel as though they are bartering sex for something else. In other words, clients are not engaging in sex for appropriate reasons; rather, they are acting out of curiosity or to affirm their attractiveness to the opposite sex. Therapists should help their clients understand what their values are regarding sexual motivations. Usually individuals who engage in sexual encounters based upon these reasons, again, usually lack self-esteem, commitment, and intimacy—characteristics most people consider important in sexual and social relationships.

During this stage the client might report specific sexual dysfunctions. At this time therapists should initially universalize and thereby detoxify these specific sexual dysfunctions. Loss of sexual desire, erectile dysfunction, premature ejaculation, and orgasmic difficulties may be present either alone or in context of the kinds of problems just discussed. The therapeutic assessment of these dysfunctions must encompass the individual's previous sexual functioning, the dynamics of the previous marriage, sexuality within the marriage, the overall impact of the divorce process on the person's sexual self-concept, and the present circumstances in which the sexual dysfunction is manifested. Regarding the extent to which the problem existed in the previous marriage and the possibility that it may have been a factor in the divorce, the therapist will have to be content with the client's version of the problem and its causes. The direction that the therapy takes will obviously depend on the overall assessment and on the therapist's level of competence for treating sexual dysfunctions.

It is only when the individual enters Stage IV of the intimacy dissolution process, the acceptance stage, that they have the acceptance and awareness of their own needs and desires to maintain a healthy social and sexual relationship. They have attained a balancing of self and relationship and at this point are probably able to enter into an intimate relationship. Although it is important for therapists working with individuals going through the intimacy dissolution process to consider the individual's sexual needs, problems, and issues, it is crucially important not to separate out the sexual areas of therapy from the psychological or emotional. Human behavior is wonderfully complex and to do so is to simplify this complexity.

One purpose of this book has been to explore the feelings and behavior of those individuals who are sexually single again. In so doing demographic data were presented in order to give therapists information on exactly how many individuals fall into this category. Socially constructed notions about psychological and sexual identity movement in terms of making the transition from a married person to a single or widowed person have been presented, including a discussion of the specific sociopsychological problems faced by single parents. Implications of specific therapy techniques were then considered, within which the specific problems of each stage of the intimacy dissolution process were then developed. For a summary of these stages and issues, please see Table 7.1.

The next section discusses HIV/AIDS and its effect on the sexually single population.

HIV/AIDS

Because of the impact of HIV/AIDS, therapy with sexually active adults in the twenty-first century is very different from therapy with sexually active adults in the 1970s and early 1980s, before people knew about AIDS. Therapists need to be aware of the disease process involved in AIDS so that they might be better able to educate their clients. The following basic information is useful for therapists when working with individuals who are sexually active.

The number of people infected with HIV in the United States is estimated to be about 1.5 million. In addition over 40,000 new AIDS cases are reported nationally every year. All of these individuals are believed to be capable of spreading the virus sexually or by sharing needles and syringes or other implements for intravenous (IV) drug use. Of these, an estimated 100,000 to 200,000 will come down with AIDS-related complex (ARC). It is difficult to predict the number who will develop AIDS, because symptoms sometimes take as long as nine years to appear. With our present knowledge, scientists predict that those infected with HIV will develop an illness that fits an accepted definition of AIDS within five years. This percentage increases with each passing year.

Numerous studies of HIV-infected people have shown that high levels of infectious HIV, viral antigens, and HIV nucleic acids (DNA and RNA) in the body predict immune system deterioration and an increased risk for developing AIDS. Conversely, patients with low levels of virus have a much lower risk of developing AIDS (Hammer et al., 1993).

The incidence of HIV infection is also difficult to estimate because new infections are largely asymptomatic and reported AIDS cases have a long and variable incubation period. However, there are indications that prevention efforts are succeeding. Since the prevalence of infection among gay men, intravenous drug users, and persons with hemophilia is high and infection persists, the prevalence of HIV is likely to remain high even without further transmission. Sexual intercourse with an infected partner, or with a risk-group member whose infection status is not known, is likely to constitute a substantial risk for the future. Simply reducing the number of partners will not be enough to avoid infection, if infection status is unknown and adequate precautions are not taken.

Transmission of HIV

Although HIV is found in several body fluids, a person acquires the virus during sexual contact with an infected person's blood, semen, vaginal secretions, or breast milk. The virus then enters the bloodstream through the rectum, vagina, penis, or mouth. Small unseen tears in the surface lining of the vagina or rectum may occur during insertion of the penis, fingers, or other objects, thus providing an entrance of the virus directly into the bloodstream. Therefore, HIV can be passed from penis to rectum and vagina and vice versa without a visible tear in the tissue or the presence of blood.

Risk Factors

What is clear and what everyone should know is that unprotected vaginal or anal intercourse is an efficient way to transmit the disease.

Although it has often been said that the virus is more easily passed during anal than vaginal intercourse, evidence to support the statement is lacking. There is no reason to doubt that a woman can acquire the disease from an infected male partner and men can contract the virus from their women partners, although probably not as easily. In Africa, the disease is primarily a heterosexual one, with the major route of transmission penile/vaginal and vice versa.

Though the risk groups for AIDS are well understood, little is known about the absolute risk of acquiring infection through sexual contact. This risk depends on two variables: the number of sexual contacts with an infected person and the likelihood of transmission of infection during sexual contact with an infected partner.

The number of sexual contacts with an infected partner will depend on the number of partners, the number of sexual contacts with each partner, and the prevalence of infection in those partners. If infection with HIV is like other sexually transmitted infections, repeated exposure to an infected person is not necessary for infection, but the probability that transmission will occur increases with the frequency of exposure. As the prevalence of infection in the population increases, the likelihood of infection in a random partner also increases. Therefore, in an epidemic, one would expect to observe an increasing risk of infection as the prevalence of infection increases.

The risk of transmission during sexual contact with an infected person depends on the type of body fluid the uninfected partner is exposed to, the anatomic area that is exposed (or the possible route of entry of the virus), and the level of infection in the infected person. Although HIV has been isolated from blood, saliva, semen, and vaginal secretions, little information is available in the relative infectivity of these body fluids. Since the virus preferentially infects lymphocytes, the concentration is probably highest in secretions containing lymphocytes, such as blood, semen, and vaginal secretions. The ease with which the virus enters the body depends on the physical properties of the exposed area. It is highly unlikely that the virus crosses intact skin. The fragility of the lining of the rectum may account for the positive association between HIV and receptive anal intercourse reported in many studies of AIDS and HIV infection in gay men. However, some infected gay men and nearly all infected heterosexuals, including the majority of infected prostitutes and other women in Africa, have no history of receptive anal intercourse, indicating that

AIDS is clearly transmissable through heterosexual penile/vaginal intercourse.

HIV seems less likely to be transmitted during a single contact than other sexually transmitted infections. The transmission rate of gonorrhea is estimated at 22 to 25 percent after a single exposure in a man to an infected woman and at 50 percent for a woman whose male partner is infected. The risk of transmission of other infections after a single exposure is less well understood. Evidence for infection is found in about 30 percent of the sexual contacts of an individual with primary or secondary syphilis, but this often includes multiple exposures and some of the contacts may represent the source rather than the spread of infection.

HIV is transmissible from men to women and from women to men, but the risk of transmission per single sexual exposure is not well defined. Two studies of the wives of hemophiliacs have each found that 2 (9.5 percent) of 21 were seropositive. As part of a study of infected male military personnel, seven of the steady heterosexual partners of these men were tested; five were infected. A fourth study tested heterosexual partners of intravenous drug abusers with AIDS or AIDS-related complex and found that 20 (48 percent) of 42 were seropositive. None of these studies can accurately quantify exposure, since the date of infection for the initial case is not known. However, since the people with HIV infection were probably infected for a much longer period of time than the people with acute hepatitis B, HIV is probably less easily sexually transmitted than hepatitis B.

Nonsexual Infection

AIDS can be transmitted nonsexually by injecting the virus directly into the bloodstream, such as that which occurs during intravenous drug use, blood transfusions, prenatally from a pregnant mother to her child, or through breast milk. The virus must be passed into the immune system cells in the bloodstream of the uninfected person. Therefore, contact must be made between the body fluids of one person and the blood of the other in order for infection to occur.

Drug Abusers

AIDS can be transmitted nonsexually to those who inject drugs into their veins. They are another population at high risk and with high rates of HIV infection. Users of intravenous drugs make up about 25 percent of the cases of AIDS throughout the country. HIV is carried in contaminated blood left in the needle, syringe, or other drug-related implements, and the virus is injected into the new victim by reusing dirty syringes and needles. Even the smallest amount of infected blood left in the needle or syringe can contain enough live HIV to be passed on to the next user of the contaminated implements.

No one should use intravenous drugs, foremost because of the risk of addiction, poor health, family disruption, emotional disturbances, and death that follow. However, many drug users are addicted to drugs and for one reason or another have not changed their behavior. For these people, the only way to avoid contracting HIV is to use a clean, previously unused needle, syringe, or other implement necessary for the injection of the drug solution.

Hemophilia

Prior to 1985, some persons with hemophilia (a blood clotting disorder that makes them subject to bleeding) were infected with HIV either through blood transfusion or the use of blood products to help their blood clot. Now, special heat processes have virtually eliminated the risk of infection for the nation's 20,000 hemophiliacs whose lives depend on regular infusions of special blood-clotting products. Receiving blood concentrate is nearly 100 percent safe now that we know how to prepare safe blood products to aid clotting. Some studies of these patients whose blood lacks a critical clotting factor have not found a single case of HIV infection since late 1984, when drug firms first began use of heat process on these blood concentrates. Hemophiliacs represent a very small percentage of the cases of HIV throughout the country.

Transfusions

There is still a very slight risk that HIV can be passed on from transfusions (about 1 in 50,000 units). That translates to about 70 transfusion-related HIV cases a year nationally. Blood-screening tests are making the nation's blood supply much safer for the 3 to 4 million patients who get transfusions each year. Currently, all blood donors are initially screened and blood is not accepted from high-risk individuals. Blood that has been collected for use is tested for the presence of the HIV antibody. However, some people may have had a blood transfusion prior to March 1985 before it was known how to screen blood for safe transfusion and some became infected at that time with HIV. Fortunately, the number of these cases today is much smaller. With routine testing of blood products, the blood supply for transfusion is now safer than it has ever been.

Still, some experts remain concerned about transfusions. Experts say the source of today's few units tainted with HIV are collected in a window period that occurs right after infection. A lag time of several months occurs before antibodies to the virus appear and tests sensitive to them can be effective. However, the risk of getting HIV from blood must be put in perspective. Transfusions are a life-sustaining therapy given only under critical circumstances. Blood is probably one of the safest parts of the lifesaving effort.

Casual Contact

No known risk of nonsexual infection can be found in most situations that we encounter in our daily lives. We know that family members living with individuals who have HIV do not become infected except through sexual contact. There is no evidence of transmission of HIV by everyday, common family contact. This includes sharing telephones, toilets, utensils, cups, and spoons that have been used by a family member infected with HIV. Although small amounts of the virus have been detected in saliva, there is a special protein in saliva that effectively kills the virus. Thus, there have been no known cases of acquiring HIV through kissing (CDC, 2003).

> The risk of health care workers being exposed to HIV on the job is very low, especially if they carefully follow universal precautions (i.e., using protective practices and personal protective equipment to prevent HIV and other blood-borne infections). Again, it is important to remember that casual, everyday contact with an HIV-infected person does not expose health care workers or anyone else to HIV. For health care workers on the job, the main risk of HIV transmission is through accidental injuries from needles and other sharp instruments that may be contaminated

with the virus; however even this risk is small. Scientists estimate that the risk of infection from a needle-stick is less than 1 percent, a figure based on the findings of several studies of health care workers who received punctures from HIV-contaminated needles or were otherwise exposed to HIV-contaminated blood.

About 2,500 health care workers who were caring for AIDS patients when they were at their sickest have been carefully studied and tested for infection with HIV. These doctors, nurses, and other health care givers had been exposed to the patient's blood, stool, and other body fluids through spills or being accidentally stuck with a needle. Upon testing, only three who had accidentally stuck themselves with a needle had a positive antibody test for exposure to HIV.

Risk Among Heterosexuals

Although the initial discovery was in the homosexual community, AIDS is not a disease only of homosexuals. AIDS is found in heterosexual people as well. AIDS is not a black or white disease. AIDS is not just a male disease. AIDS is found in women; it is found in children. Presently AIDS in increasing at alarming rates among heterosexual women. Eventually, if left unchecked, AIDS will probably increase and spread among people in the same manner as other such sexually transmitted diseases as syphilis and gonorrhea, which exist at alarming rates today.

What started out as a disease afflicting mostly homosexual men and intravenous drug users has spread into the general population. For heterosexuals, fears about the spread of AIDS through casual contact have yielded to concern to catching it in a brief sexual encounter. It is becoming clear that HIV/AIDS is a profound killer that is not going to go away soon.

In 2003, the estimated number of diagnoses of AIDS in the United States was 43,171. Adult and adolescent AIDS cases totaled 43,112 with 31,614 cases in males and 11,498 cases in females. Also in 2003, there were 59 AIDS cases estimated in children under age thirteen. The cumulative estimated number of diagnoses of AIDS through 2003 in the United States is 929,985. Adult and adolescent AIDS cases total 920,566 with 749,887 cases in males and 170,679 cases in females. Through the same time period, 9,419 AIDS cases were estimated in children under age thirteen (CDC, 2003). Some studies indicate that women do not spread HIV as easily as men do. In fact, some studies suggest that women may be acting as a buffer, slowing the spread of the virus to the general population. Other researchers refer to women as vectors, providing the connections to many areas of the population. These statistics indicate that heterosexual women then face greater danger than heterosexual men in casual sex. Many experts believe that a key factor in the course of the progression of AIDS in the United States is the efficiency of transmission from women to men.

Vaginal sex can transmit HIV to either the male or the female partner, but numerous studies in developed countries have shown that in the absence of other risk factors (like STDs) men are two to three times more likely to transmit HIV to women than vice versa. The area susceptible to infection is much larger in women (vagina, cervix, and uterus) than in men (head of the penis, exposed urethra). Women are exposed to a larger quantity of infectious fluid (ejaculate) than men (vaginal fluids). Vaginal fluids contain less HIV on the average than semen. Women retain the secretions within the body after sex while men are only exposed during the actual sex act (Winkelstein et al., 1987).

Dr. Polly Thomas, former coordinator of Pediatric HIV/AIDS Surveillance Projects at the New York City Department of Health, thinks that American women may not be efficient transmitters and may be temporarily holding back the spread of the virus into the heterosexual population. No one has any idea how many people are infected but asymptomatic, or how much transmission is going on. Men and women outside of monogamous relationships and many people in them must ask themselves, "Am I at any risk of exposure to the virus?" More frightening, since ten years can pass before someone exhibits any visible sign of infection, we must ask "Have I ever been exposed?" People falsely perceive themselves as immune and, moreover, possessed of an intuitive power that enables them to choose safe partners.

Women and AIDS

Michelle is a fifty-three-year-old administrative assistant to a top executive in a very exclusive department store. Prior to her divorce, she had been married to Paul since she was eighteen. They grew up in the same neighborhood and knew each other most of their whole lives. They had two grown children, who were both married.

About five years ago, Paul decided he wanted a divorce. Michelle was devastated, especially when she learned Paul (age fifty-seven) was seeing a twenty-three-year-old woman. She could not understand how this could happen to her at this time in her life. She had devoted herself to Paul and the children and now, without these roles to fall back on, she felt lost and alone. Her early abondonment fears were triggered, and often, terrified in the middle of the night, she would call Paul to come and hold her. She entered therapy and after about a year began to feel better about the possibilities for the future.

Although she was an attractive woman, she had no interest in other men and was extremely reluctant to begin dating. Finally, after being "dragged out by her friends," she met a man who she started dating. Herman was sixty-two, was retired, but worked part-time. He adored Michelle. They began dating and after a few months began sleeping together. Michelle was very surprised because she experienced sexual pleasure with Herman that she had never experienced with Paul. They had an excellent sexual relationship for the next year—loving and free.

One day Herman became very ill and could barely breathe. They took him to the hospital and he was diagnosed with AIDS two weeks later. He was unable to breathe because he had AIDS-related pneumonia. Apparently, he was given contaminated blood when he had bypass surgery many years before. Michelle was once again devastated; she knew he was going to die. She was also terrified; did she have it? She was tested for AIDS and spent three weeks waiting for the results in a state of chronic terror, crying constantly and feeling rage for Paul, because "it's his fault that I was out there in the first place." Fortunately, Michelle tested negative. She has to be tested again in three months just to make certain, but the doctor feels that she's probably okay.

Now she has other problems. She is terrified of catching HIV from Herman. She doesn't want to kiss him; she cringes at the thought of having him sleep in her bed, and sex is out of the question. Herman is depressed, scared for his life, lonely for Michelle's touch, guilty about the possibility of having given her AIDS. He hardly sees her anymore.

The most likely route of HIV transmission for women in the United States over the past few years has been through male IV drug abusers, but this is changing quickly. If a male is an IV drug abuser, his risk of contacting HIV is very high to begin with. When this male has intercourse with a woman, her risk increases dramatically. Almost 30 percent of women with HIV contracted the virus through a male IV drug abuser. Heterosexual transmission appears to occur more easily through IV drug use than through any other method. Women are at a phenomenal risk of getting the disease today as compared to five or ten years ago. In the United States, the transmission of HIV is more likely to occur from male to female. Although not much is known as to the reason for this, one theory is that men were likely the first round of the epidemic since they are the majority of ones infected. Men inoculate their partners with a substantial dose of the virus during intercourse (in the ejaculatory fluid), while most women do not. Therapists should keep in mind that HIV/AIDS disproportionately affects poor women, women of color, and drug users.

According to a study conducted by the CDC in Atlanta, Georgia, regarding the transmission of HIV, less than 8 percent of HIV cases are contracted from women (CDC, 1998; CDC, 1997). In sexually active couples, of the fifty men with HIV who did not use condoms during intercourse, eight passed on the virus. Out of the twenty women infected, only one male contracted HIV when not using condoms. All these people had penile/vaginal intercourse.

THERAPY STRATEGIES

Who Should Be Tested?

Therapists should recommend that anyone who is unsure about whether to get the test for AIDS ask himself or herself the following questions:

1. Are you a man who has had sex with other men that involved the exchange of body fluids at any time since 1977? A single contact may have been sufficient for infection to occur.
2. Have you shared syringes, rubber bulbs, "works," "cookers," or needles for intravenous drug use (such as shooting heroin or cocaine) at any time since 1977?
3. Could any of your sexual partners since 1977 have belonged to any one of the above groups?
4. Did you receive whole blood or blood products, donor sperm, organs, or tissues at any time before March 1985?
5. Have you or any of your sexual partners been sexually active in Haiti or central Africa (e.g., Zaire, Rwanda, Zambia, Uganda)? These are countries where the prevalence of HIV infection seems to be high among people not included in one of the acknowledged highest-risk categories in the United States (that is, gay or bisexual men and IV drug users).

If clients answered yes to any of these questions, they ought to follow the guidelines described next and consider getting tested, both to avoid exposing themselves and to avoid exposing their sexual partners. Therapists can be extremely helpful to persons worried about their HIV status. It is never too late for individuals to begin protecting themselves against HIV. Even if they have reason to believe that they have already been infected, it is always to their benefit to avoid further exposure, since multiple exposures may trigger the illness.

How Can a Person Reduce the Chance of Getting HIV?

In the absence of a vaccine or therapy, the major hope for preventing transmission is the adoption of safer-sex behavior. Control of certain behaviors can stop the further spread of AIDS. Knowing the facts about AIDS can prevent the spread of the disease. Education of those who are at risk for infecting themselves or infecting other people is the only way to stop the spread of AIDS. Certain types of behaviors lead to infection with HIV, and personal measures must be taken for effective protection. If the AIDS epidemic is to be stopped, the disease must be understood—its cause, its nature, and its prevention. Precautions must be taken.

How Can the Virus Be Stopped? What Are Some Guidelines?

The best way to fight AIDS is to prevent transmission of HIV. Transmission is known to occur only through the exchange of infected blood, vaginal secretions, or semen; it is this exchange that must be prevented. Certain actions may help avoid exposure or further exposure to HIV infection. Utilizing these behaviors may require a substantial change in sexual behavior for those at a high risk for HIV infection. Everyone should assess his or her level of risk and undertake risk reduction behavior as necessary.

Recommendations for People Who Are HIV Positive

People who have HIV should observe routine and reasonable precautions against accidental contact by others with their blood or semen. Hands or skin may be washed with soap and water. Other surfaces where blood or semen have been spilled may be cleaned with soap and water or a mild disinfectant solution, such as 10 percent bleach solution. Caution should be exercised so that toothbrushes, razors, tweezers, and other instruments which may carry blood are not shared. This is good advice not only for avoiding HIV infection but also for avoiding more common diseases. Remember that the lining of the rectum is fragile. Do not engage in activities that might damage the rectum. Unprotected oral-anal contact (rimming) should be avoided; it might spread the virus and certainly can transmit other diseases (such as amebiasis and hepatitis B).

Alcohol and nonmedical drugs impair judgment and lower the efficiency of the immune system. Avoid using nonmedical drugs and be aware of the side effects of alcohol consumption. Poppers (amyl or butyl nitrate) and inhalant drugs are immunosuppressive and may be associated with increased risk of contracting HIV. A spermicide called nonoxynol-9 is found in some diaphragm contraceptive jellies and creams as well as on some lubricated condoms. It has been shown to kill the virus and so may help prevent transmission.

General health is also important. A person with any infection will do better if he or she is well nourished, rested, exercising regularly, not smoking, not drinking to excess, and not overstressed. The same is true of persons with an HIV infection. Note that urine may contain the virus and so should not be allowed to enter the mouth or come in contact with open cuts on the body. To protect themselves and their partners, HIV-positive persons must evaluate their risk factors to determine how to modify their sexual behaviors.

Therapists can assist HIV-positive persons to follow risk-reduction behaviors in any future sexual encounter. Simply reducing the number of different sexual partners provides no protection if a person continues to have unsafe sexual relations.

If a person is not sure whether a sexual partner belongs to one of these risk groups and feels he or she cannot talk about sexual and drug use histories with his or her partner, then the individual should *always* follow the risk-reduction guidelines.

Risk-Reduction Guidelines

Risk reduction is appropriate for those with significant risk factors as just described. The following guidelines divide common sexual behaviors into three categories of risk for transmitting HIV: high risk, lower risk, and no risk. Behaviors in the high-risk category involve the contact of blood or semen with mucous membranes and are therefore extremely dangerous. High-risk behaviors should be avoided at all costs if one of the partners may be carrying HIV. No-risk behaviors involve no exchange of bodily fluids and are therefore completely safe; they can be practiced regardless of whether either of the partners is carrying the virus.

The situation is less clear cut in the case of the lower-risk category. Behaviors in this category involve some risk of the exchange of bodily fluids other than blood or semen. These fluids may contain HIV but at a low concentration that makes infection less likely. Saliva is almost certainly safe, and preliminary studies suggest that oral sex is unlikely to transmit the virus. Despite this, it is impossible to prove that lower-risk behaviors will never transmit the virus. The best that can be said is that these behaviors are much less dangerous than those in the high-risk category. In cases where one or both sexual partners may be carrying the virus, the partners should carefully discuss which activities and what levels of risk are acceptable to both of them.

What Are Some General Measures Clients or Anyone Else Can Take?

1. If a client has been involved in any high-risk sexual activities or has injected illicit drugs into his or her body, he or she might want to consider taking a blood test to see if HIV infection has occurred.
2. If the test is positive, or if the individual engages in high-risk activities and chooses not to have a test, he or she should be counseled to tell all sexual partners. If they then jointly decide to have sex, they must protect each other by always using a condom during intercourse.
3. If the client's partner has had a positive blood test showing that he or she has been infected with HIV, a condom should always be used during sexual intercourse.
4. If the client is at high risk, he or she should also avoid oral contact with the penis, vagina, or rectum.
5. The client should avoid all sexual activities that could cause cuts or tears in the linings of the rectum, vagina, or penis.
6. Clients should not have sex with prostitutes. Infected male and female prostitutes are frequently also intravenous drug abusers;

therefore, they may infect clients via sexual intercourse and other intravenous drug abusers by sharing their intravenous drug equipment. Female prostitutes can also infect their unborn babies.

In sum, the most certain way to avoid contracting HIV and to control the AIDS epidemic in the United States is for individuals to avoid promiscuous sexual practices, to maintain mutually faithful monogamous sexual relationships, to avoid injecting illicit drugs, and to use condoms.

Sexual transmission of HIV can be prevented only if precautions are taken. The need for precautions depends on whether either sexual partner is infected. If neither partner is infected then precautions need not be taken. If only one partner is infected, the most certain way to avoid transmission is to avoid having sexual intercourse. This would not preclude massage and mutual masturbation if there is no exposure of the mucous membranes (e.g., rectum, mouth, vagina, or penis) to body fluids of the infected partner. Another approach that reduces but does not eliminate the risk of transmission is the consistent use of condoms or condoms plus spermicides.

For individuals who wish to remain sexually active, the best protection against AIDS is condoms.

Condoms

Condoms have become the weapon against AIDS, recommended for use in oral sex, anal sex, and sexual intercourse. A study showed that in laboratory tests HIV cannot pass through either a synthetic or a natural skin condom (Kubic, 1997). Many experts are skeptical and believe that natural skin condoms are more porous and offer less effective protection, and therefore should be avoided. Although condoms are effective in preventing HIV transmission, it is important to note that condoms can break, leak, or be used improperly and are associated with an annual 10 percent failure rate in pregnancy prevention—and a woman is fertile only a few days of each month, whereas a person with HIV can transmit it anytime. Improper use of condoms or a tear in the condom could lead to infection.

Therapists often assume that clients know how to use condoms and that specific instruction is not necessary. This assumption is often incorrect. Women who have been in a long-term marriage, for example, and have not had experience with partners other than their former spouse may not have specific knowledge in this area. Many times men, while they have knowledge about condom usage, do not know that only specific types of condoms are effective against the AIDS virus.

How To Use Condoms Effectively

1. The use of condoms is strongly suggested. If an individual is unsure of a partner's complete sexual history, the couple should always use a condom. Condoms are useful for preventing the transmission of HIV, and also provide protection against diseases such as gonorrhea, chlamydial infections, syphilis, and herpes. Note that many other methods of birth control, such as using a diaphragm with a spermacide, do *not* provide adequate protection against the transmission of HIV infection and other venereal diseases.
2. When putting on a condom, leave about one-half inch of room at the tip to avoid semen breaking the condom upon ejaculation. If the penis is uncircumcised, retract the foreskin before putting on the condom. If intercourse is continued to ejaculation, withdraw promptly.
3. During withdrawal, hold the rim of the condom firmly against the base of the penis so that the condom cannot slip off and no semen can escape.
4. Use proper lubrication. Lubrication is important to avoid tearing the condom or abrading body tissue. Always use a water-soluble lubricant such as K-Y Jelly. Never use oil-based lubricants such as Vaseline, since these may damage the latex of the condom.

Spermicides

Spermicides containing nonionic surfactants have in vitro activity against syphilis, gonorrhea, and herpes simplex virus. One of these spermicides, nonoxynol-9, kills HIV in vitro when tested in concentrations similar to those in a commercially available spermicide product. Uncontrolled epidemiologic studies suggest that women who consistently use spermicides have some protection against gonor-rhea, but no studies have been done to evaluate whether the use of a lubricant containing nonoxynol-9 is safe or effective in preventing sexually transmissible diseases during anal intercourse. Spermicides alone should be considered inadequate to protect one from HIV infection.

If both sexual partners are infected with HIV, the risk associated with unprotected sexual intercourse is not clear. It is not known if rein-fection with the virus causes the disease to progress or if other sexually transmitted infections act as cofactors for the development of AIDS in people infected with HIV. Since such cofactors or coinfections are theoretically important, infected couples should take precautions by avoiding intercourse or by using condoms consistently.

Finally, if the infectious status of a sexual partner is not known, or if either partner is at risk (because of a history of a homosexual contact, intravenous drug use, hemophilia, or sexual contact with another person at risk), it is prudent to assume that the partner could be in-fected. Heterosexual contact with persons who have had multiple sex-ual contacts (e.g., prostitutes) would also pose a risk for heterosexual transmission, particularly in areas where there is a high prevalence of infection among heterosexuals. Prevention efforts should concentrate on therapy with people about ways to reduce the risk of transmitting HIV infection. Gay men's organizations have been advising all gay men to practice safer sex at all times.

Other efforts could include educating the general public about the risks and the way infection is and is not transmitted. People can then make informed decisions whether to have sexual contact and know how to take precautions during sexual encounters with a partner who may be infected. The use of condoms could be increased by educa-tion, easier accessibility, and use of modern marketing techniques.

Even condoms are not 100 percent reliable in preventing transmis-sion of the AIDS virus; using spermicidal jelly along with condoms is safer yet, but still not totally safe. The natural type of condom is un-satisfactory. For the time being, the latex type is more reliable.

HIV is contagious and control of this disease may be facilitated by the willingness of AIDS patients and those at risk to modify their sex-ual behavior in ways that reduce the risk of transmitting the disease to others. These behavioral modifications also have direct personal health implications for affected individuals because they reduce the risk of acquiring further infections that may exacerbate the disease. At this time, a clear distinction among the uninfected, the infectious, and the infected individual is not possible given the possible long incubation period of the disease. All sexually active individuals are counseled to alter certain aspects of their sexual behavior that may increase the risk of acquiring any of the sexually transmitted diseases. These changes include

1. reducing the number of partners,
2. avoiding anonymous sex partners,
3. modifying those sexual practices that may present a significant opportunity for the exchange of bodily fluids (stool, blood, urine, and semen), and
4. reducing use of volatile nitrites, barbituates, amphetamines, intravenous and various other illicit drugs, and alcohol because they decrease the person's ability to control behavior.

What Implications Does This Have for the Sexually Single?

The appearance of this deadly disease has far-reaching implications for the sexually single. First of all, a new type of sexual relating must take place: straightforward and open. The conversation must occur in the beginning of the relationship, not when both partners are in bed. The use of condoms must be discussed early on, and the relationship must be based on the results of that talk.

Clients must be educated about the nature of HIV and its transmission routes. They need to understand the importance of discussing all these factors with their potential sex partners prior to the bedroom scene. They need to role-play with their therapist, discussing the specific words they will use and how and when they will inform partners that they will not have sex without a condom. This is especially useful for women. Unfortunately, all too often, women are educated about HIV, say they will use condoms, go through the role-plays, and then, in the heat of the moment, fail to insist on the use of a condom. They are putting themselves at tremendous risk. Following are some typical reasons given for not using a condom:

> "Well, he's only dated three people in the last three years so he's safe."

"He's healthy and very athletic and hasn't been sick in the past
   five years."
"I was too embarrassed to ask him to use a condom."
"I asked him and he said he hates condoms, so I just went along
   with it. I'm sure I'm okay."

Sometimes, the woman will tell the man to use a condom and he will
and then, two months later, she stops asking—somehow feeling that
she "knows" him now and "knows" he's okay. These quotes, by the
way, were not made by adolescents. They were professional, educated women living in a large cosmopolitan city.

The reasons why women often do not take care of themselves are
varied and complicated, many of them having to do with socially constructed notions about assertive behavior in women or not wanting to
hurt a man's feelings. However, being sexually single in the twenty-
first century can be deadly if proper precaution is not taken.

AIDS-related fears are commonly discussed in a therapist's office.
Following are some questions the therapist can explore with the sexually single client.

1. Given that AIDS exists, what do you feel you "should" change
   sexually?
2. What do you feel you "have" to change?
3. What do you think you "will" change?
4. What do miss about sex in the good old days, the "Woodstock"
   days, when sex was free, easy, frequent, and varried? What else
   do you miss? [If the client experienced the sexual liberation of
   the 1960s and 1970s and enjoyed it, help the client to mourn
   these losses.]
5. What do you like about safer sex?
6. What are some "new" things you can do, different sexual
   practices, using safer-sex procedures?
7. What kinds of alternatives are there to traditional intercourse?
8. How would you bring up the topic of safer sex with someone?

It is also important to help them understand that they have control
over their lives, and to help women understand that they have a right
to protect themselves.

Ann, a recently separated client, accepted an invitation to dinner. After dinner, when the man drove her to her car, he passionately kissed her good night. This led to about an hour of passionate kissing in the car—nothing more. The next morning, she raced to the doctor's office, convinced that she had contracted HIV. She demanded and was given an AIDS test, which was negative. She then spent the next six months in the library reading everything she could about AIDS and had herself retested six months later. Ann is an example of the worried well.

Most sexually single people will not get AIDS, but many people worry about it. Depending upon their situation, worry is to be expected. Individuals need to learn to assess their risk realistically. If they have a significant risk factor and they are not following the risk-reduction guidelines, or if extreme anxiety is interfering with their normal living, they ought to explore this in therapy. Characteristic problems are depression, periods of celibacy punctuated by episodes of unsafe sex, and obsessive preoccupation with illness or symptoms.

SUMMARY

It is over two decades since the virus first entered the U.S. population. There is absolutely no evidence that the disease can be spread by casual contact, such as shaking hands, sharing meals, or just being near someone with the virus.

Infection can be prevented by using safer-sex practices, by having sex only with an uninfected partner, and by avoiding sex with multiple partners. The use of condoms during sex can greatly decrease the possibility of transmitting the virus. Practices that injure body tissues (such as anal intercourse) should be avoided, as should oral-genital contact. Drug users should not share needles or syringes. Those who continue to share needles are being urged to sterilize them with common household bleach.

AIDS is no longer the concern of any one segment of society; it is the concern of us all. No American's life is in danger if he or she or his or her sexual partner does not engage in high-risk sexual behavior or use shared needles or syringes to inject illicit drugs into the body. People who engage in high-risk sexual behavior or who shoot drugs are risking infection with HIV and are risking their lives and the lives of others, including their unborn children.

We cannot yet know the full impact of AIDS in our society. From a clinical point of view, new manifestations of AIDS may be appearing—for example, mental disturbances due to HIV infection in the brains of carriers of the virus. From a social point of view, it may bring an end to the free-wheeling sexual lifestyle that has been called the sexual revolution. Economically, the care of AIDS patients will put a tremendous strain on our already-overburdened and costly health care delivery system. Clinically, it is the therapist's responsibility to educate and help clients who are at risk to use safer-sex practices.

PART III:
SINGLE AGAIN AND DEALING
WITH THE LARGER SYSTEMS

Chapter 8

Interacting with School Personnel

THE PATHOLOGY ASSUMPTION

Perhaps therapist's diagnostic skills face no greater challenge than the formulation of an understanding of the school behavior and academic difficulties of a child from a single-parent family. In examining the literature on single-parent families, it was relatively easy to find research that supported a deficit model of the children living in these families. Many of the initial articles reviewed focused on the pathology and negativistic ramifications of the divorced family setting (e.g., see Walsh, 1990). Upon closer investigation, however, it became readily apparent that many methodological problems existed with this research (Emery, 1982; Marsh, 1990).

In Guttman (1988), bias by teachers and school psychologists, participants in many studies, reflects a low reliability. Since these school personnel not only participate in evaluations of children but also read and utilize the studies for educational purposes, society causes and is reinforced by figures and observations which could be seriously questionable. Flawed teacher ratings of child behaviors have "raised doubt about studies concluding that children from two parent families function better than do children of divorce" (Blechman, 1982, as cited in Guttman, 1988).

The deficit model, supported or not by research, seems to enjoy wide acceptance. Santrock and Tracy (1978) discussed moral behaviors in terms of children of divorce and children from two-parent families. They concluded that differences could be found only on teacher ratings. This is interesting to note, since other studies not using teacher ratings failed to find differences in school achievement test scores when comparing father-present and father-absent children. It is Guttman and Santrock's contention that teacher ratings are based on stereotyped variables derived from middle-class expectations. It was observed that teachers rated boys and girls of divorce lower than those children from two-parent families, although girls were rated better than boys in either case.

A very important question arises in light of Guttman's discussion. Does teacher bias in fact cause lower student functioning for children of divorce? Is lower rating a self-fulfilling prophecy? In 1978, Santrock and Tracy showed a twenty-minute video to thirty teachers. The subject was an eight-year-old boy. When teachers were told that the child was from a divorced family background, they rated him lower on happiness, emotional adjustment, and the ability to cope with stress. This evolved into Santrock and Tracy's implicit personality theory and led Guttman to conduct a further study. Teachers were asked to view a film of a nine-year-old child from Tel Aviv. Student peers were also asked to view the same film. The teachers and students were told that the child was female or male, to account for bias in terms of gender. The child was filmed to demonstrate twenty-three characteristics spanning emotional and other behaviors. Seven of the behaviors were school related. The subjects were asked to rate the students on a scale of one (lowest rating) to five (highest rating). The results concluded that children were judged less favorably if the rater was told that the child was from a divorced family. Teachers seemed to rate lower than did peer-aged members of the rating panel. Female children of divorce, overall, were rated lower in academics than their male counterparts, but boys of divorce were rated lower in the affective domain (emotions). The main point is that accurate assessment is made more difficult by the assumption often made by single parents, school officials, classroom teachers, and guidance therapists that the child's problems are always caused by the absence of one parent.

Many other questions have been raised by researchers in terms of bias. As Fassell (1991) suggests, we need to question the manner in which research in the area of divorce reflects the bias of society in favor of the two-parent family. She feels that with research carrying the implication that children of divorce are flawed, it follows by implication that these children will eventually make flawed choices themselves. This is not necessarily true.

Attempting to learn about the other side of the coin was quite difficult because initially locating citations to support the position that positive outcomes can occur for children of divorce was not an easy task. The following studies are presented not to convince the reader that divorce should be a precondition for academic achievement but rather that all children do not suffer academically from this transition. The literature and theoretical hypotheses and interpretations focus on the pathology and dysfunction in these children—in many cases serving to create self-fulfilling prophecies. It is time that the professionals working with these children examine their own assumptions so that they do no more harm. Following are some methodologically sound studies that examined academic scores and children in single-parent families. The results clearly indicate that there is no one academic consequence to living in a single-parent family: some children have problems; for some there is no effect; and for others there is an improvement.

Watts and Watts (1991) studied more than 4,000 Canadian high school students from two-parent and female-headed single-parent families. They found that the ability and educational aspirations of the student have the largest direct effect on student academic achievement, whereas the effect of family configuration (one parent versus two parent) was negligible. The authors rated academic orientation, self-concept, the involvement of significant others, the involvement of parents, and even socioeconomic status as better indicators than the marital status of their parents.

They believe that other factors, such as whether the children witnessed any physical violence in their home prior to the onset of single-parent family life and the attitude of the mother toward her status as a single parent, are more important factors in determining the outcomes of divorce for children.

McCombs and Forehand (1989) studied low-, medium-, and high-achieving adolescents and found that the two variables most accounting for the variance between low and high grade achievers were the mother's reports of conflict between her and her ex-spouse in front of the child, and the adolescent's report of the intensity of conflict between himself or herself and the mother. These findings indicate that school performance after divorce is far from uniform and possibly caused by more complex factors than the divorce itself.

In a review of studies between 1970 and 1980, Cashion (1982) concluded that children in female-headed single-parent homes are likely to have good emotional adjustment, good self-esteem, and school success, and do as well in school as children from two-parent families when socioeconomic factors are controlled.

Wood and Lewis (1990) compared thirty-two divorced mother custody families with second- and fourth-grade boys and girls with a control group from two-parent homes. They examined three variables—family structure (one parent or two parents); coparental relationship variables such as trust, frequency of contact, and quality of coparental relationship; and the children's behavioral adjustment at school. In contrast to earlier studies they found no significant differences in behavior problems between children of single- and two-parent homes. Structure of family was not found to be a significant predictor variable accounting for variance in children's school behavior. However, two of the three coparental relationship variables were selected as significant predictors. A lower frequency of coparental interaction was related to greater number of incidences of acting-out behavior in school; moreover, low-quality/high-conflict coparental relationships were significantly related to acting-out behaviors and distractibility.

These results imply that children's behavioral problems are impacted more by problems in the family system (as evidenced by difficult coparental relationships) than by divorce and single-parent status. In other words, divorce itself is neither positive nor negative, and the outcomes of divorce are at least in part a function of the behavior of the parents.

These researchers caution teachers to be aware of basing their judgment of student behavior or school performance on their assumptions about the home life of the child, in particular their status as a member of a single-parent family.

The literature also points to longitudinal studies dealing with performance and children of divorce. A 5-year study (Kaye, 1989) involving 457 students (50 percent from 2-parent homes) revealed that although achievement scores dropped in the months after divorce, the overall grades did not seem to be adversely affected. The study went on to state that a crisis model of divorce is only partially correct and needs to be complemented by a cumulative stress model which focuses on the problems that persist or gradually increase following divorce.

Perhaps the most impressive study was done by the National Center for Education Statistics (Snyder and Hoffman, 1990; NCES,

2001; National Household Survey, 1998). These researchers tracked a large representative sample of high school students. The article states that across all the various comparisons and all the different outcomes, family configuration had remarkably little effect on student growth and changes during the last two years of high school. The lack of effect of single-parent and stepparent families was also consistent for boys and girls in single-mother, single-father, mother-stepfather, and father-stepmother families. Taken together, results of the various analyses indicate that family configuration has little discernible effect during the final two years of high school.

Further research regarding effects of divorce on academic performance is cited by Beer (1989). In this study there were no significant effects for the composite score from the Iowa Tests of Basic Skills when compared to marital status of parents.

According to Gately and Schwebel (1991) divorced parents who value and use appropriate support from friends, therapists, and relatives experience a more positive post-divorce adjustment (Woody et al., 1984). The same is true of children. Support given directly to children by peers, relatives, teachers, guidance therapists, and additional caretakers can promote social competencies and reduce behavioral problems. A supportive school environment can facilitate a favorable postdivorce adjustment in children. Although having therapy resources available is beneficial, simply having a safe, orderly, and predictable school environment with high expectations and norms for achievement is associated with a positive emotional, behavioral, and academic postdivorce outcomes in children (Guidubaldi, 1983).

Children respond to expectations. Mothers, teachers, guidance therapists, and other involved adults should explore their expectations of children from single-parent families. Do adults expect these children to have problems at home and to fail in school? Or do adults expect these children to be happy and independent with good cognitive abilities and good verbal skills? Children will be guided by adult expectations and will benefit from positive expectations. Stigma is associated with low self-esteem in children and it results in defining the children as problems, even when they do not have problems. It additionally undermines their sense of confidence as well. Academic personnel can counteract possible stigmatizing effects on children in these families if they are not pessimistic about the students' success.

ACADEMIC RESILIENCE

The term *resiliency* is discussed in an article by Hetherington, Stanley-Hagan, and Anderson (1989), to state that some children exhibit remarkable resiliency and in the long term may actually be enhanced by coping with these transitions. Others suffer developmental delays or disruptions. Although the adjustment of children is related to the adaptation and behavior of parents, what may be a positive event for one family member is not necessarily positive for another. It is interesting to note that only about one-third of divorce group subjects fell into a category that is categorized as vulnerable in the academic domain. In contrast to the monolithic view that children who experience parental divorce are universally maladjusted, the majority of divorced adolescents in the sample demonstrated relatively successful academic careers. The fact that these youngsters were evidencing healthy adjustment in the classroom is interesting. They did not resemble children of divorce as they are uniformly portrayed in the literature. Instead, the data indicate that we must not make sweeping generalizations about these children in the domain of academic performance, or possibly in other areas as well.

Bonanno's (2004) research into the question of human resilience is a powerful argument against the pathology assumption. The result of this research, which began in the 1990s, is the identification of four distinct patterns of disruption following the death of a loved one or a traumatic even such as divorce. The chronic pattern is characterized by a severe disruption of normal functioning lasting at least two years; in the delayed pattern, initially moderate disruption is followed by an escalation in dysfunction; the recovery pattern shows initially moderate disruption followed by a slow but predictable return to normal functioning over time; in the resilient pattern, quite mild levels of initial disruption are followed very quickly by a return to normal functioning.

It is Bonanno's (2004) conclusion that the roots of the pathology assumption are incorrect, because loss theory has been based almost exclusively on the study of the recovery pattern. Recoverers are those who most likely seek professional help in dealing with loss-related issues. The reductionistic error to be found in the literature is the generalization to other subpopulations of what is true for recoverers. The recoverers probably have to do grief work. Recoverers probably go through a series of developmental stages in their return to equilibrium. In Bonanno's opinion, no empirical validation supports the notion that the path traveled by the resilient is the same as that of the recoverer.

Bonanno's (2004) work suggests that resiliency is far more common than the literature would suggest. Further, it is Bonanno's contention that the trajectories of recovery and resilience are different and unique. He posits that resilience is not a simple absence of pathology, but is typical of many person who "exhibit a stable trajectory of healthy functioning across time, as well as the capacity for generative experiences and positive emotions" (Bonanno, 2004, p. 21). Perhaps some of the confusion evident in the research just discussed may be explained by the differences in academic achievement between children who come from families in recovery versus those whose families are more resilient.

In this chapter, some of the more subtle factors that impact the assessment/intervention process are considered. An appreciation of these factors will help therapists avoid simplistic diagnoses.

CHALLENGING "REALITY"

Kay's divorce had been finalized six months prior to the phone call she received from her daughter's fifth-grade teacher. The girl's work had been slipping, and she tended to avoid socializing with the other children. During her meeting with the teacher, Kay mentioned the divorce. The next week, with no warning or notification, the girl found herself in a group for children from single-parent families that was conducted by one of the school's guidance therapists.

As incredible as the story sounds, it is true. It illustrates a seminal difficulty in the assessment of children from single-parent families: the belief that death or divorce causes behavioral and academic difficulties. Cognitive psychologists (e.g., Meichenbaum, 1977) and constructivist family therapists (e.g., White and Epston, 1990) suggest that people and systems of people selectively attend to and react to only some portions of reality. They use this selective attention process and language (Mince, 1992) to create a reality for themselves and to cocreate a shared reality with others. They behave, believe, and feel as if their subjectively held views are factually true. It appears as if Kay, the teacher, and the guidance therapist have cocreated a reality in which divorce begets academic problems.

Hodges (1991), in his encyclopedic work on dealing with children from divorced families, offers a significantly different reality. He writes,

> When a child from a divorced home has emotional or behavioral problems, the general assumption is that the problems were caused by the divorce. Statements such as "that child is aggressive because he comes from a two parent family" are unlikely to be made, even though they may be truer than assumptions that behavior problems in a child from a divorced family were caused by the divorce. . . . The literature and clinical experience reviewed in this chapter have not indicated that delinquency, serious academic problems, depression and suicide are likely long-term outcomes. (pp. 19, 47)

Peck and Manocherian (1988) in their discussion of divorce, as well as Walsh and McGoldrick (1991) in their consideration of the effect of parental death, also attack the pathology model of single-parent families. These authors understand death and divorce to superimpose a list of developmental demands around the issues of separation, loss, and the establishment of a new family structure upon the more normative developmental demands on the family and its individual members. If the two sets of developmental tasks are in conflict, behavioral and emotional symptomotology can occur.

Consider the fairly typical situation in which an older sibling takes on a number of functions previously carried out by the absent parent. If the family is flexible enough to allow this parental child to also be a child, the result can be beneficial to the remaining parent, the siblings, and the child herself or himself. If, however, the system demands that the child's agenda must be abandoned in deference to the needs of the parent, this parentified child can become overburdened and distracted (Brown and Samis, 1986/1987). Preto (1988) describes the situation:

> This type of control is often seen in families where . . . forces operate to keep members from leaving the system. . . . The message is given that separation is dangerous. . . . Members of families that are so tightly bound attempt to meet each other's needs, but fail to promote growth. As a result, adolescents may become stuck when they feel the urgency to grow, but stay home

to meet the parents' needs. Parents experience a similar dilemma when fears of loss interfere with their attempts to help the children grow. The dilemma is often solved by adopting symptomatic behavior.

If the adoption of a developmental view of single-parent families is one way in which therapists can avoid the pathology assumption, an appreciation of family structure and communication flow is another (Genovese, 1992). Fulmer (1983) suggests the covert rules that govern a family's interaction may result in behavioral problems in the children. He describes one family in which, through therapy, the covert rules became overt: Mother must not be allowed to cry; we children will act up in order to deflect her sadness; when the kids act up, I, Mother, will direct my attention outward to them and away from my own grief; I will label them as bad, not sad.

Knowledge of the literature will also be of value to therapists in aiding themselves and their clients from making gravely reductionistic pathology assumptions. Hodges's work (1986, 1991) and the extensive literature review done by Lowery and Settle (1984) indicate that although some research supports the idea that children of divorce are at a disadvantage, other studies point out areas in which these children do better than children from two-parent families. It is important for therapists to be aware of the very many factors that can cause academic and behavioral problems in children from single-parent families.

The stress that often accompanies the formation of a single-parent family may impact on the children and manifest as school problems. The therapist's role, however, is not to observe the correlation between family restructuring and academic performance. It is rather to do a thorough assessment of the interacting factors that give rise to and maintain symptoms. The therapist's role is to be aware that often it is not the death or the divorce which lies at the heart of the problem. In many cases other causes such as the residual effects of having lived in an anxiety-filled two-parent family prior to the death or divorce, or the impact of greatly reduced family income, or that of continued postdivorce parental conflict, or that of the existence of growth-stunting relationships with extended family members, friends, and social institutions may all play important roles in the functioning of single-parent families.

THE SCHOOL

The observation that most academic problems vary in their intensity across different situations is not lost upon scholars and educational theorists. Graduate schools insist that the proper unit of assessment is not the individual child in isolation but rather the child in the context of his or her environmental envelope. Tombari and Davis (1979) write,

> Problems may be of a social-emotional or academic nature involving attitudes, self-concepts, assertion, obedience, reading comprehension, penmanship, math computation, or creative writing. . . .Underlying behavioral consultation is the assumption that the root of the child's problems lies in the setting in which it takes place. Thus, any plans to change children's behavior must involve manifestation of immediate environmental events. (p. 288)

There is, however, commonly a gap between theory and professional practice. In dealing with academic difficulties, it is incumbent upon the therapist to assess how the school defines the child's problem. Through consultations with teachers and other school officials, and by direct observation of the child in school, the therapist can identify the school's (both administrators and classroom teachers) assumptions concerning the cause and maintenance of problematic behaviors. The work of the cognitive psychologists and constructivist family therapists provide the therapist with entry into one level of problem analysis: the school's assumptions may be powerful influences on the child's behavior because they could set up self-fulfilling prophecies.

PSYCHOEDUCATIONAL MODELS

Ysseldyke's (1979) work can be of much help to the therapist in ascertaining how the school defines problems. He describes five different theoretical positions concerning the nature of academic difficulties. The medical model is a deficit model that assumes abnormality is the result of biological factors. Environmental or sociocultural factors play no role in assessment and diagnosis within this model. In the social-system (deviance) model, the assumption is that many definitions of "normal" behaviors are valid, and these definitions are determined by social-role expectations. The model is a deficit/asset one. For example, the aggressive behavior that a boy shows at school may be abnormal from a student-role perspective, but may be highly adaptive when assessed from an abused child-role view. School interventions involve teaching the child requisite socially expected behaviors when he or she is in the student role.

The psychoeducational process model assumes that a child's academic performance is caused by an idiosyncratic pattern of strengths and weaknesses among a number of universal underlying cognitive processes. In this model, the school assessment/intervention process is deficit focused. The deficits are viewed as existing solely within the individual child. In the pluralistic model, academic problems are assumed to result from the demand that children from all sociocultural backgrounds behave as do white, middle-class children.

In the task analysis model, academic difficulties of all kinds are seen as predicated on the nonattainment of subskills which are necessary for the performance of more complex behaviors. Skills are assumed to be hierarchical, and the acquisition of complex skills is understood as dependent upon the development of adequate lower-level behaviors. Assessment involves finding the student's current position on the skill hierarchy. Intervention consists of teaching of the component subskills required for advancement through the hierarchy. In this model of assessment, the child's performance is not compared to that of a norming group but rather to his or her previous performance. Such an approach obviates the problems of validity, reliability, and inappropriate norms that plague assessments carried out by standardized tests.

Hill (1978) demonstrated the value and power of understanding skills as hierarchy. In her study of antisocial adolescent boys with long histories of academic failure, poor relationships with peers and teachers, aggressiveness, negativism, general depression and hyperactivity, and task analysis was employed to study the preconditions required for success in school. These preconditions focused on the personal interaction between the student and the tutor, and the student's acceptance of the tutor. Included were coming to and staying at the sessions; trying a game or craft; accepting primary and social reinforcements from the tutor; accepting limits with regard to acting out behavior; etc. Increases in measures of academic achievement after the attainment of the preconditions were reported.

A theoretical position taken by school personnel which combines an appreciation of both skill hierarchies and the importance of environmental factors in the maintenance of problems is prognostic of progress. One which assumes a deficit, found solely within the confines of the individual student's skin, is contraindicative of good outcome. As consultant to the school and to the single-parent family, the therapist should strive to coconstruct with all involved the most efficacious "reality" concerning the nature of the child's academic difficulties.

SELF-FULFILLING PROPHECIES

At another level of analysis, diagnosis is informed by the works of Dusek (1975), Brophy and Everston (1978), Dusek and Joseph (1983), and many others who have studied the highly complex interactions between teacher expectations and children's performance. While it would be a vast oversimplification to imply that a "self-fulfilling" prophecy on the teacher's part is the only potent variable in academic problems, it is safe to assume that the efforts of the school, the student, the family, and the therapist will be enhanced by rejecting the reductionistic assumption that single parenthood per se is the pathologic agent. Some school officials are aware that school personnel are vulnerable in this regard. Writing in the *Principal,* Ourth and Zakariya (1982) point out the desperate need for in-service training for classroom teachers, guidance therapists, and school administrators to address the questions: "Do we, in our own minds, attach a stigma to separation and divorce? Do we automatically expect the worst when we learn that a child's parents have separated? Are we sensitive to the signs, many of them subtle, that signal real confusion and stress in a child? Do we recognize, and openly acknowledge, the strength and independence many children develop when they learn to cope with that confusion and stress?" (p. 31).

In the same issue of the *Principal,* Zakariya (1982) discusses the analysis of a study that reported significantly higher achievement scores for children from two-parent families. In-depth analysis, however, indicated that the family's income and the gender of the student had greater effects on achievement scores than did the number of parents in the home. Children from single-parent homes were greatly overrepresented in the low-income group. Although only 17.5 percent of the students studied came from single-parent homes, they constituted 41 percent of the lower income group.

Henderson (1981) acknowledges the need to provide in-service training for school personnel in order to challenge certain pervasive myths: the structure of the family has a greater effect on the child than does the emotional climate of the home; having divorced parents means that the child has only one parent; the single parent's lifestyle is detrimental to the development of a child's morality; children from a "broken home" can always be identified; and to grow up properly, a child must have both male and female role models present in the home. Herderson cites evidence for the value of group therapy for single parents and for their children, which is carried out within the school district. In both the children's and the parents' groups, members were asked to share information on tasks and roles in the new family structure. The focus was on validating the new aspects of the self that each individual developed. The reality that single parenthood, for all its difficulties, represents an opportunity to grow was cocreated by the therapists, the parents, and the children.

In assessing the quality of school-based group interventions with children of divorce, the guidelines provided by Hodges (1991) are most helpful. To be effective, groups should have the full support of the school's administration, require parental permission before a student is placed, take place during regular school hours, ensure that information shared in group will be kept confidential from both teachers and parents, and include pre- and posttreatment meetings for parents. Therapists should remain aware that not all interventions will work equally well with all children.

FAILURE ANALYSIS

A central task in any sophisticated problem analysis is the understanding of why previously attempted solutions have failed. Failure analysis often leads to the formulation of more accurate hypotheses concerning the child's behavior problem.

Consider the following hypothetical situation.

Twelve-year-old Ray has been acting up in school since the beginning of the semester. In consultation with the boy's teacher and the school psychologist, Ray's mother institutes a behavior modification program. Both at school and at home, Ray's target behaviors are closely monitored. Frequency records are kept. Charts depicting the occurrence of target behaviors are displayed. Increases in the frequency of adaptive responses and decreases in problematic behaviors are positively reinforced by the teacher at school and by the mother at home. One month after the program is in effect, Ray's behavior is worse than ever. School officials and the mother are convinced that Ray's problems stem from his parents' recent divorce. The officials and the mother agree that a therapist should be consulted to help Ray deal with separation issues.

If our fictitious therapist is one who does a thorough analysis, he or she may discover that Ray's problems are not caused by the historical effects of the separation and divorce but rather by current interactional patterns. The therapist may determine that since the divorce, Ray's mother has related to the boy as her primary attachment figure (Bowlby, 1980). Her involvement with him has been extreme, as have been her subtle demands that he adopt behavior and attitudes more appropriate for an adult than for a preteenager. As a result, the boy acts in anxious and symptomatic ways.

Failure analysis indicates that the behavior modification "solution" to the problem was sure to fail. By intensifying both the school's and the mother's focus on Ray, the solution appears to magnify the interactional processes which originally gave rise to the problem.

The therapist who was consulted concerning Ray's behavior problems was called in after the family and the school had made a formal and intentional decision to attempt to solve the problem. This is not always the case.

Schools tend to respond differently to behavior problems than to other sorts of academic problems. Unlike children who are mentally retarded, learning disabled, hearing or vision impaired, etc., all children at some time act inappropriately. Usually, the essential difference between the behaviors of normal children and behavior-disordered children is in the intensity and duration of their behaviors, and not in the behaviors themselves (Kirk and Gallagher, 1989).

In cases in which the duration and intensity of a child's academic and behavior disorders have not reached severe problematic levels, the therapist is positioned to be most helpful to the child. Within the unique context of consultant to both family and school, the therapist is able to help coordinate the efforts of both systems, to aid in the clear flow of communication between the systems, to encourage the use of those school and family factors which positively impact on the child's behavior, and to intervene with regard to factors which are growth stunting. To do so, the therapist's assessment of the family must be as sophisticated as the assessment of the school environment.

THE FAMILY

Therapists who adopt a systemic view of families share a basic philosophical orientation with interactionist educational theorists: Behavior is best understood in the context within which it occurs (Nichols, 1984). A systemic epistemology allows a therapist to understand that while some symptomatic children from single-parent families are reacting to separation issues, this factor may not be the primary maintainer of the problematic behavior in all cases. The systemic approach allows for the possibility that the child who is doing poorly in school is the symptom bearer who most overtly expresses the dysfunction of the entire family (Goldenberg and Goldenberg, 1991). Analysis of this possibility results in a sophisticated approach to the assessment/diagnosis process.

Some theorists understand symptomatic behavior in children from single-parent homes as the result of an incongruity between the developmental tasks appropriate to the child's age and those of reorganizing a family's basic structure following the departure of one parent (Peck and Manocherian, 1988; Walsh and McGoldrich, 1991). An example would be the parentified child mentioned earlier: The centripetal forces at play as a family restructures may bind a teenager so tightly to his or her family that individuation is stunted. Peck and Manocherian (1988) and Hodges (1991) both provide excellent outlines of the developmental needs of children at various stages and describe how the process of transforming from a two- to a one-parent system may impact on those needs.

In assessing families from a systemic perspective, therapists move beyond the individual—the monad—to dyadic and triadic analysis. To do so effectively, an appreciation of the Bowenian concept of triangles is required (Kerr and Bowen, 1988) The concept suggests that when families become stressed, the tension between a pair of persons is diluted by bringing in a third party. This unconscious solution is short-lived. As the anxiety gets transferred from person to person to person within the triangle, more anxiety is generated than originally existed. Bowen's theory is highly articulated, and it is recommended that therapists become familiar with it and with techniques designed to detriangulate. Only a brief outline is offered here.

Bowen believes that when a dyad becomes stressed it behaves in predictable but subtle ways. His concept of the triangle is one way to conceptualize these automatic systemic phenomena.

In describing the function of the triangle, Papero (1990) makes several important clinical observations. It is not uncommon in any stressed pair for one of the two to feel the interpersonal anxiety more than the other. When the felt anxiety surpasses a tolerant level, the stressed partner will automatically form a relationship with a third person. The formation of this relationship tends to lower the experience of anxiety in the originally stressed partner. If, however, the relationship with the third partner is highly intense, the process can generate more anxiety than it absorbs. Papero (1990) gives the example of the affair: an affair of low to moderate intensity can, at least for a time, relieve the tension in a marital dyad; a high intensity affair, however, can lead to the creation of a huge degree of stress upon the marriage. Children are often the third side of a triangle and, as such, are at risk.

Guerin and Katz (1984) have used their understanding of triangles in dealing with school problems. Such families usually are involved with one or more of five factors: the symptomatic child is emotionally vulnerable within the family, and this vulnerability is played out among peers or in school; explicit conflict exists between the child and a school authority figure, usually the teacher; covert conflict between the child and one or both of the parents is displaced into a conflict between the child and the teacher; the child has a special relationship with the teacher that makes the child a target of unfavored but powerful classmates; the child is caught up in a triangle based on a conflict, overt or covert, between the parent and the teacher (p. 29). Any of these situations can lead to antisocial behavior or underachievement in school.

Guerin and Katz (1984) describe several common triangles that may, among other things, cause academic difficulties. At any moment in time, two of the three individuals are strongly connected, in either a calm or an agitated way. The third person occupies a more distant position from the other two. Triangulating emotional patterns are understood to be most damaging when the positions become relatively fixed.

Most typically, in the primary parent triangle, the emotional makeup of the family involves an overclose relationship between the mother and child, with the father in the outside position. The mother and child are oversensitive to each other's level of emotional arousal. Increases in the mother's level of anxiety from an unrelated source, such as continued stress with a former spouse, can be transmitted to the child. Problem behaviors appear as the child's anxiety increases. The child may also become the target of the parent who occupies the outsider position.

In the parent-sibling triangle, the symptomatic child usually occupies an inside position with the parent, and a sibling is on the outside. A variation of this structure is very common in single-parent families. The leadership vacuum created when the single parent leaves for work each day is filled by one of the siblings, usually the eldest daughter. Not only is this child burdened with much responsibility and with the lack of real power to carry it out, she must vacate the position when the parent returns home. When conflict between the parent and daughter arises, often the daughter overtly displaces it onto a younger sibling. The relationship with the parent becomes distant and passive-aggressive in nature. The younger child is the one most likely to express anxiety in the form of school-related problems.

In the parent-child-teacher triangle, parent-child conflict is displaced onto the relationship between the child and the teacher. Variations of this triangle include the child's acting out of the parents' anger at the teacher. This pattern is common in families when the parent is a teacher or other professional who feels that his or her expertise is not sufficiently appreciated by the teacher. In another variation, something about the symptomatic child triggers an emotional reaction from the teacher. The source of the teacher's anxiety is to be found in some relationship other than that with the child. When the parent joins with the teacher to "fix" the problem, the teacher's focus on the child intensifies, as do the problem behaviors.

Herz Brown (1988) also suggests the analysis of triangles when working with single-parent families. Central to Herz Brown's thinking is the experience of a power gap in these family systems. Feeling incapable of doing all the disciplining and nurturing required for the healthy development of his or her children, the single parent will often triangulate with the school and extended family members to fill in the perceived power vacuum.

Herz Brown (1988) describes how the economic deprivation that often accompanies the formation of a single-parent family can create troublesome triangles with the single parent's own parents. If, as in Nancy's case (see Chapter 3) of moving in or accepting financial help, the single parent and her parent(s) re-create an earlier family structure in which she is subordinate to her own parents, then the power gap between the single parent and her children will also increase.

Should single parents surrender to the school their right to discipline their children, the same loss of parental power will ensue. Isaacs (1987) believes that many symptomatic children in single-parent families have chosen to ignore their own well-being in the service of protecting and helping an overtly stressed single parent. Such a family structure creates a completely reversed power hierarchy in the family: the child becomes nurturer to the parent.

Many authors agree that often it is the continuing conflict between former spouses which leads to problems with the children (Herz Brown, 1988). Meyer's (1992) outline of various types of relationships between parents serves as a guide to assessment. In situations with one cooperative and one uncooperative former spouse, conflict is often caused and maintained by the person who feels that he or she was abandoned by the other. When both spouses are uncooperative, the level of anger is often such that they avoid direct contact. "During these recuperative periods, they work on each other indirectly through the children. Unfortunately, the children suffer from these indirect attacks, even if they themselves are not victims" (Meyer, 1992, p. 163). Meyer appears here to have identified another triadic relationship. In yet another scenario, oppositional former spouses create a love-hate relationship characterized by alternating hostile outbursts and "honeymoons." Should one of the honeymoons result in a temporary reconciliation followed by another separation, the impact on children can be devastating (Hodges, 1991).

Guerin et al. (1987) have identified the child-as-refuge triangle, the target child triangle, and the tug-of-war triangle. In each, a child may become symptomatic as a result of being drawn into parental conflict. In the child-as-refuge triangle, the parent who more acutely feels the anxiety caused by an unsatisfactory marital relationship forms a special relationship with one of the children. The move, as in all triangulations, calms the marital dyad temporarily. The target child is found in an overly close relationship with one of his or her parents. The outside parent directs anger actually meant for the spouse at the target child. While relieving dyadic tension momentarily, this deflection of hostility will often cause problems for the child. The tug-of-war triangle is common in single-parent family systems. In this situation, each parent showers the child with affection, attention, and gifts in order to become the child's favorite and to exclude the other parent. (Keep in mind that these triangles can occur in the two-parent family system as well.)

An assessment of a single-parent family is a sophisticated undertaking as is the analysis of school factors discussed. The therapist's work is made more difficult in that an analysis of the interaction between the two systems is also called for.

THE SCHOOL AND THE FAMILY

Okun (1984) observes,

> The family therapist must consider the reciprocal influences of the family and school systems and the possible impacts of these influences on the child in order to understand fully the possible impacts of these influences on the child in order to understand fully the child's behavior in terms of transactions and relationships within subsystems and the larger system. Without assessing the degree of congruence between the operating rules of the family and those of the school system, without evaluating information provided by both parents and teachers regarding the child, and without actually observing the child in both the family and classroom settings, the therapist will overlook important data. (pp. 7-8)

The therapist must also be aware of any form of miscommunication between the family and the school, even in those cases when both systems agree on certain rules.

Consider the reciprocal effects of family and school interactions on Tina's seventeen-year-old son. Tina is overwhelmed by the responsibilities of single parenthood and expects the school to effectively control her son's behavior at school. The school believes that the boy's behavior problems are related to his mother's "permissiveness." The teachers and the school disciplinarian are even vigilant for any infraction, and punishment is swift. In actuality, the boy is being punished for offenses committed by many others which go unpunished by the school. When Tina is informed of yet another problem at school, she becomes furious: the boy will be grounded for a full month, including weekends. As a result of the miscommunication between the school and the family, the boy is caught in an ever-escalating punishment paradigm.

Both the mother and the school wish to positively impact upon the boy's behavior. Each perceives an inability on the part of the other to be effective; however, the coconstructed reality is that each believes that they must work alone, and that the best strategy is to employ preventive measures. An analysis of the interaction between the two systems suggests to the therapist more potent intervention strategies than does the assessment of either system in isolation.

Jones (1987) provides another example of uncoordinated family-school interaction in the maintenance of problems. Many schools have a strong interest in promoting parental involvement in academic and behavior problems. If a single parent, either through guilt or a sense of being totally responsible for the welfare of his or her child, finds it impossible to ever say no to the large number of meetings, exercises, and evaluations suggested by the school, his or her life may soon be centered around the child. As a result, the needs of the parent and the other children may be neglected.

ROLE OF THE PROFESSIONAL THERAPIST

The role of the therapist is to coordinate the efforts of the school and family in the resolution of the problem. This is no mean task. Not only must the therapist be knowledgeable of both the educational and therapy literature, he or she must also be able to form relationships with family members and school personnel that allow for effectively joining with the two systems:

1. The therapist strives to avoid the serious error of treating the single-parent family generically (Jones, 1987).
2. The therapist strives to avoid the reductionistic pathology model of the single-parent family.

3. The therapist predicates treatment based upon a thorough analysis of school factors, family factors, and the interaction between the two systems.
4. The therapist joins both the family and the school systems in an active fashion but does not become part of a particular alliance or coalition.
5. The therapist is informed of the ways in which school systems operate and is conversant with educational jargon.
6. The therapist is informed of the ways in which family systems operate, and is able to understand family interactions, roles, rules, etc., as they relate to academic and behavior problems in the school.
7. As consultant to two systems, the therapist is vigilant with regard to confidentiality issues.
8. The therapist is aware that single parents are faced with many reality problems and takes the position that the parent actively seeks assistance with these problems. To this end, the therapist makes available to the single parent certain vital referral sources, such as the following:
   Family Court Support Collection Unit
   Personal Health Division—Women, Infants, and Children
   Community health centers
   Social Service Referral Department
   County child support services
   Day care services
   County employment programs
   Food Stamp Information Services
   Public Assistance Information
   Local women's services
   Local job service agencies
9. The therapist encourages the family to avoid viewing single parenthood as a temporary family structure (Herz Brown, 1988). The therapist explores the possibilities for growth and happiness as well as dealing with difficulties. The therapist disputes any coconstructed reality that suggests the family can wait until some ill-defined "white knight" appears and solves its problems.
10. The therapist is aware of the many theories of development to be found in the professional literature. Among others, Freud's

(1917) theory of psychosexual development, Erikson's (1963) of psychosocial development and Kohlberg's (1969) of moral development inform our work. In dealing with children, Piaget's (1952) work on cognitive development, along with clinical judgment, suggest which techniques are most appropriate with a particular youngster.

Entire family systems, as well as individuals, can be understood from a developmental point of view (Carter and McGoldrick, 1980, 1988). Walsh and McGoldrick (1991), Parkes and Weiss (1983) and Bowlby (1980) discuss the developmental course of the mourning process. Herz Brown (1988) as well as Peck and Manocherian (1988) consider the stages of development that entire family systems must negotiate following divorce, while Wallerstein and Kelly (1980) and Hetherington, Cox, and Cox (1985) trace the same journey from the perspective of the individual.

Although the number of different theoretical approaches to development is quite large, all share certain common elements. As individuals and family systems grow and develop, demands are placed upon them to respond in increasingly complex and more articulated ways. Some of these demands are primarily internal, such as when the toddler first acquires language or the ability to crawl. The development of the child, of course, engenders a demand that the family adapt appropriately. Some of the demands are initiated by the family or societal institutions: children are expected to attend school; families expect that children will exhibit greater degrees of self-control as they mature. Some of the external demands are normative. For example, families in Western societies expect to deal with the question of bladder and bowel control. Some of these demands are nonnormative in the sense that society has provided neither individuals nor family systems with adequate models for the successful negotiation of a particular set of developmental tasks. In this sense, the change from a two-parent to a single-parent family system is an example of a nonnormative developmental process.

Developmental theorists and therapists who adopt a developmental stance regard symptoms not as indicators of psychopathology but as problems in negotiating phase-specific demands. The problem— the symptom—may result from an attempt to use strategies which were adaptive in earlier stages but which no longer are appropriate for the advanced development of the entire family system and of the individuals who comprise the system. For example, the effective discipline of toddlers calls for a one-way, authoritative flow of communication from parents to children in a context of love, care, and concern for the well-being of the young ones. Parents of young children do not need the input of the children to know that running into the street is an unacceptable behavior on the part of a three-year-old. Parents who attempt democratic solutions to problems, such as by attempting to negotiate rules with children, place the children at risk. Toddlers are not ready to make this sort of decision.

Regardless of how successful the rule "Parents know best and will make decisions for the children" may be through toddlerhood, the family who tries to extend its use with adolescent children is also putting the children at risk. The mutual weaning of parents and children is the primary developmental task of adolescence. The weaning is prerequisite if the children are to become independent adults capable of forming their own relationships and if the parents will continue to grow.

The professional therapist is aware of the specific developmental tasks clients are attempting to negotiate and is able to frame problems in developmental terms.

THERAPY STRATEGIES

Assessment, unbiased by the pathology assumption, begins even before the therapist meets the family. The initial phone call provides only the merest outline of the difficulty: A child or children from a single-parent family is experiencing academic difficulties. How do we ascribe meaning to the family's story? Is our thinking directed by deficit models of the family, or do we assume an unbiased position? Hodges (1991) reflects our belief concerning best practice when he writes, "It is presumptuous to assume that every problem is due to unresolved childhood conflict" (p. 286). To this we would add: It is likewise presumptuous to assume that every problem within a single-parent family is due to unresolved loss reactions.

The Education Model

The child's problem in school may simply reflect a lack of skills or knowledge on the part of either the child or the parent with regard to the sorts of behaviors that lead to academic success. As defined by Hodges (1991), *skill* implies knowing how to do what needs to be done, and *knowledge* as knowing what needs doing. Therapists are well positioned to help families in both areas.

Consider, for example, the possible impact of parentification described earlier in this chapter. It is common, and may be growth promoting, that children in single-parent families take on additional tasks and responsibilities more than do children with two parents. There are simply fewer hands to do what needs to be done in order for the system to run smoothly. It is not growth promoting, however, should the parentification expand into areas which are beyond the child's capacity. Healthy parentification would not include putting the child in charge of all his or her own academic decisions.

Structural Moves

Herz Brown (1988) describes how many overburdened single parents tend to divest themselves of parental authority in the daily interactions with their children. Awareness of the potential impact of parentification with regard to study behaviors will allow the therapist to provide parents with the knowledge that children need their leadership and guidance in this area. The generational boundary-making techniques of Minuchin and Fishman (1981) are of value in this process; for example, the therapist and parent discuss the problem together, with the children at a peripheral position in the room; the children brainstorm solutions to the problem which are subsequently evaluated by the parent.

Sherman and Fredman (1986) suggest a number of structural moves designed to reinforce generational boundaries and to support the parental position in the family's power hierarchy. Seating the parent apart from the children during sessions; alloting different household tasks to the children and the parent; meeting alone in executive session with the parent to deal with parenting issues; asking parental permission to interact with the children; reinforcing the need for privacy by instituting a closed-door policy for the parents' and children's rooms; scheduling alone time for both parent and children; allying with the parent in matters of discipline; encouraging the parents to conference with other adults and school personnel, and not with the children, concerning the problem; encouraging mature, controlled parental behavior and discouraging frustration-propelled, regressive parental behavior; encouraging age-appropriate behavior on the part of both parent and children; and helping the parent and children contract responsibilities, duties, and consequences of behavior, are all included.

The therapist can help provide requisite skills through the use of basic behavioral principles (e.g., Franks, Wilson, and Terence, 1975). Stimulus-control procedures can be employed to set up both a particular time and a particular place when and where only studying occurs. The therapist can help with time-management procedures by having the family construct daily calendars for the children that include time for school, chores, play, and study. The concept of contingency management can be employed by having reinforcement depend upon following the negotiated schedule.

Herz Brown (1988) provides the therapist with a valuable warning. She suggests that overburdened single parents may look to others—extended family members, school personnel, friends, and therapists—to take over parenting responsibilities. While such a move may temporarily relieve the parent of some stress, it also decreases the parent's power in the family. What results is a short-term gain for long-term pain. In consulting with parents, the therapist provides insights, skills, and intervention, but does not assume responsibility for the children's academic success.

Supporting Hierarchy

Madanes (1991) has made the systemic observation that parents and children often interact in ways which lead to inversions and incongruities in the power hierarchy. Therapists must respond appropriately when one hierarchy places the children in a dependent place with regard to shelter, food, and finances while another places them in a power position concerning decisions such as whether to study. This situation is not uncommon within single-parent families with adolescents.

The existence of incongruent hierarchies manifests in several ways. The first is via communications, which suggests that the parent is unable to actively participate in therapy due to an inability to occupy an executive position within the hierarchy.

Such a belief is indicated when the parent takes the position that the solution to the problem is to be found by some external expert—a psychiatrist, therapist, etc. Madanes (1991) suggests a therapeutic response that relabels the problem as one which is in the arena of parental expertise. The child's problem is not labeled as an emotional upsetment or as the result of psychological conflict, but rather as laziness or choosing to fail.

Parents further disqualify themselves by pleading ignorance as to what is appropriate behavior on the part of their child, by using such meaningless phrases as, "I just want him to do well," or by turning to the child for advice or asking the child what is best. The therapeutic response is to frame the problem as one which was born of the child's confusion, and to demand that the parent provide simple, concrete guidelines and definitive limitations on behaviors.

Madanes (1991) suggests that families may also undermine therapy by disqualifying the therapist. At times, this takes the form of a direct attack on the therapist's competence. In this instance, a nondefensive and brief description of the therapist's qualification is necessary. At other times, the attack is more veiled, such as when the parent cites contradictory expert opinion or previous failures in therapy. Replies that suggest the therapist is aware of other theoretical positions but does not agree with them all, and those which underscore the differences between this and previous therapy experiences are called for. Labeling interventions as behavioral experiments whose outcome can be evaluated after a limited time is also helpful.

Content or Process

The therapist must remain aware that the presenting problem of academic difficulty may be a manifestation of less-than-adequate systemic functioning. The problem may be the methaphoric expression of some more fundamental family difficulty, an attempt to deflect tension onto the child by some other dyad, the result of some cross-generational coalition, the replication of issues from previous generations, etc.

It is our experience, however, that traditional approaches to family therapy will be more effective if the anxiety around the presenting problem can be rescued. The therapy techniques previously described will be helpful in this regard.

Several writers have suggested techniques for dealing with academic and school behavior problems at the systemic level. Titler and Cook (1981) propose that therapists aid in the communication between family and school by adopting the Bowenian position of insisting that all intersystem messages be clear, mutually respectful, and nonemotional. Bagarozzi (1980) states that a therapist who is prepared to assess and intervene around academic problems from the systemic, psychoanalytic, and behavioral perspectives is more effective than one who adheres only to one therapeutic ideology.

Guerin and Katz (1984), in discussing the impact of triangular relationships, suggest that these interactions be broken down into their dyadic components. If analysis indicates that difficulty between student and teacher results from a covert alliance between the single parent and the child, the therapist is advised to coach the parent to build a more explicit relationship with the child.

If the symptoms-maintaining triangle involves a former spouse, the therapist must be very careful in intervening. Only if it is apparent that the ex-spouse can put the dyadic issues aside and agree to work on parenting issues should joint sessions be considered. To allow former spouses to rehash old angers and hurts may put the child in jeopardy. Latent nonadaptive family structures may be reactivated. Rather than to allow this possibility, the therapist who is unsure of the former couple's capacity to put the needs of their children ahead of their own would be wise to coach the custodial parent around the issue of putting children "in the middle" of parental battles.

Both Weltner (1982) and Herz Brown (1988) call for therapy strategies aimed at supporting the executive functions of the single parent and at strengthening intergenerational boundaries. Weltner suggests fostering an understanding in the parent that the collective tasks facing her may be too much to deal with alone; that a parental child may be of great value if the child is well supported and not exploited; that several children may be employed to parcel out certain of the parent's executive functions. The boundary-defining techniques described earlier are applicable. The reader is directed also to the in-session and between-session interventions outlined by Minuchin and Fishman (1981), Sherman and Fredman (1986), and Sherman, Oresky, and Roundtree (1991). Herz Brown (1988) cautions that the power vacuum created at the executive level may foster the formulation of triangles which serve to keep the single parent impotent. Identification of such triangles is the first important therapy strategy. The single parent is then coached on how to "employ" children, friends, and extended family members in ways that do not disempower her or him. In the later stages of therapy, interventions are aimed at solidifying extrafamilial activities. Herz Brown (1988) is convinced of the importance of work outside the home to the single parent. This is a topic of Chapter 9.

Consultation with the School

In assessing both the family and school systems and any recursive interactions between the two, the use of the ecomap is a most helpful tool. Holman (1983) describes the ecomap as a dynamic diagram of the connections between a family and the people and institutions which together comprise the family's life space.

The construction of the ecomap begins with the family creating a family map (see Chapter 3) which depicts the relationships among the individual family members. Next, in the form of large circles, important forces outside the family's boundary are identified. These include the extended family, school, church, work, health care agencies, and more. The nature of the relationship between the family and each of these other systems is indicated by the use of different sorts of lines to graphically connect the various systems to the family:

> --------indicates a strong relationship;
> - - - - -indicates that the relationship is weak; and
> -/-/-/-/-depicts a stressful relationship.

By adding arrows to these connections, the direction of flow of energy, resources, or communication is also mapped.

Holman (1983) writes,

> The ecomap provides a visual overview of the complex ecological system of the family and shows its organizational patterns and relationships. It maps the major systems that are part of the family's environment and provides a picture of the balance between the demands and resources of the family system. In highlighting the nature of the connections between the family and its ecological system, the ecomap demonstrates the flow of re-

sources from the environment to the family as well as depriva-
tions and unmet needs. (p. 63)

The ecomap thus serves to direct the therapist to the optimum point of
intervention—the troubled student, or his or her family, or the school
environment, or the relationship among these factors.

To consult effectively with school personnel, the therapist must
join with this system as well as with the family system. An attitude
that reflects the school's position as expert in educational issues, fully
appreciates the school's conceptualization of the problem, and encourages cooperation and coordination of the effort of both systems
should provide the desired outcome.

In observing the child in class, the therapist frames the interactions
between the teacher and child, as well as those among the child and
other students in terms of his or her knowledge of behavioral psychology and systems theory. With input from the teacher, guidance
personnel, and the parent, interventions for at home and at school
are negotiated. The school is better positioned than the family to provide extra help and instruction in study skills such as active listening,
active reading, and note taking. The school is also more able to moni-
tor and modify classroom behaviors and peer interactions. The parent
has greater control over scheduling time for home study and the other
variables previously discussed. Differential task division should reflect these variations.

Chapter 9

Single Parents, Work, and Welfare

THE FEMINIZATION OF POVERTY

In the aggregate, the data that describe what has been referred to as the "feminization of poverty" are shocking. Single-parent families headed by divorced or never-married mothers are much more likely to be both poor and also dependent upon public assistance programs than are two-parent families. In reviewing the statistical picture of the economic deprivation of these families, McLanahan, Garfinkel, and Ooms (1987) and Holder and Anderson (1989) report the following:

- The average standard of living for men, postdivorce, increases by 42 percent, while that of women declines by 73 percent.
- In 1977, 67 percent of poor persons older than 16 years old were women.
- By 1985, 55 percent of all poor families were headed by women.
- Seventy-five percent of all employed women work full-time, but in 1985 their average income was only $14,404.
- In female-headed single-parent families, the mother's income accounts for 60 to 70 percent of the family's total.
- From 1960 to 1981, the number of poor, female-headed households increased by 40 percent. During that same time period, a 45 percent decrease occurred in all other categories of poor families.
- In 1988, 50 percent of children living in female-headed households were poor.
- Even among the more prosperous of divorced mothers, income was only 60 percent of the predivorce level measured one year after the divorce.

- It is estimated that of children born in the late 1970s, 45 percent of whites and 84 percent of blacks will live, for some time at least, in a female-headed single-parent family.
- In 1983, approximately 58 percent of single mothers were awarded child support payments from the courts. Of these, 50 percent received the full award, 26 percent some portion of the award, and 24 percent received none.
- The organization of programs for Aid to Families with Dependent Children can serve to keep single mothers unempowered. Poor mothers are often left with choosing between a kind of full-time work that provides only a marginal economic position or becoming dependent upon welfare.

The ultimate solutions to such problems as the feminization of poverty are to be discovered at the level of profound changes in social policies, social institutions, and attitudes. We cannot stress this enough. If we are to assist children of divorce, then we must assist their mothers. Feminists have described the problems and have called for fundamental societal changes to address questions such as those of the low earnings of single mothers, the inadequacies in child support, and the unfairness in work requirements for public assistance (McLanahan, Garfinkel, and Ooms, 1987).

That sweeping cultural change does not occur quickly leaves the professional therapist and his or her clients in a dilemma. While supporting the sort of political and cultural evolution which will serve to alleviate the problems associated with economic and therefore power inequities, the therapist and client must negotiate within the context of the current societal milieu.

The first step in one possible solution to this dilemma is to study the feminist critique of the salient societal beliefs about single parenthood. These beliefs can lead clients to form and maintain non-growth-promoting and abusive relationships with former spouses, governmental agencies, and others. The second step is to assess the degree to which the clients may have incorporated these beliefs into their own reality constructions. The third step involves exploring with clients ways in which a difficult situation may be made better.

It must be emphasized that in assessing and intervening at this level, the therapist must in no way blame the clients for their predicament. To ascertain the degree to which a client may have internalized societal myths, such as framing the single-parent family in pathological terms or assuming that single mothers cannot be effective workers, is most certainly not to imply that the client is the author or the maintainer of the myth. The purposes of the analysis, rather, are to make overt any covert agreement on the client's part with the various cultural biases that put her in a one-down and unempowered position and to aid the client in disputing the validity of these constructions.

In Chapter 8 it was suggested that the therapist should help the client dispute any belief system which suggests she should wait passively until some "white knight" comes to her rescue. The approach is similar here. To assume that one is unable to make adaptive changes in one's life until great and sweeping alterations in the cultural climate are initiated by others is to remain passive and powerless.

POVERTY AND PSYCHOLOGICAL DISTRESS

Hicks and Anderson (1989) point out that the drop in income which many single mothers incur impacts not only on finances. The degree of correlation between financial security and self-esteem implies that persons with enough money feel better about themselves than do those without. Often, impoverished people are perceived to be of less value to outside observers as well. If the single mother's predivorce status was based upon her husband's salary and position, the therapist may find a client whose negative self-images are reinforced by "friends, relatives, acquaintances and shopkeepers who regard her as less important" (Hicks and Anderson, 1989, p. 319).

As income declines, so also does the range of possible interactions with the environment. Braver et al. (1989) list common changes for divorced families. These include relocation to a less desirable abode, problems with child care, the loss of a familiar neighborhood, and the disruption of friendship networks. Even in those instances in which the custodial mothers remain in the family home, the number of positive experiences available to her and her children are generally greatly reduced. Not only does the loss of discretionary income mean fewer trips to restaurants and theaters, for some it implies worry concerning the availability of basic needs such as food, clothing, and transportation. Given the bleak current situation these mothers face, the attendant loss of self-esteem, and the likelihood that these parents hold little hope for improvement in the future (Weitzman, 1985; Braver et al., 1989), the stage is set for clinical depression. In considering clinical depression using a cognitive epistomology, Beck et al. (1979) describe the depressive triad: a belief in one's inability to cope with the world's demands; a belief that these demands are unfair and impossibly difficult; and a belief that the incongruity between the perceived enormity of the demands and one's ability to meet them will not diminish in the future. Single mothers, as described by Hicks and Anderson (1989) and Braver et al. (1989), seem to be at high risk for adopting a depressive stance.

An experimental study designed by Braver et al. (1989) examined the relationship between economic hardship and postdivorce psychological distress of custodial mothers. In comparing seventy-seven custodial mothers to a control group, several statistically significant results were reported. Perhaps of greatest import to the professional therapist was the finding that *drop* in income was related to measured psychological distress, but *actual* income level was not. The sociological term *relative deprivation* appears to be a strong factor here. The authors write,

> The finding that drop in income related to poorer psychological adjustment at all levels of current income suggests that the impact of psychological factors such as loss of status and self-definitions involving the former standard of living should not be underestimated. It may be that although wealthy women who are reduced to middle-class status do not experience great economic hardship, they nonetheless do experience disruption in social networks, life-style and self-esteem, which may cause considerable psychological distress. (Braver et al., 1989, pp. 30-31)

Given the small numbers involved in this particular study, therapists are warned against overgeneralizing its findings. There may, however, be considerable clinical value in thinking in terms of drop in income, self-esteem, and status, as well as in terms of absolute family income. While Braver and colleagues call for significant societal changes to address the problem of postdivorce drop in income, some custodial mothers have been able to design their own solutions. Their successes can be most informative as therapists work with single-parent families. For example, Flo's (whom we will meet next) artful use of various support networks was of enormous value to her as she transformed her family from an upper-middle-class, two-parent system to a single-parent family comprising five children and a mother who had never worked outside the home, and a woefully inadequate child support award.

THERAPEUTIC VALUE OF SUPPORT NETWORKS

George and Flo met during the summer between their freshman and sophomore years of college. He was a lifeguard at the swim club to which Flo's family belonged. She was immediately attracted to his aggressive and assured demeanor. He seemed to be a "can-do" sort of fellow. He was attracted to her classical beauty and refinement. The sparks flew, and for the next three years they carried on an impassioned, long-distance relationship. Perhaps the fact that George's college was in Boston and Flo's in New York served to keep their need for each other intense.

During their senior year in college, Flo and George were married in a civil ceremony. This "first" marriage was one of convenience—it served to keep George out of the Vietnam war. They were married in a religious ceremony during the summer of 1965. Both were twenty-one years of age.

George had been a prelaw student at college, Flo, a French major. Immediately after graduation, George's drive to succeed manifested itself. He simultaneously enrolled in law school at night and opened an insurance practice. He was successful in both endeavors. Although Flo was eligible for certification as a French teacher at the secondary school level, she did not follow through on the necessary paperwork.

Within a year, the first son, Rick, was born. A second son, Tommy, followed in 1967. By the time Peter was born in 1972, Flo was the mother of three sons under the age of eight. She was the wife of a successful young attorney, and she was not yet twenty-nine years of age.

Despite the social upheaval characteristic of the 1960s and early 1970s, and despite the early stirrings of the feminist movement, the young couple seemed happy, in an anachronistic way, during the early years. They seemed to be following a script, one described by McGoldrick (1988):

> Women have always played a central role in families, but the idea that they have a life cycle apart from their roles as wife and mother is a relatively recent one, and still is not widely accepted in our culture. The expectation for women has been that they would take care of the needs of others, first men, then children, then the elderly. . . . They went from being daughter, to wife, to mother, with their status defined by the male in the relationship and their role by their position in the family's life cycle. (p. 29)

The "script" is all about gender roles. Holder and Anderson (1989) succinctly restate the different stories ascribed to men and women. Women operate within the world of relationships, the most important of which is the family. Men deal with the world of work. It is as if the front door of the home divided the world into the spheres of influence as neatly as do "HIS" and "HERS" towels. "Women managed the home and children and were socialized to perform more nurturing activities. Men were schooled to actively compete in the larger community, to influence policy and norms, and to earn money" (Holder and Anderson, 1989, p. 360).

The difficulty with this view of a marriage partnership is, of course, that it is not a partnership at all. Although both husband and wife are mutually dependent upon each other's functioning for as long as the marriage continues, the disparity in economic power permits the husband to purchase what the wife provides should their union dissolve. The woman has no such option.

As George became increasingly more successful as a matrimonial attorney, the family's lifestyle and social status grew proportionately. George replaced his cars and boats more frequently, it seemed, than his brothers-in-law replaced neck ties. The homes of Flo's three sisters were filled with furnishings handed down by their well-to-do sister. But although Flo and George were financially "flush" during this period, their relationship was on the way to bankruptcy.

Over time, each began to resent the other's noninvolvement. George devoted essentially all of his energies to his practice, the social networking required to have the practice grow, and recreation. Flo felt often as if she had to play the role of the single parent. She viewed George as nonfunctional with regard to his parental role, and unsatisfactory in his role as husband. From George's perspective, Flo had opted to put all her resources into the home and children. He considered Flo to be unable or unwilling to "play." As Flo turned to her sisters for support, Geroge turned to his female office manager for companionship.

It is not uncommon for angry, distancing couples to forge temporary reconciliations. The decision to divorce, after all, is almost never an easy one. Questioning one's own ability to survive without a partner often takes on an obsessive quality. Wondering about the possible deleterious effects on the children, reminiscences of better times, and considering ways of making things "better" all add to the inertia.

Religious beliefs, antidivorce family legacies, and a simple refusal to admit failure especially daunted Flo. She felt unequal in the struggle—George had the money and the power, and he was a divorce attorney. For his part, George believed that his marriage was no different from the other areas in his life, and that if he worked on the problem with sufficient diligence, success would be assured.

It is also not uncommon for children to be born during these trying, vacillating times.

Laura was born in 1976, Kevin in 1978. When the divorce was formalized in 1980, Flo was thirty-seven years old. She was the custodial parent of five children ranging in age from fifteen to two. She received 50 percent from the sale of the matrimonial home, $100 per week in alimony, and $75 per week per child in child support. With the proceeds from the sale of the house she had shared with George, Flo bought a comfortable but somewhat rundown home for herself and her children. Her primary problem was how to maintain the household. If George were prompt with alimony and child support payments, she would receive $475 per week. George was not prompt, although the payments would ultimately be made. Flo felt that she needed to go to work if her family was to survive economically. But how does a thirty-seven-year-old French major with five children, one who has never worked outside of the home, choreograph this most difficult dance?

The divorce was a particularly bitter one, so Flo could not rely on George to provide any help, financial or otherwise, that was not court mandated. There was nothing that the courts or other societal institutions could do for her. She turned to her family and friends to provide the various sorts of support she needed. It is important to remember that Flo went through this without the benefit of therapy. She seemed somehow to sense what her needs were and was able to develop several support systems which, as a whole, provided her with what she required. In a sense, Flo's moves provide a road map for therapists who work with single-parent families.

In moving to a town in which two of her sisters and her father resided, Flo took the first step in meeting her needs for nurturance. In their family of origin, Flo and her sisters assumed the typical sorts of roles: There was a responsible one; the popular, well-liked one; the physically and emotionally weak one; and the studious one (McGoldrick, 1989). Flo was popular, and the sisters to whom she turned during the transition to single parenthood were the studious and responsible ones. The fourth sister, the weak one, was significantly less available to Flo during the time of crisis as a result of both physical and emotional distance.

The relationship between Flo and her two nearby sisters was remarkably growth promoting. In a very real sense, these women became Flo's primary attachment objects. They, thus, provided her with sort of emotional assuredness and calmness which is prerequisite for making good life choices. Flo knew that she belonged, that she was loved, and that she was not alone. Some of her most basic needs were met so she was able to focus on personal growth and other issues found higher up the needs hierarchy

(Maslow, 1970). McGoldrick (1989) refers to the unique relationship that may exist among sisters:

> Often it is not until mid-life that sisters reconnect with each other, through the shared experiences of caring for a failing or dying parent, a divorce in the family, or perhaps a personal health problem. Such events inspire them to clarify their priorities and to redefine the relationships in life that really matter to them. (p. 255)

Flo created another web of relationships among her neighbors. She became very close with a number of women who did not work outside the home. What all of these women shared with Flo was the responsibility to care for their children. Several of them became acutely aware of Flo's particular predicament. How was she to be freed of the responsibility of caring for her children while simultaneously making the sorts of decisions that would assure her economic emancipation?

This friend network supported Flo magnificently when she decided to train to become a computer programmer. With great humor and with much effort, an incredibly complex juxtaposition of time scheduling on the part of Flo and her friends allowed her to take the required courses. Within a year, Flo was a working mother with an adequate personal income. The relationship networks between Flo and her sisters and her friends maintained, albeit changed in some degree, even after her return to work. These relationships were and are mutually rewarding for all involved. Flo gives as well as takes, and in no way has she assumed a one-down, dependent, or infantilized role in her interactions with family and friends. Flo and her relationship networks ingeniously empowered her when she was needy. Now she can use her strength in the service of her friends and family. Each of Flo's support networks helped in a far more subtle but equally important way in addition to meeting her needs for nurturance, substitute parenting, and mutuality. They allowed Flo to become free of the sociological constraint, the construct, which suggests to women that to work is to be less of a mother.

Ferree (1984) describes the conflict between mothers and work:

> In the classic sociological model, the relationship of family and job for women is portrayed as one of conflict and competing demands. Family demands are assumed to have the higher priority, while work performance and satisfaction are influenced by family circumstances, with work commitment and actual labor force participation viewed as contingent upon "prior" home responsibilities. (p. 58)

Flo's case history provides an alternate construct, in other words, that a woman can be successful and happy in both her professional and family roles simultaneously.

Carter and McGoldrick (1988) point out that as a result of gender-specific socialization patterns, most women are oriented toward relationship. Hicks and Anderson (1989) underscore the need for single mothers to establish support networks:

> The development of a support network is imperative for women who live outside the boundaries of marriage. . . . A strong support network is crucial in beginning the healing process and continuing it once it has begun. . . . However it happens, if a women can become active in her community, join women's groups, develop relationships with those who have similar interests, the new single state can provide a sense of freedom, independence, or autonomy that can be very satisfying and enjoyable. (p. 12)

Professional therapists must be aware, however, that a woman's ability to form relationships does not always result in the sort of personal growth experienced by Flo. Some relationships can retard growth.

McLanahan, Wedemeyer, and Adelberg (1981) provide an outline of some of the various types of relationship networks common among single-parent families. The family-of-origin network, the extended network, and two variations of conjugal networks are described.

One response to single parenthood is for the mother to reunite with her original family. The reunion may be a physical one, as in those instances when a single-parent family moves back into the grandparental home. The reunion is essentially a psychological one in those cases in which kin become the single mother's primary attachment objects even if there is no physical move back home. Often either a female or male best friend is included in a peripheral way within this support network.

Because membership in this sort of network is limited by kinship, these relationship configurations tend to be small. Usually they include only those family-of-origin members who live near the single mother. However the degree of interaction among the members, referred to as the density of the relationship, is very high. The content of the relationship is multiplex in nature in that it is based on multiple ties within the relationship. Support tends to be divided along the traditional gender division of labor assumptions with fathers and brothers helping out financially while mothers and sisters assist with child care and personal problems. Often the assumption of future intergenerational reciprocity is implicit. These single mothers often provide to the children of the next generation the same sort of support that they themselves received.

Flo's family-of-origin network was very much as described by McLanahan, Wedemeyer, and Adelberg (1981). In addition to adding the necessary "extra hands" required for family functioning, the network provided a sense of security, a belongingness, which the authors report as typical in this form of network. Another sort of emotional support readily available from family-of-origin networks is a feeling of personal worth, of self-efficacy, of a "can-do" orientation. Single mothers who use their kinship network well often do not feel the need for a husband.

For all their value, family-of-origin networks can have a downside for single mothers. The authors identify the issues of intimacy and social integration as potentially problematic areas. At the beginning, relationships between the single mother and other members of her family tend to be asymmetrical in that she, clearly, is the needy one. Emotional asymmetry tends to limit mutual confiding and other behaviors associated with intimacy. Further, while the family network protects the single mother from becoming dependent upon outside relationships, it may also serve to isolate her from social supports and new social interactions. These mothers may be swallowed up by their intensely loyal families.

Another response to single parenthood is the creation of an extended support network based essentially upon new friendship ties. The structure of these friendship networks as well as the kinds of supports they provide to single mothers vary considerably from those of the family-of-origin networks. McLanahan, Wedemeyer, and Adelberg (1981) see these networks' heavy concentration of postdivorce women friends as their most distinguishing characteristic. In addition to individual friendships, these networks often connect single mothers to such organizations as women's support groups, community action, and social groups. Compared to family-of-origin arrangements, extended networks are quite large. While single mothers often interact intensely within many of the components of the network, interaction among the groups is quite low: the members in the car pool, for example, are unlikely to be involved with the Parents Without Partners people.

Differentiation is found among the kinds of support single mothers derive from the various network components, and this tends not to break down along stereotypical gender lines. The family of origin and the ex-spouse often provide financial support. Babysitting cooperatives, car pools, and food cooperatives help in the performance of the tasks required for family functioning. Emotional support and intimacy needs are met by others in the network who share a strong identification with the role of single parent and the commitment to autonomy and success. Those intimates often also share lofty professional and career aspirations.

As relationships within extended networks are predicated upon the ad hoc needs of members, and as the members enjoy great mobility in entering and leaving, relationships tend to be, on the whole, less permanent than in the family-of-origin paradigm. Commonly, however, a few of the networks' relationships are stable, enduring, and reliable.

The McLanahan, Wedemeyer, and Adelberg (1981) study found several interesting results. For example, while most of the women who had been involved in extended networks were quite satisfied and well functioning, a few in this group were in considerable distress. Common to the women was a nostalgic longing for the past and a belief that occupational success does not undo marital failure. To the professional therapist's ear, such affect, cognition, and behaviors are strongly indicative of the need to explore the question of mourning and relationship restructuring discussed in an earlier chapter. In Flo's case, mourning work was apparently done in the safe and secure bosom of her family-of-origin network. What emerged was a woman eager to grow, who possessed the attitudes, emotions, thinking patterns, and behavioral repertoire to forge the kind of extended network which allowed for and nurtured growth.

McLanahan, Wedemeyer, and Adelberg (1981) describe how women may incorporate a "key male" or spouse substitute into either the family-of-origin network or the extended network without altering the essential nature of either type of support. Perhaps the most interesting finding of the study was the interaction effect between the kind of support group formed and the mother's role orientation on perceived psychological distress. Women reported stress when their support network contradicted their personal orientation. Change-oriented women trapped in a close-knit family-of-origin network are not happy, nor are stability-oriented women operating within a loose-knit and somewhat unreliable extended network.

Of singular diagnostic importance to professional therapists who work with distressed single mothers is the question of what is the most appropriate level at which to intervene. In some cases, what is called for is an alteration in the existing support network, in others, it is changes in the single mother's self-definitions and role orientations. A most thorny therapy problem arises in those instances where the single mother's role orientation and support group are syntonic but nonadaptive. Often, these women are aware that something is not right in their lives, but they are unable to connect their discomfort with the fact that, although comfortable, their support networks are growth inhibiting.

Twenty-five-year-old Lana had successfully put together a family-of-origin network with Jeff functioning as a much older key male spouse substitute. With his financial support, Lana was able to live in her own apartment and raise her two children, the youngest of whom was Jeff's daughter. Lana was accepted into Jeff's close-knit extended family, and she also enjoyed a close relationship with her older sister. In addition to Jeff's financial support, Lana was receiving public assistance. Although bright and highly articulate, she had no desire to work outside the home. Her relationship to Jeff had to be kept from the authorities or she would lose her benefits. Lana most certainly is not the only single mother to be dissatisfied with her relationship with welfare-type agencies.

Tillman (1976) states starkly that Aid to Families with Dependent Children is

> a supersexist marriage. You trade in "a" man for "the" man. But you can't divorce him if he treats you bad. He can divorce you of course, cut you off any time he wants. But in that case "he" keeps the kids, not you. "The" man runs everything. In ordinary marriage, sex is supposed to be for you and your husband. On AFDC you're not supposed to have any sex at all. You give up control over your body. It's a condition of aid. . . . "The" man, the welfare system, controls your money. He tells you what to buy and what not to buy, where to buy it, and how much things cost. If things—rent, for instance—really costs more than he says they do, it's too bad for you. (in Imber-Black, 1989, p. 34)

A central tenet of this book is that single parents need not passively accept negative societal constructs of whom and what they are. They need not always behave in ways that confirm the stereotypes which are used to define them.

Lana's financial insecurity derived not only from her dependence on welfare but also from her dependence on Jeff. Here, too, she was in constant danger of being "cut off." Any movement in the direction of her own autonomy was punished by Jeff's threats of economic and personal abandonment. Lana was depressed, but she did not recognize the source of her distress. Having lost her father at age five, she had been constantly in search of relief from her fear of being emotionally and physically alone. The price she paid for the "security" derived from welfare and Jeff was enormous.

Therapy was in the service of restructuring her support network to foster autonomy while helping her in the work of mourning her many previous losses. Insight into the problem is insufficient. Action also is required. The professional therapist must be aware that when clients say they want change in their lives they are often talking about an endpoint and not the difficult process of change. In Lana's case, she wanted to be more independent financially and emotionally. However, much of the therapy was in the direction of understanding and overcoming her resistance to making the sorts of changes in her life necessary for the attainment of her goals.

The work within the therapy sessions had several foci. Lana needed to examine her relationship with her father, see him in a more realistic light, and mourn his loss. Two joint sessions with the older sister aided in the process and also enabled Lana to examine the nature of her family-of-origin network. Joint sessions with Jeff enabled the couple to understand the complementary roles each played within their relationship.

Helping Lana establish an extended network—the action side of her therapy—was difficult. Her first venture out was to join a group of adult survivors. Although she re-created her preferred dependency orientation in relationships with the members of the group at first, she soon found herself involved in more mutual interactions with the other members. Jeff showed his support for Lana's growth by babysitting during the meetings. At some level, he seemed to be relieved to have Lana less dependent upon him.

This first step back into community opened some important doors for Lana. One member of her survivors' group introduced her to a community theater organization. Now more open to begin the construction of extended networks, Lana became fully involved and fully enjoyed her small role in the company's musical presentation. It was during this period that she decided to go to school to earn a high school equivalency diploma; as her world expanded, her dependency shrank.

Another case further illustrates the point. Daniella's needs were different from Lana's when she entered therapy following a divorce.

She had endured an emotionally and physically abusive relationship until her ex-husband began to beat her two sons.

As a secondary school teacher, Daniella was not in jeopardy of becoming dependent upon the welfare system. She had, however, incorporated the societal construction that, without a partner, she could not be both a successful worker and a good mother to her boys. Her depression was fueled by irrational feelings of inadequacy.

Daniella was an aerobics instructor as well as a teacher, so a latent extended network structure was available to her. At the time when she began therapy, she was making no use of this structure, however. She had no family of her own other than her sons, and so it was in therapy that certain of the functions of the family-of-origin network were carried out. Within the context of an open, honest, and caring relationship with her therapist, Daniella was able to dispute her belief around the question of inadequacy, work, and mothering. Over time, in a process similar to the one which Flo and her sisters created, Daniella came to see her strengths and weaknesses realistically and to feel accepted and respected. The reduction in anxiety made it rather easy for this highly talented woman to make use of her extended network in ways which brought about much satisfaction for herself, her sons, and her friends.

While Flo, Lana, and Daniella have become happy and successful in their single parenthood, their lives are far from ideal. Each would prefer to be involved more intimately with one special man, but none defines her life as a failure because of this particular aspect. To a greater rather than lesser degree, each feels in control of her life and less at risk of becoming involved in abusive relationships with either other persons or social institutions. To a greater rather than lesser degree, each feels that she has more control over who and what she and her family are rather than do any societal stereotypes.

ROLE OF THE PROFESSIONAL THERAPIST

The therapist serves as a reality check for the single mother by asking her to assess the degree to which she has accepted the social system's deficit model of her and her family.

The interaction of many single-parent families with larger social systems such as social services, schools, and/or human service agencies is influenced by the expectations that these families place on larger systems and, in return, the expectations and constructs which the systems maintain about single-parent families. Quite often, it seems that the agencies as well as the families themselves perceive the single-parent family as deficient or somewhat lacking in one or more necessary components. The families may look to the agencies to augment or fill in the gaps initially created by the exiting of a parent. Single mothers may attribute difficulties with their children to the absence of the father—traditionally the disciplinarian.

For example, mothers with preteen or teenage sons often look to outside agents as potential surrogate disciplinarians. They may request a male therapist or worker with the hopes that this worker will function as a role model for their sons. Frequently, however, they are more likely to be seeking parenting assistance than role modeling from the male therapist. Too often both the single mother and the male adolescent maintain the erroneous assumption that the difficulties the family may be having with his adolescence result from an inadequacy in the family's structure rather than considering that this assumption may be a significant component of the problem.

Single parents, experiencing a sense of overload from what seems like too many roles and responsibilities, may look toward larger systems to essentially pick up some of the slack. Mothers eager to compensate for self-assessed deficiencies may be apt to become over-reliant on mental health and school professionals, organizations such as Big Brothers Big Sisters, or the local Little League coach to supplement their family system. This can be particularly taxing to a mother who is transporting two or three children to myriad support groups and activities while simultaneously attempting to hold down a full-time job.

Although any of these representatives of the larger systems may adequately fulfill the requirements of their designated roles, they are unlikely to be equipped to meet the emotional functions of the roles the family may be assigning them. In many cases, this can result in a continuous loop of social systems disappointing the single-parent family who places on these agencies excessive expectations which they inevitably fail to fulfill.

This is most likely to occur in social service systems such as public assistance or welfare. These systems are neither designed nor capable of fulfilling a coparenting function. Primarily constructed to supply emergency financial assistance, these systems can quickly become a source of frustration rather than empowerment for the single parent. Social and eligibility workers with large caseloads are not likely to address the emotional needs of their clientele. However, at times it may seem that these systems are inherently designed to deter access to the types of assistance they were created to provide. It is not surprising, therefore, to find single mothers—particularly younger single mothers—diminished by their inability to negotiate the system. Frequently, social services functions as a persistent source of stress to the family and, as the family may seem to be absorbed by social services, so may social services be absorbed into the operation of the family system. Rather than attributing these difficulties to social service systems, the family is apt to perceive these dilemmas as intrinsic to being in a single-parent family.

Unfortunately, the larger systems are likely to do the same. Despite the ever-increasing awareness of the preponderance of single-parent families as representatives of their society, larger social systems continue to approach the single-parent family as inadequate and incomplete, thereby conceivably reinforcing the family's negative self-constructions. Families which look toward social services or other larger systems to replace a missing parent may be operating from the pretense that single parenthood is a temporary status which eventually can be remedied. In doing so, they may be relinquishing the opportunity of experiencing their family system as capable and essentially complete.

The professional therapist ensures that no pathologizing of single-parent families goes unchallenged.

THERAPY STRATEGIES

In working with single mothers, McGoldrick (1988) suggests that

> Urging women to accept and move toward "male" values is not the solution to female powerlessness. It is important to validate women's focus on relationships at the same time that you empower them in the areas of work and money. (p. 65)

provides the preferred therapy milieu.

1. Therapists can arrange to have each new single-parent client put into contact with a network of other single parents. This aids in the formation of extended support networks that empower sin-

gle mothers with regard to their careers and economic well-be-ing.

2. Therapists can give clients permission to mourn their losses, and help with the work of mourning.
3. Therapists can help clients identify and dispute negative societal stereotypes concerning single mothers and their families.
4. Therapists can help clients assess how their own cognitions, af-fects, and behaviors and those of their support networks wither, promote, or retard personal and financial autonomy.
5. Therapists can encourage clients to use support networks in novel ways to have their needs met. From carpooling to joint liv-ing arrangements with other single-parent systems, any and all potential solutions may be entertained.
6. Therapists can help clients with specific issues such as self-esteem and assertiveness.
7. Therapists can help clients find training in specific skills.
8. Therapists can help with regard to financial matters. As pointed out by Hicks and Anderson (1989),

    Whether it be the stress of adjusting to a lower standard of liv-ing, the need to develop very specific skills for managing fi-nances, or the need to overcome a socially ingrained fear of money, women must be helped to get control of financial mat-ters. Without their control they will never fully experience their own power, self-esteem, pride and autonomy. (p. 331)

9. Therapists can adopt a construction of reality which suggests that single parenthood need not be understood as a problem-saturated role. Rather, the formation of a single-parent family can present a large number of options which, in sum, can lead to a most satisfying family experience. Therapists can help clients cocreate this reality for themselves.

PART IV:
SOCIAL CONSTRUCTION THERAPY
WITH THE SINGLE-PARENT FAMILY

Chapter 10

The Single-Parent Family
and Social Constructions

Prior chapters have presented therapists with research findings and traditional family therapy theory and therapy techniques applicable to the single parent. This chapter describes what some believe is a paradigmatic shift in the field of family therapy and represents leading-edge theoretical formulations in the field. This current theory is illustrated with case material. Social construction theory and therapy has profound implications for how we do therapy and how we view our clients, and provides a framework whereby we can examine our own biases and assumptions about the divorce experience (intimacy dissolution) and being a single parent.

SOCIAL CONSTRUCTIONIST THEORY

For most social constructionists, descriptions and explanations of the world and its people are socially derived products of historically and culturally situated interchanges among people (Gergen, 1999). Language derives its major significance from the way it is embedded within patterns of relationships (Gergen, 1999).

Social constructionist theory flows from the work of Kelly (1969), Berger and Luckmann (1966), and Gergen (1985). Social constructionism places emphasis on social interpretation and the intersubjective influences of language, family, and culture. As Gergen (1985) states, "From the constructional position the process of understanding is not automatically driven by the forces of nature, but is the result of an active, cooperative enterprise of persons in relationship" (p. 267). Thus, social construction theory proposes that an evolving set of meanings continually emerge from social interactions. These meanings are part of a general flow of constantly changing narratives. Language, with its grammar, syntax, and vocabulary, is the obvious instance of stability in that it provides a categorization process for symbolic interactions. Some socially constructed meanings become part of the ongoing cultural and social structural arrangements of a society and can seem highly consequential. These socially constructed meanings could prevent people from seeing other aspects or important features of their reality.

Meanings that are socially constructed tend to be constructed out of myth, propaganda, wishes, prejudices, and fears. As such a multitude of information is "left out" of a person's reality. Berger and Luckmann (1966) believe that the socially constructed meanings we have inherited are "opaque" (p. 55); in other words, the ways in which our meanings are constructed are invisible to us, as are the elements which compose it. The social world we are born into is experienced by the child as the sole reality. The rules of the world we are born into are nonproblematic, they require no explanation, and they are neither challenged nor doubted. Through socialization, socially constructed meanings are internalized; they are filtered and understood through meaningful symbols. From these meanings flow psychological meanings and scripts for behavior. A person attempts to match his or her own experience with the available meanings and scripts. The person learns the language, the appropriate behavior for his or her gender, age, and culture. In this way, a person develops an individual identity, an individual script, and, along with it, individual meanings—all of which are created by and embedded in the dominant culture.

Maines (2000) believes that the social constructionist agenda is an attempt to show that no matter how sedimented social conditions may appear or actually be, those conditions are nonetheless produced, maintained, and changed through interpretive processes.

Using this as a backdrop for therapy, it would be helpful to explore what marriage, divorce, and being part of a single-parent family mean for each family member. Figure 10.1, using this viewpoint, describes the process of the development of a worldview.

Social constructionism implies that what is real is not an objective fact; rather, what appears to be real evolves through interpersonal interaction and agreement as to what is fact. It redefines meaning systems as created by a socially interactive process rather than based on an intrapsychic process.

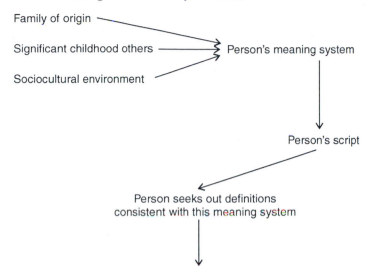

The single-parent family who sees problem as part of its meaning system seeks out information that is consistent with this view. Behaviors, interactions, and affect (the person's script) reflect this view. A cycle is set up whereby the family experiences the problem as flowing from its past, reinforced by interactions in the present, and not having a solution in the future.

FIGURE 10.1. Model of social constructionist therapy: development of a worldview.

SOCIAL CONSTRUCTIONIST THERAPY

Social constructionist therapy explores the family meanings that incidents, behaviors, and encounters with single-parent families have for individuals and how these are determined by the sociocultural environment. The sociocultural environment equips them with methods and ways of understanding and making judgments about aspects of the single-parent family, ranging from how they felt about their divorce or the death of a spouse to religious values. These ways of making sense of experiences are embedded in a meaning system that is accepted as reality by the social group and in the scripts (ways of behaving) that are a part of the individual's meaning system. The dialectical relationship between individual realities and the socially constructed meanings around the single-parent family is the focus of this chapter.

Before discussing the actual social constructionist therapy model for therapy the single-parent family, a comparison of deficit and solution-focused therapies is presented in Table 10.1. de Shazer (1985) was one of the first theorists responsible for solution-focused therapy. His work led him away from a focus on the problem in therapy to a focus on solution, which clients defined as more helpful. He stated that often the solution clients constructed had very little to do with the problems they presented, but that it "fit" with the client's definition of the problem. Consequently, the therapy moved in a direction away from the therapist trying to understand the client's problem (and therefore trying to design a solution to it) to a focus on questioning the client about his or her own goals and exploring the self as a potential resource for problem solving. While doing this, Molnar and de Shazer (1987) noticed exceptions to the client's story—times when the problem was not happening. These therapists then focused on

TABLE 10.1. Comparison of problem/deficit models of therapy with solution-focused models

Traditional approaches	Solution-focused therapy
Therapist is an expert–has special knowledge regarding the problem to which the client needs to submit (Colonialization/missionary model)	Client and therapist both have particular areas of expertise (Collaborative model)
Client is viewed as damaged by the abuse (Deficit model)	Client is viewed as influenced but not determined by the abuse history, having strengths and abilities (Resource model)
Remembering abuse and the expression of repressed affect (catharsis) are treatment	Goals are individualized for each client, but do not necessarily involve goals of catharsis or remembering
Interpretation	Acknowledgment, valuing, and opening possibilities
Past oriented	Present/future oriented
Problem/pathology oriented	Solution oriented
Must be long-term treatment	Variable/individualized length of treatment
Invites conversations for insight and working through	Invites conversations for accountability and action and declines invitations to blame and invalidation

Source: McNamee and Gergen (1992). *Therapy As Social Construction.* (p. 140). Thousand Oaks, CA: Sage. Used with permission.

what that experience was like when the problem was not happening and developed the solution-focused therapy model. White (1996, 1989), building on Bateson's (1972) notions of restraints, proposed a similar model of "alternate descriptions." As defined by Bateson (1972), restraints are the limitations that people hold—the beliefs, the values, that make it less likely for them to notice other aspects of their problem-saturated life. In so doing, he developed a narrative therapy through which people could explore their ongoing story. Therapy in this sense involves assisting individuals to reauthor their lives. Narrative therapy assumes that people's lives are strongly influenced by their storymaking and that poor relationships are embedded in these stories (Barry, 1997).

Some of the assumptions of this approach follow:

1. Every human has a biological drive to unfold and to grow—to be the fullest he or she can be (Perls, 1969). "You can let the organism take over without interfering . . . without interrupting we can rely on the wisdom of the organism" (Perls, 1969, p. 17).
2. There are no absolute truths and there are no absolute realities.
3. We coconstruct reality through language with another in a continual interaction with the sociocultural environment. Thus, what is "real" is that which is coconstructed through language and interaction by persons in continual interplay with the surrounding sociocultural environment.
4. Our inner world is a construct, colored by the past, and our past is a construction.
5. People tend to re-create an image of their world by noticing behavior in others that confirms their self-definitions and definitions of situations and by selectively ignoring disconfirmatory behavior.
6. How we "see" problems, how we "see" roles, how we "see" relationships—all these ideas do not simply reflect or elaborate on biological "givens" but are largely products of sociocultural processes.
7. People who come for therapy are experiencing problems in living. They have tried solutions—many of which have been unsuccessful. The problems they report are not seen as being functional in maintaining the system or as a manifestation of underlying pathology. They are seen as problems—problems which have nega-

tive effects for the person, couple, or family. The way that people use language to talk about problems is the way they can use language to coconstruct a new story.

8. Repetitive knowledge of behavior that is discrepant with the perceptual view of the person will result in a change in the person's perceptual view. This is accomplished by focusing on and amplifying exceptions in the person's description of the world.

9. Social constructionist therapy focuses on challenging the person's view of the problem. It accomplishes this by breaking up the meaning that the problem holds and questioning his or her behavioral script. This is achieved through the use of such techniques as metaphors and reframes, which amplify the person's process, and by finding exceptions to the person's process (deconstruction or descripting), thereby providing seeds (construction or rescripting) for transformation.

THEORETICAL CONCEPTS

Constructed Perceptions

Gergen and Gergen (1983; Gergen, 1985) used the term *self-narratives* to describe the social psychological processes whereby people tell stories about themselves to themselves and others. Self-narratives are a way to identify and preserve values for the self and the moral community (Gergen, 1988). These theorists characterize self-narratives as the way individuals establish coherent connections among life events. They believe that individuals have a set of schema by which they attempt to understand life events as meaningful and systematically related. In this way, events are rendered understandable and intelligible because they are located in a sequence or as part of an unfolding process.This process enables individuals to make "sense out of nonsense" and to interpret events in a coherent, consistent manner. Gergen and Gergen see single-parent family problems as sociocultural symbolic constructs. Inquiry into the sources, processes, and consequences of their construction and organization is the therapy that flows from this view.

The Social Construction of Meanings

These narratives or *meaning systems* are originally created and maintained by interactions with significant others. The process begins at birth and continues until death. If a person holds a particular meaning system, he or she then will seek out events and persons that are consistent with that meaning system. These meaning systems in turn lead to *states,* the emotional reaction to the meaning system, and *behaviors,* which are consistent with the meaning system.

These meaning systems are socially constructed and are embedded in the larger sociocultural environment. Berger and Luckmann (1966) describe social constructions as the consensual recognition of the realness and rightness of a constructed reality, plus the socialization process by which people acquire this reality. Social construction includes not only the routines and the mechanisms for socializing the children of the system, but also the means for maintaining the definition of reality on which it is based. Language is one way that a community reaffirms the dominant reality and discredits competing social constructions. Meanings, which are social constructions, refer to the complex and unique definitions in each individual that can influence behavior. These meanings were constructed in childhood and are maintained by ongoing sociocultural perturbations. These meanings are created, embedded in, and recognized by the larger social group and thus operate at the social, interpersonal, and intrapersonal levels.

The Social Construction of Scripts

Individuals' meaning systems determine the content of their scripts. The notion of scripts was initially introduced by transactional analysts and later by social psychologists Gagnon and Simon (1973) when they applied this notion to the area of sexuality. They believe that we are like actors with parts in plays. These parts, or scripts, exist in all areas of life, including the sexual. Scripts, they believe, are the organizers for our behaviors, involved in learning the meaning of internal states, organizing the sequences of specifically acts, decoding novel situations, setting the limits on responses, and linking meanings from different aspects of life to specific experiences (Gagnon, 1990). People develop scripts out of their meaning systems. A script is a device "for guiding action and for understanding it" (p. 6). Scripts are plans that people have about what they are doing and what they are going to do. They justify actions that are in agreement with them and challenge those which are not. Scripts are the "blueprints for behavior," which specify who one will do a behavior with, what one will do, when, and why one will do a particular behavior.

"Scripts constitute the available repertoire of socially recognized acts and statuses, and roles and the rules governing them" (Laws and Schwartz, 1977, p. 217). Scripts operate at a social, personal, and intrapsychic level. They are embedded in social institutions and as such are internalized by individuals. The overriding, dominant scripts receive most attention because of their primacy and potency among people's options. It is against the dominant social scripts that people attempt to match or reject their own personal social scripts. "It is clear that the . . . script that individuals bring to treatment exist at the intrapyschic and the interpersonal levels and most, though not all, interventions involve changes in both" (Gagnon, 1990, p. 33).

Family scripts (Atwood, 1996) can account for how individual members may disown responsibility for what happens and attribute blame to someone else in the family. Thus a change in the script can be attributed to the recognition that everyone has a potential role in creating the family situations and that alternative ways of interacting do exist. In "normal" family processes, in order for the family scripts to be helpful to the family, there have to be ways of updating them when necessary, as in life-cycle changes, e.g. birth of a baby, graduation from college. This then involves a series of reedits or revisions in which the family improvises in response to changed circumstances. Any novel, innovative behavior changes that emerge and are then repeated can over time become part of the family's expectations. The family script is rewritten in this manner and the family can adapt to developmental changes and novel situations (see also Byng-Hall, 1995).

Constructing a Timeline

The concept of time is an important part of this model (Atwood, 1991; Penn, 1985; White, 1989). For example, we can ask such questions as, "How long has this problem been around? When did you first start becoming depressed about this problem?" In doing so, the therapist introduces a historical context of a beginning, a middle, and, hopefully, an end. These types of questions give persons, couples, and families information about the origins and persistence of problems and how the trends developed over time. This also helps dispel beliefs that people are born that way, or are just like one of their parents, or are victim to any other genetic causality. The problem becomes located in time rather than in the person, and its characteristics are then examinable and observable.

Collapsing Time—The Rubber Band Backward and Forward

Couples are asked, "If I were to take a rubber band and stretch it back to when the problem was not there, what was your life like?" Asking "How long has this problem been around?" and "When did you first start having this problem?" places the person's experience of the problem within a developing trend. Asking a person about what life was like before the problem implies that there was a time when the problem was not there and further implies that perhaps at some point in the future it will also not be there. As will be discussed in a later section, the rubber band can also be used (if requested by the client) to stretch back in time to explore the person's story when he or she was a child in his or her family of origin.

Stretching the rubber band into the future allows the person to envision a future without the problem. Here persons are asked, "If I were to take the rubber band and stretch it forward, say three months from now, and the problem was gone, what would your life be like?" Questioning about development over time is an effort that not only draws attention to the fact that the intensity of the experience of the problem varies over time but also identifies that at times the problem is absent, and it presents the possibility that the problem might not be there in the future. This will lay the groundwork for ideas that the person has some control over the problem and, by implication, that at some point the problem will no longer be there. The progressive use of directional description of the time metaphor allows couples to understand their participation in the problem's persistence at different points in time (White, 1996).

Change

Watzlawick, Weakland, and Fisch (1974) describe two types of change, first-order and second-order change. Simply, first-order change is a change that occurs *within* a system, while second-order change is a change of the system itself. It is considered a *change of change.* First-order change maintains homeostasis; second-order change is a change of the premises governing the system as a whole. First-order changes are incremental modifications that make sense within an established frame (Watzlawick, 1978, 1984). Second-order change changes the frame itself. To accomplish second-order change, the therapist phases in particular material and phases out other material. First-order change is exemplified by traditional psychotherapy. Second-order change is represented by the approaches of Minuchin (1974), Haley (1967), Watzlawick (1978, 1984; Watzlawick, Weakland, and Fisch, 1974), and White (1985, 1986a,b, 1989).

Because the focus of intervention is on meaning systems and scripts, the change model adhered to in this chapter is a second-order change model. It is similar to Epston and White's (1990) recent work whereby the therapist initially assists the person in learning processes that help him or her amplify (be aware of) their process, provides techniques that he or she can use to generate new possibilities, and is someone who creates a "safe environment" in which the client can explore his or her process, generate new possibilities, consider the implications of the possibilities, and negotiate a frame around the chosen change. These ways of learning can be used by the person outside therapy. Over time, as the person learns to rely on his or her own self-healing processes, confident in the processes increases, as does confidence in his or her own abilities to generate growth and change. In this case, the result is new structures of a higher order—ones that are more connected and integrated than the prior ones. They are more complex, more flexible, and more susceptible to further change and development.

Thus, the present chapter presents the underlying assumptions and theoretical concepts of social constructionism and presents a model of social constructionist therapy with the single-parent family. The approach to therapy presented in this chapter is based on the belief that we create our own reality. Persons, couples, families make sense of their ongoing experience and it is this process of making sense that is the object of this therapy. The therapy takes as its focus the client's meaning system, viewed from the past, present, and future—both negative and positive. The initial focus of the past is affective—understanding how their meanings developed and how they believe these meanings affected them in the past. Once the past is put in perspective, the second focus of the approach is cognitive—on his or her script for behavior in the present, and on the maintenance of the meaning system; helping the person, couple, family be aware of their processes; and facilitating learning about and amplifying exceptions to the process in order to provide possibilities for new solutions. Future focus enables them to image how different meanings and the resultant scripts could affect their lives in a positive way. Revisioning their lives, their relationships, or their family is the last stage of this therapy and emphasizes future visions of life without the problem.

THERAPY STRATEGIES

Proposing the Notion of a Family Meaning System

Using this as a background for proposing a social constructionist therapy model with single-parent families, therapy around these issues can be divided into three different stories: the family's story about their families of origin (whether or not old skeletons are present), their story about their present relationships (how the problems they are experiencing are maintained), and their story about what they see for their future (how their family meanings and resultant scripts can change). Knowledge of each of these three stories helps the therapist understand the family's frame of the problem and helps the family learn about their frame of the problem. Hoffman (1990) states that

> problems are stories people have agreed to tell themselves . . . then we have to persuade them to tell themselves a different, more empowering story, have conversations with them, though the awareness that the findings of their conversations have no other reality than that bestowed by mutual consent. (pp. 3, 4)

Thus, family members are asked about what the problems associated with being a single-parent family member mean to them in their given sociocultural contexts. The notion of the single-parent family is treated as a symbol invested with meaning by society. The approach to the family problem is thus a matter of symbolic analysis and interpretation. The family problem is seen as emanating from various forms of action or practice within the family's life.

Joining the Family Meaning System

Underlying the beginning of any therapy is the importance of joining the family meaning system or constructing a workable reality. The dynamic interplay of joining and constructing a workable reality initiates the process of change. The construction of a workable reality can be defined as the process in which the view of the problem is transformed from a paradigm of individual causality to a paradigm of family interaction. It is a process analogous to socializing through which an empathic rapport develops with clients. The therapist's reflections serve to create an environment conducive to change. In this environment, the therapist listens to the family's language, learns it, and uses it to create a comfortable environment. The basic assumption is that the client is the expert in knowing what is best for them. The role of the therapist is that of curious observer—interested in learning about the family's story. The therapist interacts with the family orthogonally, so as not to become part of the system.

Exploring the Past

If the family feels unresolved past issues are contributing to the problems, the therapist can use the rubber band method to help the client move back in time: "If I were to take a rubber band and stretch it back to when you were a child, could you tell Mom/Dad what it was like for you? Could you tell Mom/Dad what you wanted from them and didn't get? Could you tell Mom/Dad what you learned about yourself from the way you were treated by them? What meanings did you give these experiences? Could you also tell Mom/Dad what you appreciated about her/him? Could you tell Mom/Dad what they taught you that was helpful for you as a very young person growing up? And Mom/Dad, could you reflect that back?"

Similar questions could be asked of the parent: "Could you tell your child what wishes, desires, hopes you had for him/her when he/she was born? And son/daughter, could you reflect that back?" This phase of therapy is not to blame the child or the parent and is used only if the family feels old unresolved issues need to be settled. Further, the focus of this phase of therapy is not to ascertain the truthfulness of the memories but rather to put the perceptions in perspective, along with recognizing that multiple perceptions of the same event exist.

Putting the Past in Perspective

After both parent and child(ren) have explored the story of the past, the past can be put in perspective. This can be facilitated by a ritual. The family members can write down all the important childhood events that relate to the explored issues, both negative and positive, and place the paper in a shoe box and bury it (i.e., symbolically burying the past). Family members may wish to write letters to one another, forgiving them for their mistakes and thanking them for the gifts they gave them. These letters could either be mailed or buried. The family members could have a ritualistic ceremony whereby they symbolically let go of their pain and the effects of the pain, by setting a balloon or kite free at the beach. They can symbolically show appreciation for early gifts from one another by doing something special for them.

Learning the Present Family Meaning System

Berger and Kellner (1964/1994) define family as a definitional process. At this point in therapy, the family members tell their present story. Here the therapist attempts to obtain as complete an understanding as possible of the family's story about the problem. Therapists can learn about the family story by paying careful attention to linguistic symbolizations such as family myths, legends, rites, and metaphors. Here then the therapist begins to uncover the family meaning system.

An individual's reality is maintained by developing a personal sense of self that is congruent with the social constructions. As stated earlier, based on early interactions and ongoing socialization, individuals construct a reality around meanings which includes a preferred way of relating to others. This then becomes the basis for how they view others and how they expect others to view them. In many ways, these perceptual sets determine predictable ways of interacting with others. Here relevant questions might be, "How do you think of the problem? Do you see any other options? What solutions have you attempted?"

When uncovering the family's story about the present, both the therapist and the family members learn what information the family selects out of their environment and how they fit that information into an already-existing meaning system so as to reinforce that system. For example, in a family with an adolescent with a problem, differentiating the fine line between being an adolescent with a problem and being an emotionally disturbed adolescent becomes particularly important. It will make a great difference for the family's general expectations and perceptions of the capabilities of the teenager. The therapist and the family learn how the family's patterned conversations and attempted solutions reflect this meaning system. When families learn about their meaning system and connect them to the way they "see" their problems, they gather information about how they have inadvertently participated in the perpetuation of the problem. For many families, telling their story invokes a revolving door image with no exits, as they begin to see themselves as going around and around in the same cycle unable to break out of the pattern. It is here that the family begins to reflect on the implications of their meaning system. Having the family's story about the family separation, single parenthood, and perhaps a new family helps to assure the family that the therapist understands their story and their experience of the story. This reflection eventually will lead to reconstructing which is crucial in social constructionist therapy. This method facilitates the relinquishment of old family sensitivities and promotes healing (see also Siegel, 1986).

Once it is accepted that a family's meaning system is socially constructed, it then becomes possible to deconstruct it. The following section elaborates on the processes by which the family's meaning system can be uncovered and then challenged in order to make room for new experiences. Techniques used to amplify the family's process can be used. These processes often help the family see where they are stuck. At this point the family meaning system is uncovered and the possibility of choice arises in terms of whether to keep the uncovered meaning system or to change it.

Some ways of amplifying the family's process are tracking and circular and reflexive questioning. Tracking is where the therapist focuses on the symbols, metaphors, themes, and language of the couple to help them better understand their transactional process. Circular questioning is where the therapist invites one member to comment on the relationship of two other members. Through circular questioning, a view of the meaning the problem holds for the family emerges that allows both the therapist and the family to appreciate its interconnectedness and circular nature. Reflexive questions are questions that enable the family's own healing processes to emerge: "If you made no changes in your relationship, what do you think the consequences would be? What would have to happen in order for you to realize that the problem was getting a little better?"

In this phase, practical issues are also explored. The therapist helps the family get unstuck by reinforcing old coping skills, teaching new skills, and providing education about the social and community services available to them. Education is provided to the family in order to enhance the family's effectiveness. Educating families about family conferences (i.e., support groups for teenagers and their parents) is another method that therapists can use at this time to assist these families. The conferences gives the families ways to discuss sharing responsibilities; they can also give family members an opportunity to express their feelings and concerns. Support groups for adolescents can be recommended to the family. They can normalize the experiences of the family members by helping them feel that they are not alone. The therapist also helps the family prioritize any overwhelming issues they may be facing. Here the therapist learns about the current situation, the family's definition of the crisis, and which decisions the family feels they must make. Family rules and roles that hinder family coping skills are explored, along with family communication styles clouding the family's definitional process. The division of labor within the family is explored here and anger expression techniques are taught and utilized.

Inviting Change in the Family's Meaning System

Once the notion of a family meaning system is accepted by the family and the individual family meaning system is uncovered, a competing meaning system can be introduced. It is not apparent to most individuals that there are alternative ways of behaving at each stage of the life cycle. Our meaning systems makes areas outside the dominant ones appear invisible. This invisibility serves to maintain and foster adherence to the dominant definitions. In fact, the function of socialization and of the sanctions against moving outside the dominant script is to keep individuals within it. To find, name, focus on, and help the family experience alternative meanings and scripts is the intention of this section.

The view expressed in this chapter is that change is normal and we have a choice in change. Our knowledge about how to behave is learned by social definitions of appropriate and inappropriate ways of behaving; however, we can choose to develop our own personal attitudes and concepts which differ from the traditional ones. Numerous scripts are avail- able to us for examination. Here the role of the therapist is to notice competing constructions or exceptions in the family's meaning system. Change requires a two-sided perspective and a therapist may seek to construct a relational definition by developing two (or complementary) descriptions of the problem (White, 1996). Complementary questions are derived and introduced to challenge or help deconstruct the dominant explanation and to assist families in achieving a relational or double description of the problem. This double description then provides the source of new responses (Atwood and Levine, 1991; White, 1996). The family's explanation, or frame, begins to overlap the frame offered by the therapist (like two overlapping Venn diagrams), and it is in this overlap that the possibility for change exists.

White's (1989) notion of "exceptions" was originally based in Bateson's idea of restraints—those ideas, events, experiences that are less likely to be noticed by people because they are dissonant with individual descriptions of the problem. Exceptions are noticing the flip side of the coin. White (1989) believes that, as a family's view of reality is challenged through questioning about these exceptions, family members ultimately recognize other aspects of their reality that do not involve the problem. In so doing they create another narrative, a second story, about their lives which does not include the problem.

De Shazer's (1991) notion of exceptions refers to times in the client's life when the problem was *not* happening, Here the therapist "seeks to find the element in the system studied (their conversation about the client's complaint, goals, etc.) which is alogical, the thread . . . which will unravel it all, or the loose stone which will pull down the whole building" (de Shazer, 1991, p. 122). The therapist reinforces alternatives to the dominant description of the problem—helping to make visible areas outside the dominant meaning system. In so

doing, he or she begins to undermine what previously had been spec-
ifying and justifying the family's reality (Amundson, 1990). Anderson and Goolishian (1988) stated that

> to deconstruct means to take apart the interpretive assumption of
> the system of meaning that you are examining, to challenge the in-
> terpretive system in such a manner that you reveal the assumptions
> on which the model is based. At the same time as these are re-
> vealed, you open the space for alternative understanding. (p. 11)

Now the therapist begins to plant new seeds and the old frame begins to break up. The old frame breaking up is the basis of a different
level of order: "Are there ever times when the problem is not there?"
The receipt of news of difference is essential for the revelation of new
ideas and a triggering of new responses for the discovery of new solutions. An exception is found. Now it must be amplified. A piece has
been found that does not fit the overall puzzle. This piece has the possibility to grow, beginning the deconstruction of the old frame (meaning system) and through amplification and activation of the new
construction—the new frame.

Here the family is encouraged to focus on the positive elements of
their interactions. They are encouraged to observe what they are doing right and to increase those behaviors. The therapist highlights and
emphasizes the smallest positive difference through obtaining thorough descriptions of exceptions, changes, or possible solutions.

Amplifying the New Meaning System

The amplification of the exception is essential for the triggering of
the new construction, which holds the possibility of new solutions
(Bateson, 1972). Here the therapist amplifies the competing constructions in the family's meaning system: "When the problem is not
there, how is your relationship? If you were to enjoy your relationship
more frequently, how would you notice? What would be different?
What else would be different? How would that be for you?" By helping the family deepen the experience of the relationship without the
problem, the therapist is facilitating a new construction—that of a
more positive relationship. This new construction holds new meanings for the family. Thus, the therapist creates an environment that
amplifies the family's strengths, resources, and solutions (Lipchick,

1988). The family therapist's perspective views clinical presentations as life transitions and opportunities for growth. He or she sees clinical problems as linguistic phenomena (rather than objectifications) that are cocreated in the context of the therapist-client relationship.

Stabilizing the New Meaning System

At this point, alternative meaning systems are available to the family and what once was invisible now holds potential for new solutions. The original meaning system which held the problem has been deconstructed and replaced by a new description. The family can now begin to focus on the future. Future focus enables them to visualize their relationship without the problem, with such questions as these: "If you could stretch the rubber band three years into the future and the problem was gone, what would that look like? How would your relationship be different? How else would it be different?"

By asking questions about future trends and choices, the therapist is making that future more real and more stable. As Penn (1985) suggests, when faced with questions about the future—even if that future is only hypothetical—"the system is free to create a new map" (p. 300). Questions such as "How will your future without the problem be different from the future with the problem?" require speculation about difference and help consolidate the emerging new meaning system for the family. Often rehearsal precedes performance. Here, a version of de Shazer's (1991) Miracle Question can be used: "If a miracle were to happen tonight while you were asleep and tomorrow morning you awoke to find that this problem were no longer a part of your life, what would be different? How would you know that this miracle had taken place? How could your Mom/Dad be able to know without your telling them?"

Another way of stabilizing the new meaning system is put forth by Epston and White (1990) when they discuss how they invite family members to a special meeting where, through questioning, they discuss the family's stories of their therapy adventure. The family members are asked to recount how they became aware of their problem and what steps they took to solve it. They can recount how and which resources they mobilized as they generated solutions to their problems. Epston and White (1990) believe that here the therapist can ask the family members to recount their transition from a problematic status to a resolved one. In addition, the therapist also can provide his or her own story of the therapy adventure, and they can then discuss their collaborative efforts, thereby helping reinforce the notion of a new meaning system. The following illustration outlines the constructionist approach to therapy:

Joining the Family Meaning System

↓

Proposing the Notion of a Family Meaning System

↓

Learning the Family's Meaning System

↓

Inviting Change in the Family's Meaning System

↓

Amplifying the New Meaning System

↓

Stabilizing the New Meaning System

Carol is a thirty-seven-year-old single parent. She has been divorced from her husband, Edward, for four years. She is the custodial parent of their two children, Dawn, age fourteen, and Mark, age fifteen. They came for therapy because Mark was sent to the school principal's office after he cursed at his soccer coach. Carol reported to the therapist that Mark had failed three subjects the past quarter and, although he never was a straight-A student, he usually managed to receive Cs or better. Also fighting with his sister had increased over the past few months.

Because Carol was having a difficult time living on the money Edward gave her for child support, she took a job locally as a bank teller. The job helped, but the family had to tighten their belts. This was difficult because before the divorce, they had a very comfortable lifestyle. Mark was no longer able to go skiing with his friends during winter break, and he had to wait until Carol saved up the money before he could get new soccer equipment. Dawn had to stop taking dance lessons and was only able to buy one new outfit in September when school started. This was very different from what it used to be like before the divorce, and the children were often resentful. They complained bitterly about their financial straights and blamed Carol for the divorce. The culmination of their bitterness occurred when they had to sell their home, where the children had lived all their lives. They moved into an apartment. Although Carol tried to make it into a nice home, she felt that no matter what she did they would never be happy. The children hated the fact that their dog, Snuffy, had to be given away because the new apartment rules allowed no pets. They hated that they had to go to a new school where they had no friends. They hated that all their friends lived on the other side of town. They hated that they only saw their dad every other weekend. They hated that they had to help their mom with the household chores. They hated each other, and they hated their mom. They hated the idea that their parents were divorced and were ashamed to tell anyone about their family situation. So, they didn't invite any of their friends over after school for fear that someone would learn of their single-parent status. They felt that the only sane person was their dad who, when he picked them up for the weekend, bought them presents and let them stay up very late watching television.

After the divorce, but before Carol began working, the family was very bad off financially and at one point Carol had to apply for food stamps, much to the embarassment of her children. They felt as if they were now lower class and it was all Carol's fault. Carol was exhausted. She was tired from trying to keep the family together only to listen to the children argue incessantly during dinner. When she began working, she was tired of working all day and then having to cook dinner. She caught a glimpse of herself in the mirror one day and saw an old woman. At first she almost didn't recognize herself. Her sister encouraged her to date, or to at least occassionally go to the movies, but Carol was simply too tired. She could not see any solution to these problems and was very resentful of Edward. Edward was an attorney who could well afford to give the family extra money; instead, he paid only what the court mandated, which was not enough money for even one person to live on, let alone three. At times, she almost felt as if she made the wrong decision to divorce Edward, but then she would remember the humiliation of his countless affairs and knew better. Carol felt she had no life. She didn't see any hope for the future. As far as dating or going out with her friends, she had no energy left at the end of a long day and felt that even if she did no one would be interested in a "tired old hag."

When Carol came in for therapy, she expressed great concern over the tension and hostility that existed within the home. She also reported that she was experiencing depression because of having "no life." In the first stage of therapy, the therapist joined with the family's meaning system. As a curious observer, the therapist listened to and learned the family's language and story about the problem and then used this language to join and create a comfortable environment.

The second stage of therapy involved proposing the notion of a family meaning system. To do this the therapist needed to understand the family's frame of the problem. Each member was asked to tell his or her story about personal perceptions of the problems, about present family relationships, and about what each saw for the future. It was learned through Carol's story that she had been a housewife since her marriage, just as her own mother had. Carol's story contained the belief that "children need their mother at home." Her story was entrenched with feelings of guilt, incompetence, and anger at Edward for causing this situation. She felt the need to defend herself and her role in the family to Mark and Dawn. A belief present in Carol's story was "a good mother is judged by the amount of time she spends with her children." When Carol told her story about her family of origin, she shared with her children the controversy that existed and still does between herself and her mother. She was never close to her mother and still felt like a disobeying child even now when she is around her, and she fears that this will happen with her own children. Mark's story repeated the theme: "My mother is never around anymore. And even when she is, she's so miserable that no one wants to be around her." He too, like Dawn, wishes that Karen would stay home with them, even though rationally they both know that financially she can't afford to.

The children believe that Carol "overreacted" to their father's affairs, although they did admit that he "sometimes" went too far. When asked to tell their story about the "Carol's depression" they all agreed that it stemmed from the loss of the marriage. They could not predict when it would hit Carol, but when it did, it bothered everyone. Carol would "hardly speak to anyone and she would remain in bed sometimes for days."

The third stage of therapy involved learning about the family's story in the present. The goal was to identify what information the family was selecting from the environment to fit into each of their meaning systems and how it was reinforcing the present system. It is at this time that the family learned about how each one of them inadvertently participated in the perpetuation of the family's problem. Mark was asked, "How do you think of the problem?" His story was that his mother was going through a hard time without his dad and that she should reconsider her position about divorce: "If she would go back to Dad for a little while, things would be better for her and us. Mom has always been involved with her family and in doing for others, and this is what makes her happy. It's no wonder she gets tired from working and depressed with all the fighting and tension in the house. Everyone is always fighting. It never used to be this way when we lived with Dad." Dawn was asked to answer the same question. She said, "The problem is not that I don't appreciate Mom's help, it's just that she isn't there enough. We're always alone!" Dawn believes the fighting starts when Carol comes home from work and asks the children to either help with dinner, see to their homework, or clean up their mess. Carol's rule is that they are to do their homework when they return home from school before they go out or watch television. What often happens instead is that they call their father to ask his permission to go out and he says, "Sure, go out and play and have fun. You're only young once. You can do your homework later." Then Carol comes home, sees their homework not done, starts yelling, and then calls Edward to yell at him also. By the time they all sit down to dinner, the tension level is high. And their homework is still not done. After dinner, she's too tired to yell at them to study, so she goes in her room and falls asleep. The principal said that Mark hands in about one out of every five homework assignments and that this is the main reason for his failures. Carol says that at this point they fight almost every day over similar incidents and she feels completely alone because Edward never supports her with the children. Edward is resentful about the divorce and feels that Carol overreacted to his indiscretions. "After all," he says, "I was still a good father and husband." The only times when he at all supported her was when Mark cursed at his soccer coach and when he failed three subjects on his report card. Then he came over and the two parents had a long talk with Mark. But Carol feels that instead of things getting better after the talk, they seem to have gotten worse. Now every time Mark gets into trouble at school, he shouts, "Go ahead, Mom, why don't you call Dad? Can't you handle things?" The therapist believed that at least some of Mark's problem behavior was serving to keep Edward involved in the family.

For the future, Dawn wishes that Carol could just "be a mother." When asked to define this, Dawn said, "Someone to spend time with us, not work, and to be there after school." Carol believes that the problem is Edward's. She feels that she has done everything she could think of and that now it's Edward's turn. If he would give them more money, or support her with her decisions, then the problems would cease. She should not have to come home from work to a house filled with yelling. Carol stated, "Edward should be more adamant with Mark about staying home after school and doing his homework." Carol told stories about her own role as a caretaker. She was very proud of the job she did caring for her family. Now Carol does not think of herself as being a good mother and caretaker. When asked to define a "good mother," Carol said, "A good mother is there for her kids emotionally and physically until they are older and more independent, and even then she is still there if they need her." Carol believes that if she were a better mother and not working so much, then she would be able to spend more time "mothering the children." The family agreed that the construct "mothering" had different meanings for each of them and because of their different views, each was perpetuating the problem in the family.

Challenging the family's meaning system was the fourth stage of therapy. Mark was grateful for all his mother did. He also stated, "Mothers need to be appreciated and respected for all the work they do." Mark was questioned and confronted on this belief, because Carol was not feeling appreciated or respected by him. Mark's reply was, "I guess I never thought about it that way because her mothering now is different than it used to be." Carol believes she is not a good mother because she is not spending time with her children. She was then asked who was taking that quality time from her. She replied, "No one."

The therapist asked, "When the children do not have their homework done before dinner, who helps them?"

She replied, "Most of the time it winds up being me after dinner."

"So then is that considered quality time?"

Carol replied, "Yes."

"So, in essence, Carol, the children not doing their homework when they return home from school is actually supplying you with the opportunity for more quality time when you come home so you can be a good mother?"

After a long pause Carol answered, "If you look at it that way, then yes." Carol then added, "Most of the fighting happens during the week. We seem to get along better on weekends."

Carol was then asked, "Is this because you spend more quality time over the weekend?"

"Yes."

"I'm sorry, Carol. I'm confused. Which is more important to you, the quality of time or the quantity?"

Carol said, "The quality of time."

Carol's beliefs about mothering and caretaking were also challenged. Carol stated that she has been a mother practically her whole adult life and considered herself an expert at it. She defines an expert mother as someone who can provide for her children's needs—both physically and emotionally. The belief that she had reached expert mother status was then challenged because Carol, although a very good and accomplished mother and caretaker, had forgotten recently to take care of one person: herself. Carol agreed that she would like to be a little selfish and care for herself sometimes. She was told to go slowly with this idea because once she starts to take care herself, this could be scary. Carol disagreed: "I can take care of myself first and still use any extra time to spend with the children." The family was then asked to talk about times when they were not fighting and what were they doing instead that made the problem disappear.

The fifth stage of therapy focused on amplifying the new meaning system. The therapist amplified the exceptions found in the family's original story. The goal here was to deepen the family's experience of their relationships without the problem. The family and therapist conversed about times when the family was "problemless." Each member described how it would be for them in the future and how it is for them now when the problem is not there. By doing this the family cocreated a new and more positive construction of their family.

The last stage of therapy is to stabilize the family's new meaning system. The family now was focusing on the future. The rubber band method was used with the family and they each were asked to stretch it two years into the future. Carol saw herself participating in single activities at the church and taking up offers from friends to go out. She also saw herself managing her job and family. She felt she would be secure and confident and maybe have a polite relationship with Edward. Mark saw himself spending more time with his father. He felt that the quality time he and his mother spent together would strengthen their relationship. Mark and Dawn are both happy and proud of Carol that she is now "doing for herself" and they both appreciate what she adds to their lives.

By speaking of the future, the family formed a new and more positive family map. Their future without the problem was becoming more stable and realistic and was within their control and reach. The family cocreated through language a new family meaning system and has come to realize that each is in control of his or her own future.

SUMMARY

Changes in the narratives that families hold about their meaning systems can lead to other opportunities for change. Social constructionist therapy focuses on helping clients reconstruct what is important to them, in order to provide them with more options for action (Viney et al., 1988). This therapy focuses on the meanings clients place on the events they experience. Also, it provides clients with alternative perspectives of those events to enable them to change their behaviors if they choose to do so. The aim of the social constructionist therapist is to see the client's world through the client's eyes not to change his or her view, but to help the individual develop a variety of alternative perspectives (Viney et al., 1988).

This chapter outlined the typical problems occurring with single-parent families and proposed a social constructionist model for assisting these families. This therapy explored the role of narrative (the family's story about its problem) in maintaining the family meaning system with the problem, and presented ways of challenging this meaning system. In so doing, a six-stage model of therapy was proposed:

1. Joining the family meaning system
2. Proposing the notion of a family meaning system
3. Learning the family's meaning system
4. Inviting change in the family's meaning system
5. Amplifying the new family meaning system
6. Stabilizing the new meaning system

The successful functioning of single-parent families requires a flexibility in structure and roles and the development of responses to new developmental needs and challenges. Patterns that may have been functional in earlier stages may no longer fit and new options must be explored. Social constructionist therapy is a helpful method for assisting family members through this life-cycle transition.

Chapter 11

Conclusions

Whether or not the single-parent household, or any other kind of family arrangement, for that matter, becomes a personal or social disaster depends upon the availability of sufficient material resources, supportive social networks, and the quality of culturally shared beliefs toward it.

No single-family form produces an optimal milieu for a growing child. No family type is more "natural" to the human species than any other. Children need to have their emotional and physical needs met, but this can be accomplished by a wide variety of social arrangements. It is not necessary that this be done exclusively by biological parents in a nuclear family structure.

Children of divorce are often viewed in the social science literature as pathological creatures, victims of an inherently deviant event, destined to suffer a lifetime of failure. The same view holds true for their divorcing parents. These deficit models of divorce present a pathological picture, citing prominent studies where divorce is deviant and its effects deleterious. The literature does, however, present research which alludes to healthy reactions to and because of divorce. For example, a growing body of research suggests that the consequences of divorce are far from uniform, and that many adults and children appear to be able to cope well with the stressful events that we generally associate with divorce. Even the early studies demonstrated that, although they may be the minority, a sizable portion of the population appears to be able to emerge from the periods of transition resulting from the divorce psychologically healthy, and even possibly stronger, for having successfully mastered the challenge caused by the breakup of the home. More and better studies methodologically are sure to follow, and the message is an important one that we need to get out to parents via the schools and public agencies, as well as through an informed population of therapists.

The positive evidence beginning to accumulate in clinical, empirical, and theoretical studies suggests that children of divorce often experience outcomes less or no more difficult than those faced by children from two-parent family structures. Based on the research cited in this book, it appears recognition is growing that the effects of family configurations which differ from the model two-parent nuclear family need not be negative, and that the stigmatization associated with this phenomenon appears to (or at least should) be lessening. In light of this body of research, it is becoming more apparent that a rethinking of the social value system which fuels the thought that divorce is bad and shameful be addressed.

In American society, romantic love is not only an expectation for a potential marriage partner but a demand. Combined with socially transmitted, unrealistically based, sets of expectations around the institution of marriage and marital roles, it is not surprising that the divorce rate is approaching 60 percent for first marriages. The natural outcome of this combination is profound disappointment when individuals fall in love with the man or woman of their dreams and find they are not living happily ever after. The reality is that the *Father Knows Best* traditional two-parent family, where Dad works and Mom stays home with the kids, represents a clear minority (less than 10 percent) of all American households. If we continue to accept the concept that those who do not achieve the ideal are failures, then we are a society of failures. It is these very same socially constructed definitions that create the legacies of "broken homes" and "broken dreams"—responding to social definitions that no longer reflect the world and in so doing help create self-fulfilling prophecies in millions of people in the United States.

It is hoped that in writing this book, we have shown or at least presented the possibility that the effect of divorce can be a positive, even healthy move toward growth and maturity. Divorce may represent a transition from an unhealthy or untenable situation, for not only are adults and their children not necessarily negatively impacted by the ensuing single-parent status, but a sizable number of our "broken home" population appears to be happy.

As we have shown, a body of research is beginning to emerge that demonstrates the outcomes of divorce for children and their parents can be positive and growth enhancing. As professional therapists, we can help single parents recognize that the difficulties associated with the one-parent family are part of the life experience of a single head of a family and not because they are part of a "deviant" family structure. We can assist them in handling these difficulties—whether they struggle with social definitions or the associated psychological reactions—and in so doing play a crucial role in helping these families adjust to this transition. However, we also need to be certain that we are sending a clear message to these families—that one-parent families can be healthy, vital, nurturing family systems. We can encourage the understanding that different kinds of family structures are okay and that transitions can create stronger, better families.

We have stressed the theme that therapists must be alert to the probability that single-parent families themselves, the professionals who work with them, and the institutions they encounter have defined these families in some way as deficient. The crucial issue from a therapy perspective is simply stated: If the response to a single-parent family through death or divorce is pathologically defined, then family members are relieved by these professionals of the responsibility of making any adaptive changes. If the locus of power to make change is assumed to be always outside the family system, in other words, society's definitions about what it means to be a single parent or a child living in a one-parent household, then family members will address their situation with a passive perspective. They will learn to be helpless, much like Seligman's famous dogs (1975). They will think, feel, and behave as if they have no personal power or authority to control their own lives. It is the responsibility of therapists to be aware of the effects of these negative assumptions about the single-parent system and to understand the negative impact that these might have on the family. It is also the responsibility of the therapist to vigorously investigate and dispute any constructions adopted by themselves and by the family which suggest powerlessness.

THE MYTH OF PATHOLOGY

We list here several of the most common of these nonadaptive cognitive structures. These myths cluster around the central issues we have considered: raising children; redefining relationships; maintaining a sexual self; interacting with larger systems; creating constructs of reality. Should the actions, beliefs, or affects of family members appear to be shaped by one or more of them, the therapist is urged to refute them through the use of the research presented in this book within the context of a systemic behavioral approach to therapy (Atwood, 1992a).

1. *Children in single-parent families always have deficits.* This myth is pervasive in our society and is based on the assumption that the physical and/or psychological loss of one parent ensures long-term negative effects. It is also based on the assumption that the loss is irretrievable and cannot be dealt with. It is also predicated on the assumption that the new one-parent situation is inferior to the old.

2. *Single parents cannot be both parents (nurturers) and bread-winners. One role suffers.* This myth is based on the assumption that single parents may either be the providers of nurturance and guidance to their children or they may be the provider of material goods by being workers. They cannot be both.

3. *Single parents themselves must be psychologically traumatized.* This myth is based on the assumption that the psychological trauma associated with the divorce or death of the spouse leads to a diminution in the ability to parent, to work effectively outside of the home, and to interact with friends, family, and social institutions. Further, the effects of this trauma last forever.

4. *The single-parent family is only a temporary situation until the custodial parent finds a new spouse.* Again, this myth is based on the assumption that the two-parent model is better and that all single parents would opt for marriage if it were available to them.

5. *Single parents have forfeited their right to be sexual beings.* Because individuals are only permitted to practice sex within a marital situation, should a single parent act out their sexual needs, not only are they considered promiscuous but also selfish. Further, single-parent sexual activity traumatizes children.

6. *Children in single-parent families are expected to do poorly in school and to suffer emotionally and behaviorally.* This myth is based on the assumption that the one-parent family structure denies these children both proper role models and sufficient disci-

pline to allow them to accommodate to the demands of their academic schoolwork. It also assumes that, as a result of the loss of one parent, the children will be affected psychologically and therefore suffer psychological problems.

7. *Economic deprivation, absolute or relative, has very little to do with the problems encountered by single parents.* This myth is based on the notion that it is the psychological poverty of the single-parent families which causes the difficulties.

8. *Being a single parent means that life is horrible.* This myth is based on the assumption that being in a two-parent family is the best possible family system for adults and children. It is also based on the assumption that single parents have little or no control over their environment; that single-parent systems which thrive are the rarity or are lucky; and that nothing could be done to improve the lot of the single parent.

These myths are but a few that single parents encounter every day. We have presented information throughout the book that challenges these myths.

INTERPERSONAL AND SYSTEMIC CIRCULARITY

The therapy approach described in an earlier chapter is a systemic-behavioral one. We think in terms of family systems and the interrelationship among their components. We believe "insight" can be helpful, but it alone is not enough. For change to occur action in client's behavior is required. However, we have not, in the adoption of this position, lost sight of the individual as he or she interacts with family, friends, and society. This was the focus of the chapter on social constructionism. We understand the quality of a person's well-being to be the result of a complex and mutual reciprocity among several interacting variables (Bandura, 1978).

In a pure pathology model, behavior is seen as the external manifestation of internal characteristics, traits, and conflicts. Just as the delusions of a paranoid schizophrenic are deemed to result from the projection of his or her own unacceptable sexual and aggressive drives, the pathology model suggests that the behavior of single parents results from a poor psychological adjustment to the loss of the previous partner. The inability to neutralize the effects of loss is considered to be the dominant personal characteristic which causes nonadaptive behavior in a linear fashion:

Personal Characteristic ⟶ Behavior

The pathology model has been criticized by behaviorists as simplistic in that it ignores the impact of environmental factors on behavior. Radical behaviorists take the position that internal constructs are unobservable and not subject to direct therapeutic intervention. A functional analysis of those environmental stimuli which maintain problematic behaviors is the key to behavioral interventions. Behavioral therapy aimed at two underachieving students, for example, would probably not be influenced by the fact that one was from a single-parent family and the other from a two-parent system. The internal reaction to loss would not be dealt with as the radical behavioral model posits behavior to be caused, linearly, by environmental factors such as the nature and rate of reinforcement contingent upon particular behaviors:

Environment ⟶ Behavior

Cognitive-behaviorists take a more interactive stance. From this position, environmental factors are filtered by a person's belief systems, which attach subjective meaning to the events. For example, if our underachieving student believes himself or herself to be "less" than peers with two parents, failure on a single examination may be interpreted as evidence that failure on all future tests is inevitable. Such a combination of an event and the personal belief about the event can cause the kinds of behavior that result in failure:

Personal Characteristic

Behavior

Environment

Our position suggests that behavior may influence both environment and traits as well as being caused by them:

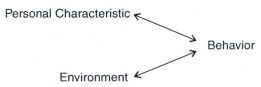

Personal Characteristic

Behavior

Environment

For example, if in therapy the therapist can assist the single parent in shifting his or her personal belief system from passive to active, it is likely that behavior will change. Changes in his or her behavior will impact on the environmental response to the single-parent family. If a single mother comes to believe that her child's difficulty in school is the result of the interplay among the student, the teacher, the guidance therapist, the administration of the school, and the family, and not because the child is from a "broken" home, then she will take a more active role in addressing the problem. Armed with the attitude of an informed consumer, she will insist that the family and the school work together to assess and intervene at the most appropriate level to best serve the child's needs. In the face of a parent who demonstrates this sort of strong personal conviction and goal-directed behavior, it is more likely that the social institution, the school, will respond in an appropriate way. As the number of these sorts of interactions grows, so do the feelings of self-worth and "can-do" attitudes within the family. And "can-do" beats waiting for the "white knight" hands down.

Part of the experience of the divorcing process is structured by the expectations of the professionals one encounters. In therapy with divorcing adults or one-parent families, it is important to help clients be realistic about the negatives that can result from divorce. Equally important is the other side of the story: assisting clients to understand that one-parent families can help children grow emotionally as well as provide needed support for parents. Therapists and educators can help by informing their colleagues and their clients that divorce does not necessarily result in negative outcomes for children or adults. They can caution them about making unfair and inappropriate assumptions about children from one-parent homes.

SUMMARY

In summary, we need to examine our own assumptions about the one-parent family system. Only in this way can we help single parents learn to draw on their own strengths and assist them in not seeing themselves as having failed so that they might greet their futures with hope and new confidence.

In contrast to our cherished fantasies about romantic love and marriage, the norm in our society is now or is fast becoming the single and/or single-parent family home: more than 21 percent of all American households consist of adults living alone; another 3 percent are cohabitations with another adult partner; 13 percent are single-parent homes. Add to that the number of two-parent homes that are remarriages, and it becomes apparent that our definition of what is "normal" could use some updating.

It is important that we continue to assist children of this and future generations as different family situations arise. Until a time when equilibrium is achieved, we must search out and support families experiencing difficulty. Through a reeducation of society, the currently widespread negative views and connotations could be addressed.

On a macro sociological level, we need to rethink the function of marriage in the twenty-first century and beyond into the new society of tomorrow. Changes in economic, religious, educational, and moral values and an extended life span will all transform our relationships and extend into the family structure. This can be seen as influencing children in many positive ways.

With more than 57 percent of all first marriages ending in divorce, we need to rethink the notion that marriage is a failure when it ends in divorce. Rather, we need to look at the social institutions of marriage and the family and the associated socially constructed norms, values, and definitions as part of our analysis. As divorce occurs, we need to look at the problems caused by the writing of new scripts and in turn construct new stories offering healthy solutions. Divorce as a concept must become a psychological shift away from deviance to if not normative behavior then one possible normative life-cycle transition.

Bibliography

Achtenberg, R. and Ricketts, W. (1990). Adoption and foster parenting for lesbians and gay men: Creating new traditions in family. *Homosexuality and Family Relations, 14*(3-4), 83-118.

Adams, G. R. (1982). The effects of divorce on adolescents. *The High School Journal,* March, 205-211.

Adams, M. (1976). *Single blessedness: Observations on the single status in married society.* New York: Basic Books.

Ahrons, C. (1980). Redefining the divorced family: A conceptual framework. *Social Work,* November.

Ahrons, C. R. and Rodgers, R. H. (1987). *Divorced families: A multidisciplinary developmental view.* New York: W.W. Norton & Co.

Alan Guttmacher Institute (1976). *Eleven million teenagers: what can be done about the epidemic of adolescent pregnancies in U.S.?* New York: Author.

Alan Guttmacher Institute (1994). *Sex and America's teenagers.* New York: Author.

Alan Guttmacher Institute (1999). *Facts in brief: Teen sex and pregnancy.* New York. Author.

Albeck, S. and Kaydar, D. (2002). Divorced mothers: Their network of friends pre- and postdivorce. *Journal of Divorce and Remarriage, 36,* 111-138.

Albert, R. (1971). Cognitive development and parental loss among the gifted. *Psychological Reports, 29,* 19-26.

Amato, P. R. and Ochiltree, G. (1987). Child and adolescent competence in intact, one-parent, and step-families: An Australian study. *Journal of Divorce, 10*(3/4), 75-95.

Amundson, J. (1990). In defense of minimalism: Making the least out of depression. *Family Therapy Case Studies, 5*(1), 15-19.

American Psychiatric Association (1968). *Diagnostic and statistical manual of mental disorders.* Second edition. Washington, DC: Author.

American Psychiatric Association (1980). *Diagnostic and statistical manual of mental disorders.* Third edition. Washington, DC: Author.

American Psychiatric Association (1987). *Diagnostic and statistical manual of mental disorders.* Third edition-revised. Washington, DC: Author.

American Psychiatric Association (1994). *Diagnostic and statistical manual of mental disorders.* Fourth edition. Washington, DC: Author.

American Psychiatric Association (2000). *Diagnostic and statistical manual of mental disorders.* Fourth edition-text revised. Washington, DC: Author.

Anderson, H. and Goolishian, H. (1988). Human systems as linguistic systems: Preliminary and evolving ideas about the implication for clinical theory. *Family Process, 27,* 371-393.

Araoz, DL (1982). *Hypnosis and sex therapy.* New York: Brunner/Mazel.

Atchley, R. C. (1975). *Social forces in later life.* Belmont, CA: Wadler.

Atwood, J. (1981). The role of masturbation in socio-sexual development. *Dissertation Abstracts.*

Atwood, J. D. (1991). Killing two Mr. Slumpos with one stone: Therapy with a depressed man and his family. *Family Therapy Case Studies, 5*(2), 43-50.

Atwood, J. D. (1992a). *Family therapy: A systemic behavioral approach.* Chicago: Nelson Hall.

Atwood, J. (1992b). A systemic-behavioral approach to therapy the single-parent family. In J. Atwood (Ed.), *Family therapy: A systemic-behavioral approach.* Chicago: Nelson-Hall.

Atwood, J. D. (1993). Social constructionist marital therapy. *The Family Journal,* in Press.

Atwood, J. D. (1996). *Family scripts.* Chicago: Taylor Francis, Inc.

Atwood, J. D. and Donnely, Joseph W. (1993). Adolescent pregnancy: Combating the problem from a multi-systemic health perspective. *Journal of Health Education, 24*(4), 219-231.

Atwood, J. D. and Gagnon, J. H. (1987). Masturbation in college youth. *Journal of Sex Education and Therapy, 13*(2), 35-42.

Atwood, J. D. and Kasindorf, Susan (1992). A Multi-systemic approach to adolescent pregnancy. *The American Journal of Family Therapy, 20*(4), 65-84.

Atwood, J. D. and Levine, L. (1991). Ax murderers, dragons, spiders, and webs: Therapeutic metaphors in couple therapy. *Contemporary Family Therapy, 13*(3), 201-217.

Bagarozzi, D.A. (1980). Wholistic family therapy and clinical supervision: Systems, behavioral and psychoanalytic perspective. *Family Therapy, 7,* 153-165.

Balswick, J. and Peck, C. (1971). The Inexpressive Male: A Tragedy of American Society. *The Family Coordinator, 20,* 363-368.

Bandura, A. (1969). *Principles of behavior modification.* New York: Holt, Rinehart, & Winston.

Bandura, A. (1978). The self-system in reciprocal determinism. *American Psychologist, 32*(4), 344-358.

Barrett, J. (1978). *Individual goals and organizational objectives: A study of integration mechanisms.* Ann Arbor, MI: Center for research on Utilization of Scientific Knowledge, University of Michigan Press.

Barry, A. (1979). A research project on successful single-parent families. *The American Journal of Family Therapy, 7*(3), 65-74.

Barry, D. (1997). Telling changes: From narrative family therapy to organizational change and development. *Journal of Organizational Change Management, 10*(1), 30-46.

Bateson, G. (1972). *Steps to an ecology of mind.* New York: Ballantine Books.

Bateson, G. (1979). *Mind and nature: A necessary unity.* New York: Dutton.

Baydar, N. (1988). Effects of parental separation and reentry into union on the emotional well being of children. *Journal of Marriage and the Family, 18*(3), 149-159.

Beal, E. (1980). Separation, divorce, and single-parent families. In E. Carter and M. McGoldrick (Eds.), *The family life cycle: A framework for family therapy* (pp. 241-264). New York: Gardener Press, Inc.

Beck, A. (1970). Cognitive therapy: Nature and relation to behavior therapy. *Behavior Therapy, 1,* 184-200.

Beck, A. T., Rush, A. J., Shaw, B., and Emery, G. (1979). *Cognitive therapy of depression.* New York: Guilford Press.

Becker, G. S. (1974). A Theory of Marriage: Part II. *The Journal of Political Economy, 82*(2), S11-S26.

Becker, H. S. (1973). *Outsiders: Studies in the sociology of deviance.* New York: Free Press.

Beer, J. (1989). Relationship of divorce to self-concept, self-esteem, and grade point average of fifth and sixth grade school children. *Psychological Reports, 65,* 1379-1383.

Berger, P. and Kellner, H. (1964/1994). Marriage and the construction of reality: An exercise in the microsociology of knowledge. In G. Handel & G. G. Whitchurch (Eds.), *The psychosocial interior of the family* (4th ed.) (pp. 19-36). New York: Aldine De Gruyter.

Berger, P. and Luckmann, T. (1966). *The social construction of reality.* New York: Irvington.

Berman, W. and Turk, D. (1981). Adaption to divorce. Problems and coping strategies. *Journal of Marriage and the Family, 43,* 179-189.

Bilge, B. and Kaufman, G. (1983). Children of divorce and one parent families: Cross-cultural perspectives. *Journal of Applied Family and Child Studies, 32*(1), 59-72.

Blades, J., Gosse, R., McKay, M., and Rogers, P. (1984). *The divorce book.* Oakland: New Harbinger Books.

Blauner, R. (1996). Death and social structure. In B. L Newgartin (Ed)., *Middle age and aging* (pp. 531-540). Chicago: University of Chicago Press.

Bloom, B. L., White, S. W., and Asher, S. J. (1979). Marital disruption as a stressful life event. In G. Levinger & O. C. Moles (Eds.), *Divorce and separation: Context, causes, and consequences.* New York: Basic Books.

Blumenthal, M. (1989). A courage born of broken promises. *The New York Times,* July 23, pp. 14, 25.

Bolton, F. G. (1980). *The pregnant adolescent: Problems of premature parenthood.* Beverly Hills, CA: Sage.

Bonanno, G. A. (2004). Loss, trauma and human resilience. *American Psychologist, 59*(1), 20-28.

Boonstra, H. (2002). Teen pregnancy: Trends and lessons learned. *The Guttmacher Report on Public Policy, 5*(1).

Bornstein, P. E. and Clayton, P. J. (1972). The anniversary reaction. *Dis. Nerv System., 33*: 470-472.

Bornstein, P. E., Clayton, P. J., Halikas, J. A., Maurice, W. L., and Robins, E. (1973). The depression of widowhood after thirteen months. *British Journal of Psychiatry, 122,* 561-566.

Boss, P. (1991). Ambiguous loss. In F. Walsh and M. McGoldrick (Eds.), *Living beyond loss: Death in the family.* New York: W.W. Norton.

Bowen, M. (1978). *Family therapy in clinical practice.* New York: Jason Aronson.

Bowlby, J. (1969). *Attachment and loss,* Vol 1: *Attachment.* New York: Basic Books.

Bowlby, J. (1980). *Attachment and loss,* Vol. 3: *Loss.* New York: Basic Books.

Bramlett, M. D. and Mosher, W. D. (2002). Cohabitation, marriage, divorce, and remarriage in the United States. *Vital Health Statistics, 23*(22).

Braver, S. L., Gonzalez, N., Wolchik, S. A., Sandler, I. N. (1989). Economic hardship and psychological distress in custodial mothers. *Journal of Divorce, 12*(4), 19-33.

Brody, J. E. (1991). A new look at children and divorce. *The New York Times.*

Bronfenbrenner, U. (1979). *The Ecology of Human Development: Experiments by Nature and Design.* Cambridge, MA: Harvard University Press.

Brophy, J. and Everston, C. (1978). Context variables in tracking. *Educational Psychologist, 12,* 310-316.

Brown, C. A., Feldberg, R., Fox, E. M., and Kohen, J. (1976). Divorce: Chance of a new lifetime. *Journal of Social Issues, 32,* 119-133.

Brown, J. H., Eichenberger, S. A., Portes, P. R. & Christensen, D. N. (1991). Family functioning factors associated with the adjustment of children of divorce. *Journal of Divorce and Remarriage, 15*(1/2), 81-95.

Brown, N. D. and Samis, M. D. C. (1986/1987). The application of structural family therapy in developing the binuclear family. *Mediation Quarterly, 14/15,* 51-69.

Byng-Hall, J. (1995). *Rewriting family scripts.* New York: Guilford Press.

Byrne, R. (1990). The effectiveness of the beginning experience workshop. *Journal of Divorce, 13,* 101-120.

Cargan, L. (1981). Singles: An examination of two stereotypes. *Family Relations, 30,* S.377-385.

Cargan, L. and Melko, M. (1982). *Singles: Myths and realities.* Beverly Hills, CA: Sage.

Carr, D. and Utz, R. (2002). Late life widowhood in the United States: New directions in research and theory. *Aging International, 27*(1), 65-88.

Carter, B. and McGoldrick, M. (Eds.) (1980). *The changing family life cycle: A framework for family therapy.* New York: Gardner Press.

Carter, B. and McGoldrick, M. (Eds.) (1988). *The changing family life cycle: A framework for family therapy,* Second edition. New York: Gardner Press.

Cashion, B. G. (1982). Female-headed families: Effects on children and clinical implications. *Journal of Marital and Family Therapy, 8,* 77-85.

Center for Health Communication Harvard School of Public Health (2004). Reinventing aging: Baby boomers and civic engagement. Boston: Author.

Centers for Disease Control and Prevention (1994-2000). The second longitudinal study of aging. National center for health statistics and National Institute on aging. Unpublished data. Available online http://www.cdc.gov/nchs/about/otheract/aging/lsoa2.htm.

Centers for Disease Control and Prevention (1997). Update: HIV/AIDS and women in the United States. Fact sheet. Author.

Centers for Disease Control and Prevention (1998). HIV/AIDS Surveillance report. Author.

Centers for Disease Control and Prevention (2002). Fact sheet. Preventing occupational transmission to healthcare personnel. Available online http//www.cdc.gov.

Centers for Desease Control and Prevention (2003). *HIV/AIDS Surveillance report: HIV infection in the United States.* Division of AIDS prevention, National Center for HIV, STD, and TB Prevention. Author.

Cherlin, A. J. (1992). *Marriage, divorce, and remarriage.* Revised edition. Cambridge, MA: Harvard University Press.

Cherlin, A. and Furstenberg, F. F. Jr. (1989). Divorce doesn't always hurt the kids. *The Washington Post,* March 19, pp. C3.

Children's troubles may precede divorces (1991). *The Wall Street Journal,* June 7, p. B1.

Clapp, G. (1992). *Divorce and new beginnings.* New York: John Wiley & Sons, Inc.

Clayton, P. J., Halikes, J. A., and Maurice, W. L. (1971). The bereavement of the widowed. *Dis. Nerv system., 32*(9), 597-604.

Cleveland W. P. and Gianturco, D. T. (1976). Remarriage probability after widowhood: A retrospective method. *Journal of Gerontology, 31*(1), 99-103.

DeFrain, J., Fricke, J., and Elmen, J. (1987). *On our own: A single parent's survival guide.* Lexington, MA: Lexington Books.

Demo, D. and Acock, A. (1988). The impact of divorce on children. *Journal of Marriage and the Family, 50,* 619-648.

DeNavas-Walt, C., Proctor, B. D., and Mills, R. J. (2003). Income, poverty, and health insurance coverage in the United States: 2003. U.S. Census Bureau, current population reports. Washington, DC: U.S. Government Printing Office.

de Shazer, S. (1985). *Keys to solution in brief therapy.* New York: W.W. Norton & Co.

de Shazer, S. (1991). *Putting difference to work.* New York: W.W. Norton & Co.

Ditzion, S. (1978). *Marraige, morals and sex in America: A history of ideas.* New York: W. W. Norton & Co.

Dinkmeyer, D., McKay, G. D., and McKay, J. (1987). *New beginnings: Skills for single parents and stepfamily parents.* Champaign, IL: Research Press.

Duffy, M. E. (1994). Testing the theory of transcending options: Health behaviors of single parents. *Scholarly Inquiry for Nursing Practice, 8*(2), 191-202.

Durkheim, E. (1951). *Suicide: A study in sociology.* New York: Free Press.

Dusek, J. (1975). Do teachers bias children's learning? *Review of Educational Research, 45,* 661-684.

Dusek, J. and Joseph, S. (1983). The bases of teachers expectancies: A meta-analysis. *Journal of Educational Psychology, 75,* 327-346.

Ehnenreich, B. (1999). Farewell to a fad. *The Progressive,* March, pp. 17-18.

Ellis, A. (1962). *Reason and emotion in psychotherapy.* New York: Lyle Stuart.

Emery, R. (1982). Interparental conflict and the children of discord and divorce. *Psychological Bulletin, 92*(2), 310-330.

Emery, R. E., Hetherington, E. M., and DiLalla, L. F. (1984). Divorce, children, and social policy. *Child Development Research and Social Policy,. 1,* 189-266.

Emery, R. and O'Leary, K. D. (1984). Marital discord and child behavior problems in a non-clinic sample. *Journal of Abnormal Child Psychology, 12,* 411-420.

Epstein, J. (1974). *Divorced in America.* New York: Dutton.

Epston, D. and White, M. (1990). Consulting your consultants: The documentation of alternative knowledges. *Dulwich Centre Newsletter,* p. 4.

Erikson, E. H. (1963). *Childhood and society.* New York: Norton.

Everett, C. A. (Ed.) (1989). *Children of divorce: Developmental and clinical issues.* Binghamton, NY: The Haworth Press.

Fassell, D. (1991). *Growing up divorced: A road to healing for adult children of divorce.* New York: Pocket Books.

Federal Interagency on Aging-Related Statistics (2000). Older Americans 2000: Key indicators of well-being. Washington, DC: Government Printing Office.

Ferree, M. M. (1984). The view from below: Women's employment and gender equality in working class families. In B. B. Hess and M. B. Sussman (Eds.), *Women and the family: Two decades of change.* Binghamtom, NY: The Haworth Press.

Framo, J .L. (1992). *Family of origin therapy: An intergenerational approach.* New York: Brunner and Mazel.

Franks, Cyril M., Wilson, G., and Terence (1975). *Annual Review of Behavior Therapy: Theory and Practice.* Volume 3. New York: Brunner/Mazel.

Frantz, T. T. (1984). Helping parents whose child has died. In J. Hansen (Ed.), *The family therapy collections.* Rockville, MD: Aspen Systems Corporation.

Freud, S. (1917). *A general instruction to psychoanalysis.* Translated by J.Riviere. New York: Washington Square Press, 1952.

Freud, S. (1937). Mourning and melancholia. In *The standard edition of the complete psychological works of Sigmund Freud,* Vol. 14. London: Hogarth Press. (original work published 1917).

Fulmer, R. H. (1983). A structural approach to unresolved mourning in single parent family systems. *Journal of Marital and Family Therapy, 9*(3), 259-269.

Furstenberg, F. F., Brooks-Gunn, J., and Morgan, S. P. (1987). Adolescent mothers and their children in later life. *Family Planning Perspectives, 19*(4), 142-151.

Gagnon, J. H. (1990). Scripting in sex research. *Annual Review of Sex Research, 1,* 1-39.

Gagnon, J. and Simon, W. (1973). *Sexual conduct: The social sources of human sexuality.* Chicago: Aldine.

Gander, A. M. (1991). After the divorce: Familial factors that predict well-being for older and younger persons. *Journal of Divorce & Remarriage, 15*(1), 175-192.

Ganong, L. H. and Coleman, M. (1984). The effects of remarriage on children: A review of empirical literature. *Family Relations, 33,* 389-407.

Ganong, L. and Coleman, M. (1999). *Changing families, changing responsibilities: Family obligations following divorce and remarriage.* Mahwah, NJ: Lawrence Erlbaum Associates.

Garber, R. J. (1991). Long-term effects of divorce on the self-esteem of young adults. *Journal of Divorce & Remarriage, 15*(1/2), 131-137.

Gardner, R. A. (1991). *Psychotherapy with children of divorce.* Lanham, MD: Jason Aronson Inc.

Garfield, R. (1982). Mourning and its resolution for spouses in marital separation. In J. Hansen (Ed.), *The family therapy collections.* Rockville, MD: Aspen Systems Corporation.

Gately, D. W. and Schwebel, A. I. (1991). The challenge model of children's adjustment to parental divorce: Explaining favorable postdivorce outcomes in children. *Journal of Family Psychology, 5*(1), 60-81.

Gebhard, P. H. (1968). Human sex behavior research. In M. Diamond (Ed.), *Perspectives in reproduction and sexual behavior* (pp. 391-410). Bloomington: Indiana University Press.

Gebhard, P. H. (1970). Postmarital coitus among widows and divorcees. In P. Bohannon (Ed.), *Divorce and after* (pp. 81-96). New York: Doubleday.

Genovese, F. (1992). Family therapy and bereavement therapy. In J. Atwood (Ed.), *Family therapy: A systemic-behavioral approach.* Chicago: Nelson-Hall.

George, V. and Wilding, P. (1972). *Motherless families.* London: Routledge & Kegan Paul.

Gergen, K. (1985). The social constructionist movement in modern psychology. *American Psychologist, 40,* 266-275.

Gergen, K. J. (1988). Narrative and the self as relationship. *Advances in Experimental Social Psychology, 21,* 17-56.

Gergen, K. J. (1999). *An invitation to social construction.* London: Sage.

Gergen, K. L. and Gergen, M. M. (1983). The social construction of narrative accounts. In K. L. Gergen and M. M. Gergen (Eds.), *Historical social psychology,* Hillsdale, NJ: Erlbaum Associates.

Gerstel, N., Reissman, C. H., and Rosenfield, S. (1985). Explaining the symptomatology of separated and divorced women and men: The role of material conditions and social networks. *Social Forces, 64,* 84-99.

Gibbs, R. W. Jr. (1979). Contextual effects in understanding indirect requests. *Discourse Processes, 2,* 149-156.

Gilchrist, L. D. and Schinke, S. P. (1983). Teenage pregnancy and public policy. *Social Service Review, 57,* 307-322.

Ginter, E.J., Ellis, A., Guterman, J., Ivey, A. Lock, D.C., and Rigazio-Diglio, S. (2001). A social constructivism model of ethical decision making in counseling. *Journal of Counseling and Development, 79*(1), 39.

Glasner, B. (2000). Where meanings get constructed. *Contemporary Sociology, 20*(4), 590-594.

Glick, P. and Norton, A. (1971). Frequency, duration and probability of marriage and divorce. *Journal of Marriage and the Family, 33,* 307-313.

Glick, P. and Norton, A. (1979). Update: Marrying, divorcing and living together in the United States today. Washington, DC: Population Reference Bureau.

Glick, I. O., Weiss, R. S. and Parkes, C. M. (1974). *The first year of bereavement.* New York: Wiley.

Goldenberg, I. and Goldenberg, H. (1991). *Family therapy: An overview,* Third edition. Pacific Grove, CA: Brooks, Cole.

Goldsmith, J. (1982). The postdivorce family system. In F. Walsh (Ed.), *Normal family process* (pp. 297-330). New York Guilford Press.

Goldstein, J. R. (1999). The leveling of divorce in the United States. *Demography, (36),* 409-414.

Gorer, S. (1979). Marrying, divorcing and living together in the U.S. today. *Population Bulletin, 32,* 1-40.

Greenberg, J. B. (1979). Single parenting and intimacy: A comparison of mothers and fathers. *Alternative Lifestyles, 2*(3), 308-331.

Greenwald, H. (1974). Treatment of the psychopath. In H. Greenwald (Ed.), *Active Psychotherapy.* New York: Jason Aronson.

Guerin, P. and Katz, A. (1984). The theory in therapy of families with school related problems: Triangles and a hypothesis testing model. In B.F. Okun (Ed.), *Family therapy with school related problems.* Rockville, MD: Aspen.

Guerin, P. J., Fay, L .F., Burden, S. L., and Kautto, J. G. (1987). *The evaluation and treatment of mental conflict: A four stage approach.* New York: Basic Books.

Guidon, A. (1977). *The sexual language.* Ottawa, Canada: University of Ottawa Press.

Guidubaldi, J. (1983). Divorce research clarifies issues: A report on NASP's nation-wide study. *Communique, 11*(8), 1, 6-7.

Guidubaldi, J. (1993, November). Divorce and Father Absence as Critical Factors in Child Adjustment. Presentation at the University of Rhode Island, Kingston, RI.

Guidubaldi, J. and Chiarella, D. L. (1985, August). Cognitive mediator variables as predictors of adjustment for divorce-family males and females. Paper presented as part of a symposium entitled Effects of divorce on children: The NASP-KSU_longitudinal study_at the annual convention of the National Association of School Psychologists, Las Vegas.

Guidubaldi, J., Cleminshaw, H. K., Perry, J. D., and McLoughlin, C. S. (1983). 'The Impact of Parental Divorce on Children: Report of the Nation-Wide NASP Study'. *School Psychology Review,* 12: 300-323.

Guidubaldi, J. and Perry, J. D. (1985). Divorce and mental health sequelae for children: A two-year follow-up of a nationwide sample. *Jounal of the American Academy of Child Psychiatry, 24*(5), 531-537.

Guttman, J. (1988). Teacher's and school children's stereotypic perception of "The child of divorce." *American Educational Research Journal, 25*(4), 555-571.

Haley, J. (1967). Toward a theory of pathological systems. In G. H. Zuk and I. Boszormenyi-Nagy (Eds.), *Family therapy and disturbed families.* Palo Alto: Science and Behavior Books.

Haley, J. (1973). Uncommon therapy: *The psychiatric techniques of Milton H. Erickson, M.D.* New York: W. W. Norton.

Haley, J. (1977). *Problem solving therapy.* San Francisco: Jossey-Bass.

Hall, T. (1991). Breaking up is becoming harder to do. *The New York Times,* March 14, pp. C1-C10.

Hammarskjold, Dag (1966). *Uncommon therapy: The psychiatric techniques of Milton H. Erickson, M.D.* New York: Norton.

Hammer, et al. (1993). Use of virologics assays for detection of human immunodeficiency virus in clinical trials: Recommendations of the AIDS clinical trials group virology committee. *J. Clin. Microbiol., 31*(10), 2557-2564.

Hansen, J. C., and Lindblad-Goldberg, M. (1987). *Clinical issues in single parent households.* Rockville, MD: Aspen Publishers.

Hanson, S. H. M. (1986). Healthy single parent families. *Family Relations, 35,* 125-132.

Hanson, S. H. M. and Sporakowski, M. J. (1986). Single parent families. *Family Relations, 35,* 3-8.

Hartman, S. (1989). Single mothers: Making it their way. *The New York Times,* January 12, p. C1.

Hayes, S. C. (1987). *Risking the future: Adolescent sexuality, pregnancy and childbearing.* Washington, DC: National Academy Press.

Henderson, A. J. (1981). Designing school guidance programs for single-parent families. *The School Therapist, 29*(2), 124-131.

Herz Brown, F. (1988). The impact of death and serious illness on the family life cycle. In B. Carter and M. McGoldrick (Eds.), *The changing family life cycle: A framework for family therapy, second edition.* New York: Guilford Press.

Hess, R. D. and Camara, K. A. (1979). Post-divorce family relationships as mediating factors in the consequences of divorce for children. *Journal of Social Issues, 35*(4), 79-95.

Hetherington, E. M. (1989). Coping with family transitions: Winners, losers, and survivors. *Child Development, 60,* 1-14.

Hetherington, E. M. (1991). The role of individual differences in family relations in coping with divorce and remarriage. In P. Cowan and E. M. Hetherington (Eds.),

Advances in family research: Family transitions Vol. 2 (pp. 165-1941). Hillsdale, NJ: Erlbaum.

Hetherington, E. M. (1993). An overview of the Virginia Longitudinal Study of Divorce and Remarriage with a focus on early adolescence. *Journal of Family Psychology, 7,* 39-56.

Hetherington, E. M., Cox, M., and Cox, R. (1982). Effects of divorce on parents and children. In M. Lamb (Ed.), *Nontraditional families* (pp. 233. 288). Hillsdale, NJ: Erlbaum.

Hetherington, E. M., Cox, M., and Cox, R. (1985). Long-term effects of divorce and remarriage on the adjustment of children. *Journal of the American Academy of Child Psychiatry, 24,* 518-530.

Hetherington, E., Stanley-Hagan, M., and Anderson, E. (1989). Marital transitions: A child's perspective. *American Psychologist, 44,* 303-311.

Hetherington, M. (Ed.) (1999). *Coping with divorce: A risk and resiliency perspective.* Mahwah, NJ: Lawrence Erlbaum Assoc.

Hetherington, M., Cox, M., and Cox, R. (1976). Divorced fathers. *The Family Coordinator, 25,* 417-428.

Hetherington, M. and Kelly, J. (2002). *For better or for worse.* New York: WW Norton.

Hicks, S. and Anderson, C. M. (1989). Women on their own. In M. McGoldrick, C.M. Anderson, and F. Walsh (Eds.), *Women in families: A framework for family therapy.* New York: W.W. Norton.

Hill, E. L. (1978). Goal analysis for problem learners. *Academic Therapy, 13*(3), 289-299.

Hiltz, S. R. (1975). Helping Widows: Group Discussions as a Therapeutic Technique, *The Family Coordinator,* Vol. 24, No. 3 (July), 331-336.

Hodges, W. F. (1986). *Interventions for children of divorce: Custody, access, and psychotherapy.* New York: John Wiley and Son.

Hodges, W. F. (1991). *Interventions for children of divorce: Custody, access, and psychotherapy,* Second edition. New York: John Wiley and Sons.

Hodgson, J., Dienhart, A. and Daly, K. (2001). Time joggling: Single others' experience of time press following divorce. *Journal of Divorce and Remarriage, 35,* 1/2.

Hoffman, L. (1981). *Foundations of family therapy: A conceptual framework for change.* New York: Basic Books.

Hoffman, L. (1990). Constructing realities: An art of lenses. *Family Process, 29*(1), 1-12.

Holder, D. P. and Anderson, C. P. (1989). Women, work and the family. In M. McGoldrick, C. M. Anderson, and F. Walsh (Eds.), *Women in families: A framework for family therapy.* New York: W.W. Norton.

Holman, A. M. (1983). *Family assessment: Tools for understanding and intervention.* Newbury Park: Sage.

Holmes, T. H. and Rahe, R. H. (1967). The social readjustment rating scale. *Journal of Psychosomatic Research, 11,* 213-218.

Horowitz, J. A. (1995). A conceptualization of parenting: Examining the single parent family. *Marriage and Family Review, 20*(1/2), 43-70.

Hoult, T., Henz, L., and Hudson, J. (1978). *Courtship and marriage in America.* Boston: Little, Brown.

Hulicka, I., Morganti, J., and Cataldo, J. (1975). Perceived latitude of choice of institutionalized and noninstitutionalized elderly women. *Experimental Aging Research, 1*(1), 27-39.

Hunt, M. (1974). *Sexual behavior in the 1970's.* Chicago: Playboy Press.

Hunt, M. and Hunt, B. (1977). *The divorce experience.* New York: Signet.

Hutchinson, R. L., Valutis, W. E., Brown, D. T., and White, J. S. (1989). The effects of family structure on institutionalized children's self-concepts. *Adolescence, 4*(94), 303-310.

Imber-Black, E. (1989). Women's relationships with larger systems. In M. McGoldrick, C. M. Anderson, and F. Walsh (Eds.), *Women in families: A framework for family therapy.* New York: W.W. Norton.

Inhinger-Tallman, M. (1995). Quality of life and well being of single parent families. *Marriage and Family Review, 20,* 513-532.

Isaacs, M. B. (1987). Dysfunctional arrangements in divorcing families. In M. Lindblad-Goldberg (Ed.), *Clinical issues in single-parent households.* Rockville, MD: Aspen.

Isaacs, M., Montalvo, B., and Adelsohn, D. (1986). *The difficult divorce: Therapy for children and families.* New York: Basic Books.

Jacobson, D. and Margolin, G. (1979). *Marital therapy: Strategies based on social learning and behavioral exchange principles.* New York: Basic Books.

Jacobson, G. F. (1983).*The multiple crises of marital separation and divorce.* New York: Grune & Stratton.

Jacobson, N. (1978). Specific and nonspecific factors in the effectiveness of a behavioral approach to marital discord. *Journal of Consulting and Clinical Psychology.*

Jenkins, J. E. et al. (1988). Parental separation effects on children's divergent thinking abilities and creativity potential. *Child Study Journal, 18*(3), 149-159.

Jones, C.W. (1987). Coping with the young handicapped child in the single parent family: An ecosystem perspective. In M. Lindblad-Goldberg (Ed.), *Clinical issues in single-parent households.* Rockville, MD: Aspen.

Kalter, N., Alpern, D., Spence, R., and Plunkett, J. W. (1984). Locus of control in children of divorce. *Journal of Personality Assessment, 48,* 410-413.

Kaslow, F. W. (1981). Divorce and divorce therapy. In A. Gurman and D. Kniskern (Eds.), *Handbook of family therapy.* New York: Brunner and Mazel, Inc.

Kaslow, F. and Hyatt, R. (1981). Divorce: A potential growth experience for the extended family. *Journal of Divorce, 5,* 115-126.

Kato, P. M. and Mann, T. (1999). A synthesis of psychological interventions for the bereaved. *Clinical Psychology Review, 19,* 275-296.

Kavanaugh, (1974). Issues and needs in research. *Language, Speech, and Hearing Services in the Schools,* 5(4), 258-262.

Kaye, S. (1989). The impact of divorce on children's academic performance. *Journal of Divorce, 12,* 283-289.

Kelly, G. (1969). Man's construction of his alternatives. In R. Maher (Ed.), *Clinical psychology and personality: The second papers of George Kelly.* New York: Wiley.

Kelly, J. (1988). Longer term adjustment in children of divorce: Converging findings and implications for practice. *Journal of Family Psychology, 2,* 119-140.

Kerr, M. E. and Bowen, M. (1988). *Family evaluation.* New York: W.W. Norton.

Kinsey, A., Gebhart, G., Pomeroy, W., and Martin, C. (1948). *Sexual behavior in the human male.* Philadelphia: Saunders.

Kinsey, A., Gebhart, G., Pomeroy, W., and Martin, C. (1953). *Sexual behavior in the human female.* Philadelphia: Saunders.

Kirk, S. A. and Gallagher, J. J. (1989). *Educating exceptional children, Sixth edition.* Boston: Houghton Mifflin.

Kirk, S. and Kutchins, H. (1992). *The selling of the DSM: The rhetoric of science in psychiatry.* New York: Aldine de Gruyler.

Klein, J. (1992). Whose values? *Newsweek,* June, pp. 19-27.

Kohen, J. A. (1981). From wife to family head: Transitions in self-identity. *Psychiatry, 44,* 230-240.

Kohlberg, L. (1969). Stage end sequence: The cognitive developmental approach to socialization. In D. A. Goslin (Ed.), *Handbook of socialization theory of research.* Chicago: Rand McNally.

Kohn, J. B. and Kohn, W. K. (1978). *The Widower.* Boston: Beacon Press.

Krantzler, M. (1973). *Creative divorce.* New York: M. Evans & Co.

Krantzler, M. (1975). *Creative divorce.* New York: New American Library.

Kraus, A. S. and Lilienfeld, A. M. (1959). Some epidemiologic aspects of the high mortality rate in the young widowed group. *J Chronic Dis.* Sep; 10: 207-217.

Kries, B. and Pattie, A. (1969). *Up from grief: Patterns of recovery.* New York: The Seabury Press, 1969.

Krupp, G. (1965). Identification as a defense against anxiety in coping with loss. *International Journal of Psychoanalysis,* 46.

Krupp, G., Genovese, F., and Krupp, T. (1986). To have and have not: Multiple identifications in pathological bereavement. *Journal of the American Academy of Psychoanalysis, 14*(3), 337-348.

Kubic, M. (1997). New ways to prevent and treat AIDS. *FDA Consumer,* January-February.

Kulka, R. A. and Weingarten, H. (1979). The long-term effects of parental divorce in childhood on adult adjustment. *Journal of Social Issues, 35*(4), 50-77.

Kurdek, L. A. (1981). An integrative perspective on children's divorce adjustment. *American Psychologist, 36(*8), 856-866.

Kurdek, L. A. and Siesky, A. E. (1980). Children's perceptions of their parents' divorce. *Journal of Divorce, 3,* 339-378.

Lamb, M. E. (1977). Effects of divorce on children's personality development. *Journal of Divorce, 1(*2), 163-175.

Laws, J. L. and Schwartz, P. (1977). *Sexual scripts: The social construction of female sexuality.* Washington, DC: University Press of America.

Lee, J. and Hett, G. (1990). Post-divorce adjustment: An assessment of a group intervention. *Journal of Therapy, 24,* 199-209.

Leslie, F. and Leslie, F. (1977). *Unplanned parenthood. The social consequences of teenage childbearing.* New York: Free Press.

Lino, M. (1995). The economics of single parenthood: Past research and future directions. *Marriage and Family Reivew, 20(*1/2), 99-114.

Lipchik, E. (1988). *Interviewing.* Rockville, MD: Aspen.

Lopata, H. Z. (1972, 1973). *Widowhood in an American city.* Cambridge, MA: Schenken Publishing.

Lopata, H. Z. (1973). Self-identity in marriage and widowhood. *The Sociological Quarterly, 4,* 407-418.

Lopata, H. Z. (1975). On widowhood. Grief work and identity re-construction. *Journal of Geriatric Psychiatry, 8(*1), 41-55.

Lopota, H.Z. (1996). *Current widowhood: Myths and realities.* Thousand Oaks, CA: Sage.

Lowenthal, M. F. and Robinson, B. (1976). Social networks and isolation. In R. H. Binstock and E. Shanas (Eds.), *Handbook of aging and the social sciences,* First edition (pp. 432-456). New York: Van Nostrand Reinhold.

Lowery, C. and Settle, S. (1984). Effects of divorce on children: Differential impact of custody and visitation patterns. *Family Relations, 34.*

MacKinnon, C. E., Stoneman, Z., and Brody, G. H. (1984). The impact of maternal employment and family form on children's sex-role stereotypes and mother's traditional attitude. *Journal of Divorce and Remarriage, 8(*1), 51-60.

MacNamee, S. and Gergen, K. (1993). *Therapy as social construction.* New York: Sage.

Madanes, C. (1991). *Strategic family therapy.* San Francisco: Jossey-Bass.

Madden-Derdich and Leonard, D. (1999). Boundary ambiguity and co-parental conflict after divorce: An empirical test of a family system. *Journal of Marriage and the Family, 61(*3), 588.

Maddison, D. and Raphael, B. (1975). Conjugal bereavement and the social network. In B. Schoenberg, I. Gerber, A. Weiner, A. H. Kutscher, D. Peretz, and A. C. Carr (Eds.), *Bereavement: Its psychosocial aspects* (pp. 26-40). New York: Columbia University Press.

Magrab, P. R. (1978). For the sake of the children: A review of the psychological effects of divorce. *Journal of Divorce, 3,* 233-245.

Mahler, M., Pine, F., and Bergman, A. (1975). *The psychological birth of the human infant: Symbiosis and individuation.* New York: Basic Books.

Maines, D. (2000). Charting futures for sociology: Culture and meaning. *Contemporary Sociology, 20,* 4.

Mandel, H. P. and Marcus, S. I. (1988). *The psychology of underachievement: Differential diagnosis and differential treatment.* New York: John Wiley and Sons.

Margolin, G. and Jacobson, N. S. (1981). Assessment of marital dysfunction. In A. S. Bellack and M. Hersen (Eds)., *Behavioral assessment: A practical handbook* (Second edition) (pp. 389-426). New York: Pergamon Press.

Marsh, H. (1990). Family configurations. *Journal of Educational Psychology, 82,* 327-340.

Maslow, A. H. (1970). *Motivation and personality.* Second edition. New York: Harper and Row.

May, E. T. (1988). *Homeward bound: American families in the Cold War era.* New York: Basic Books.

May, R. (1975). *The courage to create.* Toronto: Bantam.

McCombs, A. and Forehand, R. (1989). Adolescent school performance following parental divorce: Are there family factors which can enhance success? *Adolescence, 24,* 639-646.

McGoldrick, M. (1988). Women and the family life cycle. In B. Carter and M. McGoldrick (Eds.), *The changing family life cycle,* Volume 2. New York: Gardner Press.

McGoldrick, M. (1989). Sisters. In C.M. Anderson and F. Walsh (Eds.), *Women in families: A framework for family therapy.* New York: W.W. Norton.

McGoldrick, M. (1992). *The future of family therapy: Inserting culture, class, race and gender.* Dallas.

McGoldrick, M., Anderson, C., and Walsh, F. (Eds.) (1991). *Women in families: A framework for family therapy.* New York: Norton & Co.

McLanahan, S.S., Garfinkel, I., and Ooms, T. (1987), Female-headed families and economic policy: Expanding the clinician's focus. In M. Lindblad-Goldberg (Ed.), *Clinical issues in single-parent households.* Rockville, MD: Aspen.

McLanahan, S.S., Wedemeyer, N.V., and Adelberg, T. (1981). Network structure, social support, and psychological well-being in the single-parent family. *Journal of Marriage and the Family, 43* (Aug.), 601-611.

McNamee and Gergen, (1992). *Therapy as social construction.* Thousand Oaks, CA: Sage.

McPhee, J. (1985). Ambiguity and change in the post-divorce family. Towards a model of divorce adjustment. *Journal of Divorce, 8*(2).

Meichenbaum, D. (1977). *Cognitive behavior modification: An integrative approach.* New York: Plenum Press.

Mendes, H. A. (1979). Single-parent families: A typology of life styles. *Social Work, 24,* 3.

Merton, T. (1968). *Thoughts in solitude.* New York: Doubleday.

Meyer, G. (1992). Family therapy with divorcing and remarried families. In J. Atwood (Ed.), *Family therapy: A systemic-behavioral approach.* Chicago: Nelson-Hall.

Mince, J. (1992). Discovering meaning with families. In J. Atwood (Ed.), *Family therapy: A systemic-behavioral approach.* Chicago: Nelson-Hall.

Minuchin, S. (1974). *Families and family therapy.* Cambridge: Harvard University Press.

Minuchin, S. and Fishman, H. C. (1981). *Family therapy techniques.* Cambridge: Harvard University Press.

Molnar, A. and deShazer, S. (1987). Solution-focused therapy: Toward the identification of therapeutic tasks. *Journal of Marital and Family Therapy, 13,* 349-358.

Morawetz, A. and Walker, G. (1984). *Brief therapy with single-parent families.* New York: Brunner/Mazel.

Morgan, L. A. (1967). A reexamination of widowhood and morale. *Journal of Gerontology, 31*(6), 687-695.

Morris, J. (1989). *Pressures of a tangled life.* New York: Random House.

Morris L., Warren, C. W., and Aral, S. (1993). Measuring adolescent sexual behaviors and related health outcomes. Public Health Reports, 108 (suppl 1), 31-36.

Mulholland, D., Watt, A., and Sarlin, N. (1991). Academic performance in children of divorce: Psychological resilience and vulnerability. *Journal of Psychiatry, 54,* 268-280.

National Center for Education Statistics (2001). The 1998 high school transcript study tabulations: Comparative data on credits earned and demographics for 1998, 1994, 1990, 1987, and 1982 high school graduates. Author.

National Council on the Aging (1998). Healthy Sexuality and vital aging. Executive summary. Washington, DC: Author.

National Household Education Survey (1998). The condition of education. NCES 98-013. Author.

Neimeyer, R. A. (2000). Searching for the meaning of meaning: Grief therapy and the process of reconstruction. *Death Studies, 24,* 541-558.

Neimeyer, R. A. (2001). The language of loss: Grief therapy as a process of meaning reconstruction. In R. A. Neimeyer (Ed.), *Meaning reconstruction and the experience of loss.* (pp. 261-292). Washington, DC: American Psychological Association.

Newman, G. and Nichols, C. R. (1960). Sexual activities and attitudes in older persons. *JAMA, 173,* 33-35.

Nichols, W. C. (1984). Therapeutic needs of children in family system reorganization. *Journal of Divorce, 7*(4), 23-44.

Norton, A. and Glick, P. (1986). One parent families: A social and economic profile. *Family Relations, 35,* 9-17.

O'Hanlon,W. and Weiner-Davis, M. (1988). *In search of solutions: A new direction in psychotherapy.* New York: Norton.

Okun, B. F. (1984). Family therapy and the schools. In B. F. Okun (Ed.), *Family therapy with school related problems.* Rockville, MD: Aspen.

Olson, S.L. and Banyard, V. (1993). Stop the world so I can get off for a while: Sources of daily stress in the lives of low-income single mothers of young children. *Family Relations, 42,* 50-56.

Osterweis, M., Solomon, F., and Green, F. (1984). *Bereavement: Reactions, consequences and care.* Washington, DC: National Academy Press.

Ourth, J. and Zakariya, S. B. (1982). The school and the single parent student: What schools can do to help. *Principal,* 62(September), 24-38.

Papero, D. V. (1990). *Bowen family systems theory.* Boston: Allyn and Bacon.

Parkes, C. M. (1972). Determinants of outcome following bereavement. *Omega Journal of Death and Dying, 6*(4), 303-323.

Parkes, C. M. and Weiss, R. S. (1983). *Recovery from bereavement.* New York: Basic Books.

Parkes, K. (1975). Adolescent pregnancy: Implications for prevention strategies in educational settings. *School Psychology Review, 17*(4), 570-580.

Parsons, T. and Bales, R. (1955). Family, socialization and interaction process. New York: Free Press.

Peck, J. S. and Manocherian, M. S. (1988). Divorce in the changing life cycle. In B. Carter and M. McGoldrick (Eds.), *The changing family life cycle: A framework for family therapy,* Second edition. New York: Gardner Press.

Penn, P. (1985). Feed foward: Future questions, future maps. *Family Process, 24,* 299-311.

Perls, F. (1969). *Gestalt therapy verbatim.* Lafayette, CA: Real People Press.

Persson, G. (1980). Life event ratings in relation to sex and marital status in a 70-year-old urban population. *Acta Psych. Scand.* 62(2), 112-118.

Petrowsky, M. (1976). Marital status, sex, and the social network of the elderly. *Journal of Marriage and the Family, 38,* 20-131.

Pfeiffer, E. and Davis G. (1972). Determinants of sexual behavior in middle and old age. *Journal of American Geriatric Soc., 20*(4), 151-158.

Pfeiffer, E., Verwoerdt, A., and Davis, C. (1972). Sexual behavior in middle life. *American Journal of Psychiatry, 128*(10), 262-267.

Piaget, J. (1952). *The origins of intelligence in children.* New York: International University Press.

Pollock, G. H. (1975). *The mourning process and creative organizational change.* Plenary Session Post-Presidential Address, American Psychoanalytic Association.

Portes, P. R., Haas, R. C., and Brown, J. (1991). Identifying family factors that predict children's adjustment to divorce: An analytic synthesis. *Journal of Divorce & Remarriage, 15*(3/4), 87-103.

Preto, N. (1988). Transformation of the family system in adolescence. In B. Carter and M. McGoldrick (Eds.), *The changing family life cycle: A framework for family therapy, second edition.* New York: Gardner Press.

Rainwater, L. and Yancey, W. (1967). The *Moynihan report and the politics of controversy: Critical essays on the 1965 Report by Assistant Secretary of Labor Daniel Patrick Moynihan on the Crisis of the Black Family.* Cambridge, MA: The MIT Press.

Rando, T. A. (1984). *Grief, dying and death: Clinical interventions for caregivers.* Champaign, IL: Research Press Company.

Rathers, S. A. and Nevid J. D. (2002). *Adjustment and growth: The challenges of life.* New York: John Wiley and Sons, Ltd.

Reissmann, C. K. (1990). *Divorce talk.* New Brunswick: Rutgers University Press.

Rich, S. (1989). A generation alters notion of U. S. family. *The Washington Post,* September 5, p. A12.

Richards, L. and Schmiege, C. (1993). The problems and strengths of the single parent families. *Family Relations, 42,* 227-285.

Ricketts, W. and Achtenberg, R. (1990). Adoption and foster parenting for lesbians and gay men: Creating new traditions in family. *Marriage and Family Review, 14*(3-4), 83-118.

Roe, A. (1953). The making of a scientist. New York: Dodd, Mead, & Co.

Rogers, C. R. (1951). *Client centered therapy.* Boston: Houghton Mifflin.

Rosenberg, M. and Guttmann, J. (2001). Structural boundaries of single-parent families and children's adjustment. *Journal of Divorce and Remarriage,* 36.

Rosenthal, K. and Keshet, H. (1978a). The impact of childcare responsibilities on the part-time or single father. *Alternative lifestyles, 1*(4), 165-492.

Rosenthal, K. and Keshet, H. (1979b). The not-quite stepmother. *Psychology Today,* July, 82-88.

Rynearson, E. K. (1987). Psychotherapy of pathologic grief: Revisions and limitations. *Psychiatric Clinics of North America, 10*(3), 487-499.

Sanders, C. M. (1989). *Grief: The mourning after.* New York: John Wiley and Sons.

Sank, M. M. and Mauldin, T. (1986). Single versus two parent families: A comparison of mother's time. *Family Relations, 35,* 53-56.

Santrock, J. W. and Tracey, R. L. (1978). Effects of children's family structure on the development of stereotypes by teachers. *Journal of Educational Psychology, 20,* 754-757.

Santrock, J. W. and Warshak, R. (1979). Father custody and social development in boys and girls. *Journal of Social Issues, 35,* no. 4: 112-125.

Schlesinger, B. (1982). Children's viewpoints of living in a one-parent family. *Journal of Divorce, 5*(4), 1-23.

Schlesinger, B. (1986). Single parent families: a bookshelf: 1978-1985. *Family Relations, 35,* 199-204.

Schwebel, A. I., Barocas, H. A., Reichman, W., and Schwebel, M. (1990). *Personal adjustment and growth.* Dubuque, IA: W. C. Brown.

Seligman, D. (1973, March). How equal opportunity turned into employment quotas. *Fortune,* pp. 158-168.

Seligman, M. E. P. (1975). *Helplessness: On depression, development and death.* San Francisco: Freeman.

Sewell, K. W. and Williams, A. M. (2001). Construing stress: A constructivist therapeutic approach to posttraumatic stress reactions. In R.A. Neimeyer (Ed.), *Meaning reconstruction and the experience of loss* (pp. 293-310). Washington, DC: American Psychological Association.

Sherman, F. and Fredman, N. (1986). *Handbook of structured techniques in marriage and family therapy.* New York: Brunner and Mazel.

Sherman, R., Oresky, P., and Roundtree, Y. (1992). *Solving problems in couples and family therapy: Techniques and tactics.* New York: Brunner and Mazel.

Siegel, J. (1986). The multidimensional anger inventory. *J. Pers. Soc. Psychol., 51*(1), 191-200.

Silverman, D. (1977). First, do no more harm: Female rape victims and the male therapist. *American Journal of Orthopsychiatry, 48*(1), 166-173.

Silverman, P. and Englander, S. (1975). A widow's view of her dependent children. *Omega Journal of Death and Dying, 6,* 3-20.

Simon, J. (1990). The single parent: Power and the integrity of parenting. *The American Journal of Psychoanalysis, 50*(2), 187-198.

Snyder, T. D. and Hoffman, C. (1990). Digest of Education Statistics. NCES Number 91660. Washington, DC: National Center for Education Statistics.

Starr, B. D. and Weiner, M. B. (1981). *The Starr-Weiner Report on Sex and Sexuality in the Mature Years.* New York: Stein & Day.

Stein, P. (1976). *Single.* Englewood Cliffs, NJ: Prentice Hall.

Stolberg, A. and Bush, J. (1985). A path analysis of factors predicting children's divorce adjustment. *Journal of Clinical Child Psychology, 14,* 49-54.

Stolberg, A. and Garrison, K. (1985). Evaluating a primary prevention program for children of divorce. *American Journal of Community Psychology, 13*(2), 111-124.

Stolberg, A. L. and Ullman, A. J. (1985). Assessing dimensions of single parenting: The single-parent questionnaire. *Journal of Divorce, 8*(2), 31-45.

Stroebe, M. S. and Schut, H. (2001). Meaning making in the dual process model of coping with bereavement. In R.A. Neimeyer (Ed.), *Meaning reconstruction and the experience of loss* (pp. 55-73). Washington, DC: American Psychological Association.

Strong, P. M. (1979). Mirrors and masks: The search for identity/anguish: A case history of a dying trajectory. *Sociology Health and Illness.*

Tannahill, R. (1980). *Sex in history.* New York: Stien & Day/Scarborough.

Taylor, P. (1991). Children of divorce may be hurt before separation. *The Washington Post,* July 7, p. A10.

Thiriot, T. L. and Buckner, E. T. (1991). Multiple predictors of satisfactory post divorce adjustment of single custodial parents. *Journal of Divorce & Remarriage, 15*(1/2), 27-49.

Thomas, W. (1993). The definition of the situation. In B. Byers (Ed.), *Readings in social psychology* (pp. 173-174). Needham Heights: Allyn and Bacon.

Tillman, J. (1976). Welfare is a woman's issue. In R. Baxandall, L. Gordon, and S. Reverby (Eds.), *America's working woman: A documentary history—1600 to the present.* New York: Vintage Books.

Titkin, E. and Cobb, C. (1983). Treating post-divorce adjustment in latencyage children. *Social Work with Groups, 6,* 53-66.

Titler, B. I. and Cook, V. J. (1981). Relationships among family, school and clinic: Towards a systems approach. *Journal of Clinical and Child Psychology,* fall, 184-187.

Tombari, M. and Davis, R. A. (1979). Behavioral consultation. In G. O. Phye and D. J. Reschly (Eds.), *School psychology: Perspectives and issues.* New York: Academic Press.

Tschann, J. M. (1989). Family process and children's functioning during divorce. *Journal of Marriage and the Family, 51*(2), 431-444.

United States Bureau of the Census (2000). Statistical abstract of the United States 2000. Washington, DC: Author.

United States Department of Commerce, Economics and Statistics Administration, Bureau of the Census (2001). Statistical Brief. Sixty-five plus in the United States SB/95-8. Available online http://www.census.gov/population/socdemo/statbriefs/agegrief.html.

VanCoevering, V. (1973). An exploratory study of middle-aged and older widows to investigate those variables which differentiate high and low life satisfaction. PhD dissertation, Wayne State University.

Van Den Hoonaard, Deborah Kestin (2001). *The widowed self: The older woman's journey through widowhood.* New York: Willfred Laurier University Press.

Veevers, J. E. (1990). Trauma versus strengths: A paradigm of positive versus negative divorce outcomes. *Journal of Divorce & Remarriage, 14*(1), 99-126.

Ventura, S. J., Mosher, W. D., Curtin, S. C., Abma, J. C., and Henshaw, S. (2001). Trends in pregnancy rates for the United States, 1976-97: An update; National vital statistics reports. June 6, vol. 49. no. 4, p. 5 (Hyattsville, MD: National Center for Health Statistics).

Viney, L., Benjamin, Y., and Preston, C. (1988). Constructivist family therapy with the elderly. *Journal of Family Psychology, 29*(20), 241-258.

Vinick, B. (1978). Remarriage in old age. *The Family Coordinator, 27,* 359-363.

Visher, E. B. and Visher, J. S. (1990). Dynamics of successful stepfamilies. *Journal of Divorce & Remarriage, 14*(1), 3-12.

von Bertalanffy, L. (1968). *General systems theory: Foundations, developments, applications.* New York: George Braziller.

Wall Street Journal 4/17/78 from *Commerce Department Survey.*

Waller, W. (1967). *The old love and the new: Divorce and readjustment.* Southern Illinois University Press.

Wallerstein, J. and Kelly, J. (1975). The effects of parental divorce: Experiences of the preschool child. *Journal of Child Psychiatry, 14,* 600-616.

Wallerstein, J. and Kelly, J. (1976). The effects of parental divorce: Experiences of the child in later latency. *Journal of Child Psychiatry, 14,* 256-269.

Wallerstein, J. S. (1984). Children of divorce: Preliminary report of a ten-year fol-low-up of young children. *American Journal of Orthopsychiatry, 54*(3), 444-458.

Wallerstein, J. S. (1985). Children of divorce: Recent research. *American Academy of Child Psychiatry, 24,* 518-530.

Wallerstein, J. S., Kelly, J. B. (1980). *Surviving the breakup: How children and parents cope with divorce.* New York: Basic Books.

Walsh, F. (Ed.) (1982). *Normal family process.* New York: Guilford Press.

Walsh, F. and McGoldrick, M. (1991). *Living beyond loss: Death and the family.* New York: Norton.

Walsh, F. and McGoldrick, M. (1991). Loss and the family: A systemic perspective. In F. Walsh and M. McGoldrick (Eds.), *Living beyond loss: Death in the family.* New York: W.W. Norton.

Walsh, P. (1990). Family functioning among separated and divorced families. Dis-sertation from Virginia Commonwealth University.

Warren, N. and Amara, I. (1985). Educational groups for single parents: The parenting after divorce programs. *Journal of Divorce, 9*(2), winter.

Warren, N., Ilgen, E., Grew, R., Konanc, J., and Amara, I. (1982). Time since sepa-ration: Another perspective on the NASP study of divorce. *School Psychology Review, 14*(3), 373-337.

Watts, D. S. and Watts, K. M. (1991). The impact of female-headed single parent families on academic achievement. *Journal of Divorce & Remarriage, 15*(1/2), 97-114.

Watzlawick, P. (1978). *The language of change: Elements of therapeutic com-munication.* New York: Basic Books.

Watzlawick, P. (1984). *The invented reality.* New York: Norton & Co.

Watzlawick, P., Weakland, J. H., and Fisch, R. (1974). *Change: Principles of problem formation and problem resolution.* New York: W.W. Norton.

Weinstein, E., Rosen, E., and Atwood, J. (1991). Adolescents' knowledge of AIDS and behavior change: Implications for education. *Journal of Health Education, 22*(5), 313-318.

Weiss, R. (1980). Strategic behavioral marital therapy: Toward a model of assess-ment and intervention. In J. Vincent (Ed.), *Advances in family intervention. As-sessment and Theory.* Greenwich, CT: JAI Press.

Weiss, R. S. (1975). *Marital separation.* Basic Books.

Weiss, R. S. (1979). Growing up a little faster: The experience of growing up in a single-parent household. *Journal of Social Issues, 35*(4), 97-111.

Weitzman, L. J. (1985). *The divorce revolution. The unexpected social and eco-nomic consequences for women and children in America.* New York: Free Press.

Weltner, J. S. (1982). A structural approach to the single parent family. *Family Process, 21*(2), 203-209.

White, M. (1985). Fear busting and monster taming: An approach to the fears of young children. *Dulwich Centre Review,* 29-34.

White, M. (1986a). Family escape from trouble. *Family Therapy Case Studies, 1*(1), 29-33.

White, M. (1986b). Negative explanation, restraint and double description: A template for family therapy. *Family Process, 25*(2), 169-184.

White, M. (1989). The externilization of the problem. *Dulwich Centre Newsletter,* Summer.

White, M. (1996). Negative explanation, restraint and double description: A template for family therapy. *Family Process, 25*(2), 169-184.

White, M. and Epston, D. (1990). *Narrative means to therapeutic ends.* New York: W.W. Norton.

Winkelstein, W. J., Lyman, D., Padian, N., et al. (1987). Sexual practices and risk of infection by the human immunodeficiency virus. The San Francisco Men's Health Study. *JAMA, 257,* 32.

Wood, F. and Smith, C. (1985). Assessment of emotionally disturbed/behaviorally disordered students. *Diagnostique, 10,* 40-51.

Woody, J., Colley, P., Schlegelmilch, J., and Maginin, P. (1984). Parental stress and adjustment following divorce. *Crisis Intervention, 13,* 133-147.

Wood, J. I. and Lewis, G. J. (1990a). The coparental relationship of divorced spouses: Its effect on children's school adjustment. *Journal of Divorce & Remarriage, 14*(1), 81-95.

Wood, J. I. and Lewis, G. J. (1990b). Divorcing parents: Guidelines to promoting children's adjustment. *Child & Family Behavior Therapy, 20*(3).

Yankelovich, D. (1981). *New rules.* New York: Random House.

Yawkey, T. D. and Cornelius, G. M. (Eds.) (1991). *Single parent families: For helping professionals and their parents.* Lancaster, PA: Technomics Publishing.

Ysseldyke, J. E. (1979). Issues in psychoeducational assessment. In G. O. Phye and D. J. Reschly (Eds.), *School psychology: Perspectives and issues.* New York: Academic Press.

Zakariya, S. B. (1982). Another look at the children of divorce: Summary report if school needs of one-parent children. *Principal, 62*(September), 34-37.

Zeiss, R. A. and Zeiss, A. M. (1979). The role of sexual behavior in the post-divorce adjustment process. Paper presented at the annual meeting of the Western Psychological Association, San Diego.

Annotated Bibliography and Internet Resources

Annotated Bibliography

Alexander, Shoshana (1993). *In praise of single parents: Mothers and fathers embracing the challenge.* Boston, MA: Houghton Mifflin. 380 pages.

This book presents single parenting in the voices of the real experts—the parents themselves. Shoshana Alexander weaves her firsthand account as a single mother with the personal stories of many other men and women who, by choice or by circumstance, are raising children by themselves. The challenges these parents face in their individual lives are those faced by all families in our nation, revealing that the issue is not only how one parent can raise children alone, but also how we as a society are raising our children. (*Source:* BarnesandNoble.com)

Atlas, Stephen L. (1984). *Official Parents Without Partners source book: The world's largest organization for single parents gives you positive, practical solutions to the questions and challenges of single parenting.* Philadelphia: Running Press. 192 pages.

This book is from the organization Parents Without Partners (see Helpful Internet Information for Web site) and discusses the issues, questions, and challenges of single parents. (*Source:* BarnesandNoble.com.)

Baldock, Carole (1999). *How to succeed as a single parent.* London: Sheldon Press. 129 pages.

A guide for single parents on bringing children up. It focuses on the difficult issues faced by divorced parents, and combines a realistic understanding of both the practical and personal problems to be faced. (*Source:* BarnesandNoble.com.)

Barnes Jr., Robert G. (1992). *Single parenting.* Carol Stream, IL: Tyndale House. 294 pages.

This book compassionately addresses topics such as communication, self-esteem, finances, remarriage, and more. Barnes offers practical, in-depth answers to many questions that single parents have in raising their children. Invaluable reading for singles who take parenting seriously! (*Source:* Familyhaven.com.)

Bowers, Keri (1996). *Single pregnancy, single parenting: Creating a positive, fulfilling experience.* Los Angeles: Park Alexander Press. 297 pages.

Single Pregnancy, Single Parenting is an essential resource and guide-book for single pregnant women and single mothers. It offers a variety of important resources as well as information, tools, and practical advice to help women through the challenges and difficulties of having and raising children without a partner. This book will provide much needed support and resources for women venturing through single pregnancies and parenting. (*Source:* BarnesandNoble.com.)

Britt, Viola (1997). *Raising responsible children in a single parent home.* Kirkwood, MO: Impact Christian Books. 224 pages.

Help for the single parent! A well-documented program employing common sense and practical suggestions to help you attain the kind of family you always wanted, and children for the Lord. Vi Britt has been a single parent since November 1978. She has worked as a teacher both inside and outside of the home. Read her candid testimonies of how she set biblical truths in motion during seventeen intriguing years for James, Gala, and herself. (*Source:* Amazon.com.)

Brott, Armin A. (1999). *The single father: A dad's guide to parenting without a partner.* New York: Abbeville Press. 303 pages.

An indispensable resource for all single dads by the author of Abbeville's best-selling New Father series. In this groundbreaking volume author Armin Brott gives single dads the knowledge, skills, and support they need to become and remain actively involved fathers. With the same thoroughness, accessibility, and humor that have made the books in his critically acclaimed New Father series the best and most popular fatherhood guides in the country, Brott steers divorced, separated, gay, widowed, and never-married men through every aspect of fathering without a partner. Incorporating the advice of top psychologists, lawyers, and other experts, *The Single Father* offers a wealth of essential information and practical tips. Illustrated with cartoons that underscore the challenges and, yes, even the satisfactions of single parenting, and complete with an extensive list of resources for divorced, widowed, and gay dads, *The Single Father* is one book no single dad can afford to do without. (*Source:* BarnesandNoble.com.)

Brown, Susan, and Simmons, Monica (1998). *365 positive strategies for single parenting.* Macon, GA: Smyth & Helwys Publishing. 209 pages.

In the twenty-first century, single parenting is fast becoming the dominant parenting style in the United States. But that does not make the task any easier! One parent must juggle multiple roles in the family, alone. *365 Positive Strategies for Single Parenting* can help single parents face and overcome the challenge successfully.The book discusses
- positive one-minute strategies for maintaining balance between the needs of a child and oneself,
- developmental stages of children,
- parenting tips related to the developmental stages,
- visitation from the absent parent,
- abandonment by a parent, and
- and parenting for the future.

Brown and Simmons will help single parents become more efficient and prepared for the unexpected while creating a family of important values, strength, end love. *365 Positive Strategies for Single Parenting* is an ideal resource not just for custodial parents but also for noncustodial relatives, school counselors, ministers, or anyone working with children of single-parent families. (*Source:* BarnesandNoble.com.)

Burkett, Larry (1997). *The financial guide for the single parent.* Chicago: Moody Press. 235 pages.

The number of single-parent families has grown tremendously over the past twenty-five years. The average income for a single mom is less than $15,000 annually. Single-mother families have the highest rate of poverty across all demographic groups. The statistics are startling. The problems are real. Whether male or female, divorced, widowed, or never married, the single parent encounters unique financial problems. Financial expert Larry

Burkett offers practical help for all of these groups as they struggle financially with raising kids all alone. (*Source:* BarnesandNoble.com.)

Bustanboy, Andy and Bustanboy, Andre (1992). *Single parenting.* Grand Rapids, MI: Zondervan. 292 pages.

Advice for the single parent that covers the needs of children from infancy to adulthood. Bustanboy addresses ways in which the church can support and encourage single parents and shows how the single-parent family can be a healthy, strong environment for raising children. (*Source:* BarnesandNoble.com.)

Card, Emily W. and Kelly, Christie Watts (1996). *Single parent's money guide.* London, England: Macmillan Publishing Company. 240 pages.

Whether you're a single parent by choice or because of unexpected family circumstances, you may not be prepared for the many legal and financial responsibilities you must confront. This book will help you manage one of the hardest jobs in the world. Using her own experiences as a single parent as well as her professional skills as a lawyer, Emily Card will help you better manage your family's financial life. With useful quizzes, checklists, and advice for you and your children, this book will show you how to negotiate alimony and child support, save money on household expenses, cope with emergencies such as job loss or medical catastrophe, find out what insurance coverage you need for your family, involve your children in setting financial goals, name a guardian for your children, and write a will. (*Source:* BarnesandNoble.com.)

Curtis, Carla (2001). *Single woman's parenting journey: Survival tidbits.* Birmingham: University of Alabama, TRC Communications. 100 pages.

One reader states that this is "a book that covers life and its joyous and not so joyous moments. I felt as if I was having a personal conversation with the author. I purchased this book for the single women in my family and decided to read it as well. As a male I found this book to be a great tool to use in life's journey. I love it. A must-read for all single-mother and young teenage parents." (*Source:* BarnesandNoble.com.)

Cynaumon, Greg and Cynaumon, Dana (1994). *Empowering single parents: Ten ways to increase tour effectiveness.* Chicago: Moody Press. 239 pages.

The stress of raising children alone can be a struggle and a challenge for single parents. The Cynaumons assure readers that it is possible to maintain healthy relationships with children and find appropriate solutions to everyday problems. Their solid, practical advice teaches single parents how to become competent, loving caregivers. (*Source:* BarnesandNoble.com.)

Dinkmeyer, Don C., McKay, Joyce L., McKay, Gary D., and McKay, Joyce (1987). *New beginnings: Skills for single parents and step family parents.* Champaign, IL: Research Press. 210 pages.

Focuses on the unique challenges of being a single or stepfamily parent. Contains numerous case examples and helpful illustrations. Covers areas such as self-esteem, relationships and behavior, communication skills, and discipline. (*Source:* BarnesandNoble.com.)

Dreilinger, Marilyn (1998). *How to be a confident single parent.* New York: Bureau for At Risk Youth. 16 pages.

A guide to the problems and challenges of bringing up children on your own, this book focuses on the difficult issues faced by divorced parents and combines a realistic understanding of the problems, both practical and personal, with the author's sympathetic approach. Issues include coping on your own, feelings about guilt and responsibility, receiving adequate support, bringing up children, and dealing with work pressures at the same time. (*Source:* At-Risk.com.)

Ellison, Sheila A. (2001). *Courage to be a single mother: Becoming whole again after divorce.* San Francisco: Harper. 272 pages.

Addressing an unfortunately common situation, this unique book guides newly divorced mothers through the paralyzing doubt, guilt, fear, and anger to the practical rebuilding of their lives. Refreshingly real and honest, Sheila Ellison uses the journey through her own devastating divorce from a professional athlete, as well as stories told by dozens of others, to empower women struggling to combine the realities of divorce with the pressing demands of child rearing. Though filled with practical, reassuring advice on single parenting in the modern world, this is much more than a book on coping—it is an invaluable guide for women to discover the strength they never knew they had to nurture their children, resurrect their spirits, and ultimately create the life they want. (*Source:* BarnesandNoble.com.)

Foust, Linda (1996). *The single parent's almanac: The real-world answers to your everyday questions.* New York: Crown Publishing Group. 427 pages.

   The Single Parent's Almanac shows parents how to balance their children's needs with their own desires, responsibilities, and goals. It throws out life preservers to parents who need some guidance in the areas of taking care of themselves, surviving the holidays, dating, and sex. (*Source:* BarnesandNoble.com.)

Gilbert, Sara Dulaney (1998). *Complete idiot's guide to single parenting.* East Rutherford, NJ: Penguin Group. 352 pages.

   This compassionate guide offers indispensable advice to single parents trying to keep it all together. Learn how to find affordable day care, arrange work schedules, keep up with homework, deal with exes, and find time for new relationships, too. (*Source:* BarnesandNoble.com.)

Green, Daryl (1998). *My cup runneth over: Setting goals for single parents and working couples.* Knoxville, TN: Performance Management & Logistics Associates. 112 pages.

   Through Green's book and new consulting company called Performance Management & Logistics Associates, parents learn to communicate more openly, create written long-term and short-term family goals, and stay dedicated to priorities. (*Source:* BarnesandNoble.com.)

Hardey, Michael and Crow, Graham (Eds.) (1992). *Lone parenthood: Coping with constraints and making opportunities in single-parent families.* Toronto: University of Toronto Press. 208 pages.

   This book is about single parents, who make up an increasingly important and controversial group in Western society. The growth in the number of single-parent households is linked to debates about the "decline of family values" and questions about state involvement in family life. Their economic and social deprivation relative to two-parent households is now a persistent theme of political and academic debates about social policy. *Lone Parenthood* sets out to explore the nature of the challenge that single parents present to social policy and conventional thinking about families. Contributions from a group of authors from a range of disciplinary backgrounds bring together important current research and theory on this major aspect of modern society. A central theme of the book concerns the particular difficulties faced by single parents bringing up their children without a partner in the household. While the authors recognize that individuals have entered single parenthood through various routes, and have different ways of coping with the problems they may encounter, they also see that single parents are united by the common experience of having to make their own lives and those of their children without the support of a partner and with limited support from the state. This timely study of single parents is essential reading for students and researchers of family sociology, the sociology of gender, women's studies and social policy, and professional social, community, and voluntary sector workers. (*Source:* BarnesandNoble.com.)

Hoerner, Thomas (Denise Thurston-Newton, Illustrator) (1999). *Bachelor parents and their functional families: A guide to successful parenting for the single male.* Dallas: Author. 200 pages.

Bachelor Parents is written entirely for single fathers who have custody or are active in their children's lives. *Bachelor Parents* is answer driven for fast referencing with just a taste of off-the-wall men's humor. Best of all, it's filled with all the popular topics from the self-help section in bookstores. (*Source:* BarnesandNoble.com.)

Holyfield, Lori (Foreword by Hilary Rodham Clinton) (2002). *Moving up and out: Poverty, education, and the single parent family.* Philadelphia: Temple University Press. 192 pages.

Single-parent families in the United States have almost tripled in number in the past few decades. A huge majority of these families are female headed. In American culture, it is not so important that we all be equal so much as it is that we all have equal opportunities. Yet sometimes we turn a blind eye to those who need us most. In fact, when it comes to single-parent families, it is as if the barriers are too great, the issues too complex. We wind up reducing the debate to its lowest common denominator. Ironically, it is the families who are most affected that get tangled in the political barbed wire and hidden behind numbing statistics. Moreover, community responses, those small grassroots organizations who care deeply and give wholeheartedly, are seldom celebrated, seldom recognized for their empowering efforts. *Moving Up and Out* focuses on just such a program, the Arkansas Single Parent Scholarship Fund, which has since 1984 provided scholarships for single parents interested in obtaining their postsecondary education. In this story of a highly successful nonprofit, Lori Holyfield, herself a recipient of a scholarship, draws upon the voices of single parents to consider the barriers and struggles faced as they attempt to obtain secondary education and change the lives of both themselves and their children. The help this program has brought to Arkansas residents is needed throughout the country. (*Source:* BarnesandNoble.com.)

Horner, Steve (1998). *Single parenting from a father's heart: A back-to-basics guide for both sexes.* St. Paul, MN: Bang! Press. 329 pages.

Children who grow up without a father's positive influence, regardless of the circumstances (that might include divorce, death of a spouse, out-of-wedlock birth, or adoption), are five times more likely to be poor, twice as likely to drop out of high school, three times more likely to become unwed teen mothers, more likely to end up in foster care or juvenile-justice facilities, and more likely to grow up unemployed, incarcerated, or uninvolved with their own children. Is it true that a father's positive influence is essential to the welfare of his children? If so, why? What are his parenting values, his traditions, and his beliefs? Steve Horner, a full-time single parent of two boys from their diaper days to their high school years shares a father's point of view straight from the frontline trenches of single parenting-and straight from the heart. He leaves nothing out. (*Source:* Amazon.com.)

Hunt, Jeanne (2003). *When you are a single parent.* Cincinnati: Saint Anthony Messenger Press & Franciscan Communications. 47 pages.

Parenting is a blessed but challenging vocation—even in a home with two parents. Those who find themselves parenting alone, whether from divorce or separation, the death of a spouse, or the lengthy absence of a partner, have a daunting mission. How can you make time for handing on the faith when there are bills to pay, a house to clean, clothes to wash, and a thousand other demands on your time? *When You Are a Single Parent* tackles this important question with practical advice for doing it all without forgetting why you are doing it. Jeanne Hunt offers specific ideas to help you create a support network, set limits and priorities, plan household tasks, and celebrate family moments. Use her insights to transform your home from a battlefield where the war for your time is fought to a spiritual sanctuary.

Rather than another set of obligations to fulfill, your faith can be a powerful ally in creating a happier, healthier home. (*Source:* BarnesandNoble.com.)

Isenhart, Dawn (2000). *Surviving single parenting.* USA: Writer's Showcase Press. 108 pages.

An informative tool for anyone faced with the role of single parenting. With the growing number of single parents each year, Dawn Isenhart provides insight into the world of raising a child on your own. Whether you are a single mother or single father, the basic principles of this book will offer inspiration, wisdom, and courage that applies to all single parents. In *Surviving Single Parenting,* you will follow a path that will show you how to

- strengthen yourself,
- deal with your emotions,
- be aware of your child's feelings,
- structure your life as a single parent,
- survive the difficult times,
- show gratitude for your blessings, and
- learn how to make your child and yourself the best you can be. (*Source:* BarnesandNoble.com.)

Israeloff, Roberta and Ginsberg, Barry G. (2002). *50 wonderful ways to be a single-parent family.* Oakland, CA: New Harbinger Publications. 128 pages.

Single-parent families are now more common than their so-called nuclear counterparts. But single caretakers, whether mother, father, or grandparent, experience special challenges and stresses that are not always easy to address. This slim, accessible guide written by a well-known family therapist provides practical ideas for facing and overcoming these challenges. Easy-to-use techniques include sharing decision making with children, developing family rituals and traditions, listening effectively to children of different ages, balancing the pressures of work and home, making the family a team, finding time to play, discovering common ground, and negotiating and establishing boundaries. (*Source:* BarnesandNoble.com.)

Jordan, Diane-Louise (John Byrne, Illustrator) (2003). *How to succeed as a single parent.* London: Hodder and Stoughton. 208 pages.

Diane-Louise Jordan draws from her own experiences as a single parent to offer encouragement to others in this positive guide. With a mixture of practical advice and real-life stories, this volume is designed for those faced with these problems, regardless of how or when they became a single parent. It provides guidance on defining your role as a single parent, teaching your child self-discipline, setting boundaries, and learning to praise your child. On the practical side, it also discusses juggling time and money, managing finances, and introducing a new partner into the family unit. (*Source:* BarnesandNoble.com.)

Kissman, Kris and Allen, Jo A. (1993). *Single parent families,* Volume 24. Newbury Park, CA: SAGE Publications. 160 pages.

A host of misconceptions about single parenting is explored in this volume, which also discusses the implications of single-parent families in our society. Clearly written and gender sensitive, it provides concrete suggestions to enable single parents obtain necessary resources, including personal resources. Topics examined include the interface between the family and the external environment, transitional stages in the life of the family, and support from the extended family. Attention is also paid to special categories of families: families of ethnic minorities, father-headed families, adolescent parents, and noncustodial parenting. (*Source:* BarnesandNoble.com.)

Klumpp, Mike. (2003). *The single dad's survival guide: How to succeed as a one-man parenting team.* New York: Random House. 179 pages.

You may be single, but you're not alone. Being a great dad is challenging enough when you're part of a two-person team. But now you're raising your kids single-handedly. How can you provide the emotional, physical, and spiritual support your children need, cover all the details of running a household, and still earn a living to support your family? Being a solo dad could easily be the toughest job of your life. The good news is you're not alone. Inside this book you'll find the support, advice, and encouragement you need to succeed. Here are practical solutions for everything you're facing from conflicting emotions to day-to-day time management. You'll find useful pointers on a daughter's unique needs, a son's inner struggles, and even how to recruit trusted friends to pitch in. With plenty of humor and real-world insight, *The Single Dad's Survival Guide* will show you how to expand on your natural, built-in abilities so you can come out on top as a parenting team of one. (*Source:* BarnesandNoble.com.)

Lofas, Jeannette (1998). *Family rules: Helping stepfamilies and single parents build happy homes.* New York: Kensington Publishing Corporation. 164 pages.

Lofas incorporates lessons for making house rules work and shows how to establish guidelines and enforce them from the beginning. According to *Parenting Magazine,* this book "gives you the tools you need to create a well-run family and the skills to develop character." (*Source:* BarnesandNoble.com.)

Lorenz, Patricia (1996). *Stuff that matters for single parents.* Atlanta, GA: Charis Books. 238 pages.

Lorenz addresses myriad issues that can baffle even the most even-keeled. Having single-handedly raised four kids, Lorenz knows all about life's little ups and downs. She assures us, for those who keep a sense of humor, the experience is never boring. One reader states, "Absolutely the best book written on parenting . . . A must-read for all!" (*Source:* BarnesandNoble.com.)

Mackall, Dandi Daley (2000). *Just one of me: Confessions of a less-than-perfect single parent.* Lincoln, NE: IUniverse. 212 pages.

How often do you feel the stress of parenthood? For single parents, it's a constant struggle to be both father and mother, playmate and authority, bottle washer and financial provider. The author knows the ups and downs: for every complex question there is a simple answer—and it is always wrong. She shares secrets about how to avoid superparent burnout, who should be first or last on the priority list, and when that position changes. She discusses emotions, remarriage, and visitation rights. (*Source:* BarnesandNoble.com.)

Mattis, Mary C. (1986). *Sex and the single parent: How you can have happy and healthy kids and an active social life.* New York: Henry Holt & Company. 336 pages.

The somewhat frivolous title aside, this is a serious attempt by a family therapist to help single parents establish a balance between their own sexual and social needs and the emotional and psychological health of their children. Mattis begins with an overview of child development stages as they relate to dealing with unfamiliar people and situations. The tone is open-minded as to personal preference, while strongly advocating the emotional and physical safety of children. The issues presume a high level of maturity and are generally beyond the scope of the growing population of teenage parents. (*Source:* BarnesandNoble.com.)

McCreary, Rene D. (2002). *A single parents guide to raising literate children.* Lincoln, NE: Writer's Club Press. 124 pages.

Welcome to an opportunity to learn how to make reading an adventure for your children! *A Single Parents Guide to Raising Literate Children* will provide you with creative ideas for using events in your daily routine to encourage your children to read. You can turn your routine into exciting opportunities to encourage literacy as a way of life for your children. (*Source:* BarnesandNoble.com.)

Miller, Naomi (Susanne Van Duyne, Designer) (1992). *Single parents by choice: A growing trend in family life.* New York: Plenum Press. 239 pages.

With almost one child in four currently living with a single parent, one-parent families have become a significant and growing presence in America today. Naomi Miller, a clinician and expert in family relations, looks at a new and emerging group of single parents, namely, those who, not unlike couples, came to their decision for single parenthood intentionally. In contrast to teenage mothers, these men and women are, for the most part, older, educated, professionally successful, and financially secure. By offering relevant demographic, research, and sociocultural data, as well as a series of intensely personal and revealing interviews, *Single Parents by Choice* investigates what led these people to make such a decision. These new family constellations involve four separate groups: single biological mothers; single adoptive mothers or fathers (including those who have adopted older children as well as infants); divorced parents (i.e., the active parent who has decided not to remarry); and gay and lesbian parents (a relatively new category of alternative parenting). Listening to the poignant stories of those who have chosen single parenthood, we learn about their family backgrounds and how these played a significant role in shaping the hopes and aspirations for creating their own families. We hear about their ambitions, social lives, and love relationships, and what ultimately led them to decide to take on the responsibilities of parenthood outside the bonds of marriage. They talk about their experiences as parents and what impact their single status as parents and what impact their single status has had on their children, as well what kinds of responses they have received from family, friends, and society at large. Some important questions are raised: What are the psychological implications for the children, and how do they compare to children of two-parent families? (*Source:* BarnesandNoble.com.)

Nelsen, Jane and Delzer, Carol (1999). *Positive discipline for single parents.* New York: Crown Publishing Group. 256 pages.

As a single parent in our complex world, you face the challenge of doing alone a job that was meant for two people. In addition, self-doubt and guilt may dampen the joy you experience raising your child. What do you do? Over the years, millions of parents have come to trust Jane Nelsen's classic Positive Discipline series for its consistent, commonsense approach to child rearing. In this completely revised and updated edition of *Positive Discipline for Single Parents* you'll learn how to succeed as a single parent in the most important job of your life: raising a child who is responsible, respectful, and resourceful. (*Source:* BarnesandNoble.com.)

Noel, Brook and Klein, Art (1998). *The single parent resource.* Beverly Hills, CA: Champion Press. 274 pages.

Finally, a book that truly addresses the top concerns of single parents. Brook Noel and Art Klein conducted an unprecedented survey of 500 single parents. They asked them about their top concerns, questions, and needs. The results of this survey became the basis of the subject covered in *The Single Parent Resource.* Klein and Noel cover how to build a solid financial foundation in both the present and future; how to manage the day-to-day challenges of single parents; how to work with and release complicated emotions of anger, sadness, depression and jealousy; the "ins and outs" of dating; how to manage a household effectively, and much more. A perfect resource for any single parent or busy parent looking to maximize effectiveness and create a stronger family unit. (*Source:* BarnesandNoble.com.)

Paterson, Wendy Anne (2000). *Unbroken homes: Single-parent mothers tell their stories.* Binghamton, NY: The Haworth Press. 410 pages.

This book is a story quilt of personal narratives constructed from in-depth, case study interviews of five single-parent mothers. *Unbroken Homes* chronicles their journeys as mothers, daughters, and women, in relationships and in solitude, displaying their stories in their own words like the squares of a multicolored quilt. As a feminist work, *Unbroken Homes* breaks through the stigma associated with broken homes, and provides a new perspective on the reorganization of American families. (*Source:* BarnesandNoble.com.)

Pearson, Carol Lynn (1991). *One on the seesaw: The ups and downs of a single-parent family.* New York: Random House Value Publishing. 224 pages.

The Pearson household consists of two girls and two boys and their mother, a single parent. The story of the author's marriage, which ended in divorce and AIDS-related death, was the subject of *Good-bye, I Love You.* Now, Pearson recalls the ten years during which she combined a writing career with single parenting, experiencing the trials and joys that accompany the rearing of a typically lively brood. She celebrates family in all its permutations so evident in contemporary society. Her children's problems at school, their scrapes with authority, and their successes despite detours along the way are microcosms of other families' experiences, distinguished only by the loneliness of a father's absence. Yet buttressed by strong faith and the practical support of the Mormon community in the San Francisco Bay Area, Pearson exemplifies the spirit that keeps a family together as she shares her one-parent viewpoint. (*Source:* BarnesandNoble.com.)

Peterson, Marion and Warner, Diane (2003). *Single parenting for dummies.* New York: Wiley Publishing. 360 pages.

If you're one of the millions of single parents, this encouraging, practical book is for you. You'll find helpful solutions to balancing work and family life, developing strong relationships with your kids, managing your time (and money), and dealing with such challenges as dating and remarriage—along with insightful, inspiring real-life single-parent success stories. (*Source:* BarnesandNoble.com.)

Pickhardt, Carl E. (1996). *Keys to single parenting.* Hauppauge, NY: Barrons Educational Series. 180 pages.

Here's help for parents who must cope with the details of raising children in the often-demanding contemporary environment. Detailed advice covers such subjects as making the transition to single parenthood, helping children recover from the trauma of parents' separation, and more. (*Source:* BarnesandNoble.com.)

Read, Bobbie (1992). *Single-parent journey.* Anderson, IN: Warner Press.

Provides thirteen full sessions that address the challenges single parents face and offers biblical solutions. Each study features guides and options for leaders, reproducible handouts, exercise and activities, Bible studies, and discussion questions. Topics include good family communication, roles and responsibilities, effective time management, dating, and blending families. (*Source:* GospelPublishing.com.)

Richmond, Gary (1990). *Successful single parenting.* Eugene, OR: Harvest House Publishers. 256 pages.

With compassion and down-to-earth suggestions, Richmond encourages parents and assures them that single-parent homes can produce healthy, well-adjusted children. (*Source:* BarnesandNoble.com.)

Robson, Janet (1995). *Growing as a single parent.* St. Louis, MO: Concordia Publishing House.

Janet Robson's interest in family issues spans many years. Janet expresses her appreciation to "the many single parents who shared their frustrations, triumphs, and faith in the preparation of this Bible study." Her sensitivity for single parents is evidenced throughout. (*Source:* BarnesandNoble.com.)

Schneider, Meg A. and Byer, Martine J. (2002). *Sex and the single parent: A guide for parents who find themselves back in the dating game.* New York: Perigee Trade. 256 pages.

Schneider and Byer, both prolific authors with MSWs and experience working with families, here offer solid guidelines on dating for single parents and widows/widowers. Parents, they believe, deserve and need a love life, but at the same time they must protect children from further loss and confusion. The authors treat the whole spectrum of dating, from casual dates through serious relationships and remarriage. They openly confront problems (e.g., hostile teenagers, power plays by children to try to derail a parent's relationship, and the need to find time for passion), offering realistic and varied solutions, and in separate chapters deal with dating after the death of a spouse and after children have left home. Although divorce and parenting books generally provide some coverage of romance, this is the only extended treatment of the topic—one certainly on the minds of many parents today. (*Source:* BarnesandNoble.com.)

Strong, Dina (1999). *Singular ingenuity: Reflections on being a single parent.* Chicago: ACTA Publications. 119 pages.

The responsibilities of parenting can weigh heavily on a single parent, but the wonder of a child and the faithful presence of God can renew the spirit. More than 100 single-page reflections probe the delights and dilemmas that come with parenting alone. (*Source:* BarnesandNoble.com.)

Tankersley, Ressie Lester (2001). *By grace and alone: Single parenting with God's help.* Lincoln, NE: Writer's Club Press. 108 pages.

Single parenting with God's help. Advice, encouragement, and guidance from someone who has been there. Includes money-saving ideas. (*Source:* BarnesandNoble.com.)

Wagonseller, Bill R. and Rosen, Ruth C. (1992). *Coping in a single-parent home.* New York: Rosen Publishing Group. 113 pages.

A self-affirming volume written in an easy, conversational style. Through the use of statistics and a description of the genesis of the family nucleus, the authors attempt to provide young adult readers with good answers to specific problems and challenges that arise in single-parent families. Survival skills are discussed and suggestions are offered for long-term solutions. Ancillary discussions include custody agreements, alimony and child support, parental dating, searching for birth parents, tracking an absent parent, life-stage approaches to death and the grief process, support groups, and parental medical care both at home and in a hospital. The final two chapters address the psychological nuances of the single-parent family. Totally encouraging while stressing the realistic aspects of the specific situations, this title shows the need for facing up to one's problems and moving forward rather than wallowing in negativism and despair. (*Source:* BarnesandNoble.com.)

Whiteman, Thomas and Wright, Norman (2003). *Fresh start for single parents.* Colorado Springs: Cook Communications Ministries.

Full of helpful ideas for single-parent families, the workbook format lets you apply the material to your own situation. Whether you are a custodial parent or a long-distance mom or dad, *A Fresh Start for Single Parents* will help you and your children adjust to the challenges that come with a family breakup.

Wolverton, Carrol (2001). *Serious survival: Skills for single parents.* Internet: Booklocker.com. 144 pages.

If you are a single parent, you need this book. If you are a support group moderator, it's a must have. Survival topics are arranged in alphabetical question-and-answer format. One reader states, "What a delight to find a fresh new voice that speaks the language of single parents. Carrol Wolverton takes a hard look at the problems they face. Her helpful ideas about dealing with day-to-day problems are the strength of the book. The question-and-answer format in alphabetical order makes it easy to read. This is a book that will inspire struggling parents to rethink and keep trying to survive in today's world." (*Source:* Amazon.com.)

Worth, Jill and Tufnell, Christine (1997). *Journey through single parenting: A practical guide to finding fulfillment.* London: Hodder and Stoughton. 165 pages.

This book tackles the problems frequently met by single parents, shows how to cope with the pressures they face, and describes how to deal with anger, loneliness, money, time, sexuality, remarriage, and children. Based on numerous case studies.

Worth, Jill and Tufnell, Christine (2002). *All alone: Help and hope for single parents.* Waynesboro, GA: Authentic Media. 160 pages.

Offering help and hope to single parents, taking the reader from initial loss and hurt to the recovery of positive attitudes and action. (*Source:* Amazon.com.)

Worth, Richard (1992). *Single-parent families.* London: Watts Franklin. 128 pages.

Worth begins with an abbreviated history of the family in the United States, emphasizing the role that families have played in society. The changing relationships between men and women, the rising divorce rate, and the changing role of women, both in the home and in the workplace, have all contributed to the rise of the single-parent family. He then looks at single-parent families by type: those caused by divorce or by the death of a parent, and teenage single mothers. Worth touches on such issues as the long-term effects of divorce, teen parents dealing with their own parents, and the grieving process. He concludes with a general discussion of the difficulties facing all single parents and the need for surrogates to provide additional care and emotional support. Worth includes statistics and easy-to-read tables, balancing them with fictional stories that depict real-life situations, composed from interviews and research. The stories make interesting reading while the source notes and bibliography make the book a useful tool for more in-depth study. For another view of single parenting, see Rosenberg's *Living with a Single Parent*. (*Source:* BarnesandNoble.com.)

Yoder, Sharon and Abbott Candace (Eds.) (2001). *The single parent guidebook: Up, up and away to personal fulfillment.* Georgetown, DE: Fruit-Bearer Publishing. 176 pages.

Help is on the way for single parents who are seeking more fun, more freedom, and personal fulfillment. Dr. Sharon Yoder shows you how in her book, *The Single Parent Guide Book: Up, Up And A Way To Personal Fulfillment.* Sharon offers 163 ways you can change your single parenting lifestyle from monotonous, exhausting and over whelming obligations to live the life of your dreams. If you are expecting this to be a book on child raising, forget it! This book is all about you and includes tips ranging from selection of friends to realizing your dreams . . . to setting aside time for yourself . . . to getting along with difficult people in your life. Each chapter concludes with practical to-do lists to make it easy to make new things happen. Sharon passes on her experiences and solutions as a single mother of five for sixteen years after twenty-one years of marriage. (*Source:* keynotesandseminars.com.)

Helpful Internet Information

http://www.thesingleparentfamily.com

Thesingleparentfamily.com is an Internet site that provides resources for single-parent families, specifically single-parent families in the Charlotte, North Carolina, area. In addition to local information, the site offers information and articles on single parent issues, such as raising kids, finances, dating, and getting organized. Unique to this site is an online single-parent community where members can chat and message one another about issues and advice.

http://www.singleparentcentral.com

Thesingleparentcentral.com is an online resource for single-parent families. This site has personals, book resources, and articles, in addition to various channels such as articles, careers, celebrate the family, child care, child support, government resources, kid central, facts and stats, links, money, news and info, and quotes. Most unique to this site is it's free dating service and links to other dating sites.

http://www.parentswithoutpartners.org/Support1.htm

This link has many national statistics about divorce and single-parent families.

http://www.singleparents.org/

Singleparents.org is the Web site of the Single Parent Association Group: Supporting Parents and Children in Arizona. While this site is based out of Arizona, parents can join the virtual chapter and group online from all over the world. The resource has FAQs and testimonials about the organization, parenting tips, resources, books, and an activity calendar.

http://www.theallengroup.com/members/Fr_mccloy.html

This is an article by Marsha McCloy titled "Information About Adolescents Living in Single-Parent Families" that discusses how adolescents are affected by living in single-parent families.

http://www.parent.net/article/archive/family.shtml

This is the Web site of the Single Parent Family Resources, an international organization dedicated to equipping leaders for effective ministry to single-parent families. Single Parent Family Resources provides leadership training to churches, teachers, the military, and mental health professionals around the globe. Single Parent Family Resources offers a unique partnership with churches to enable them to begin and maintain Just Me and the Kids: a twelve-week program to begin single-parent families on the journey toward healing, wholeness, and hope. Single Parent Family Resources also offers seminars, workshops, and conferences to single parents and their children, offering encouragement and hope as they begin this journey.

http://www.parent.net/articvle/archive/family.shtml

This site is an article titled "Single Parent Families: Quality Without Shame."

http://www.thefamilyworks.org/Parenting/SinglePa.htm

This article is written by single parent Georgia Lewis, and is titled "Successful Single Parent Families." It details nine tips for single-parent families.

http://www.fww.org/famnews/single-parents.html

This article, written by Genero Armas, discusses single-parent families around the world and trends and differences of single-parent families in other countries.

http://www.pearsoncustom.com/link/socialscience/bgsu/eng112/singleparentfamilies.html

This site has six public Web sites that are resources and links for single parents. Links include Parents Without Partners, Unique Strengths, Growing Up in Single Parent Families, and Effects of Work and Welfare.

http://www.baycongroup.com/education/car_single_parent.htm

This site is about single-parent families and career help.

http://singleparents.timewithkids.com/

This article by Shelley Taylor is titled "New Year's Resolution for the Single Parent" and discusses ways to make a single parent's year better than the last.

http://www.fww.org/famnews/0418c.htm

This article by Tyler Gray is titled "The Dilemma of the Single Parent Who's Dating" and discusses issues that arise when single parents date.

http://oldfraser.lexi.net/publications/forum/2000/01/section_01.html

This article by Chris Sarlo compares key characteristics of single parent families in 1973 to single parent families in 1996. The article titled "Single

Parent Families: Then and Now" discusses issues such as poverty rate and average family income of single parent families in 1973 and 1996 and displays results in an easy to read chart.

http://talkaboutparenting.com/group/alt.adoption/messages/380722.html

This link is a population-based study titled "Children Growing Up in Single Parent Families." The authors' findings suggest that children who grow up in single-parent families are twice as likely as their counterparts to develop serious psychiatric illnesses or addictions later in life. The authors' offer ways to prevent issues from arising.

http://www.students.dsu.edu/kleinjap.single_parent_families.htm

This link is for teachers who work with students of single-parent households and explains basic information about single-parent families and what teachers can do to help a single-parent family through the academic year.

http://www.divorcewizards.com/top10singleparenting.html

This article, titled "How to Be the Best Single Parent You Can" by Shellee Darnell, a licensed marriage and family therapist, details ten strategies on how single parents can succeed and raise good kids. This link also has more helpful "top ten" articles attached to it, such as "Top Ten Ways to Cope with Separation and Divorce" and "Top Ten Ways to Help Your Child Through a Divorce."

http://herkules.oulu.fi/isbn9514259416/

This study, titled "The Association Between Single-Parent Family Background and Physical Morbidity, Mortality, and Criminal Behaviour in Adulthood," by Anu Sauvola, investigates the long-term effects that single-parent family households may have on morbidity, mortality, and criminal behavior. In this study it was shown that young adults with single-parent families in childhood experienced a more stressful pathway from late adolescence to adulthood. However, most of the children of single-parent families did well during the follow-up time.

http://www.theparentreport.com/resources/ages/preteen/family_life/534.html

This article expresses the importance of a single parent taking care of himself or herself. Titled "Single Parenting: Why It's Important to Take Care of Yourself . . . for Kids' Sake!", this article discusses ways in which single parents can care for themselves so as to improve the quality of their children's lives. Suggestions include rewarding yourself for tasks completed and managing your finances.

http://www.thebeehive.org/external_link.asp?r=/family/parenting-single.asp&3=http%3A%2F%2Fwww%2Emakinglemonade%2Ecom%2F&language=1

Making Lemonade: The Single Parent Network is a great Web site that provides numerous online resources for single parents and individuals who may be facing single parenthood. There is a newsletter, social and dating links, financial resources, legal resources, and other information that can help single parents. With the motto "When you have lemons just make lemonade. With single parent support an extended family is made," this resource looks at the positives in single parenting.

http://www.ssdan.net/kidscount/backgrounders/sph.shtml

This site is part of the SSDAN (Social Science Data Analysis Network) and has great information and a figure regarding the percent of families with children headed by single parents, 1998.

http://www.rlrouse.com/single-parent.html

This article, written by Danielle Hollister, discusses seven strategies of success in single-parent households. Titled "Surviving As a Single Parent: Seven Suggestions to Make Your Life Easier," the link discusses helpful tips such as "Forgive even if you'll never be able to forget" and "Make the best of everything you have."

http://www.divorcesource.com/CA/ARTICLES/nightingale6.html

This article by Dr. Lois Nightingale is titled "Dating As a Single Parent" and discusses the qualities that a single parent should look for in someone he or she is deciding to date.

http://edis.ifas.ufl.edu/BODY_HE339

This article by Millis Ferrer is a great time-management, interactive article for single parents. Titled "Success and the Single Parent: A Flash of Time," the worksheet-type article is a great way for single parents to display and attempt to manage their time better.

http://www.divorcecentral.com/parent/handbook/9.html

This link is to an article by Terry Hillman and Pam Weintraub titled "The Art of Single Parenting" that discusses issues faced by the custodial parent, the noncustodial parent, and the children in a single-parent home.

http://www.solveyourproblem.com/artman/publish/article_242.shtml

This article by Debbie Eisenstadt Mandel titled "Single Parent: 7 Tips for Handling the Double Load" discusses seven ways a single parent can manage his or her workload.

http://www.healthscout.com/news/68/8005301/main.html

This link is to a short article titled "Risks for Single-Parent Children" and is based on a Swedish study on the health risks associated with children raised by single parents.

http://fl.essortment.com/singleparentfa_rcsc.htm

This article written by Victoria Walker is titled "Being a Positive in a Single Parent Family" and discusses how a single-parent family can remain positive and demonstrate positive qualities for kids to model.

Index

Page numbers followed by the letter "e" indicate exhibits; those followed by the letter "f" indicate figures; and those followed by the letter "t" indicate tables.

Order a copy of this book with this form or online at:
http://www.haworthpress.com/store/product.asp?sku=5540

THERAPY WITH SINGLE PARENTS
A Social Constructionist Approach

_____in hardbound at $49.95 (ISBN-13: 978-0-7890-0294-5; ISBN-10: 0-7890-0294-9)

_____in softbound at $34.95 (ISBN-13: 978-0-7890-0407-9; ISBN-10: 0-7890-0407-0)

Or order online and use special offer code HEC25 in the shopping cart.

COST OF BOOKS_____

POSTAGE & HANDLING_____
*(US: $4.00 for first book & $1.50
for each additional book)*
*(Outside US: $5.00 for first book
& $2.00 for each additional book)*

SUBTOTAL_____

IN CANADA: ADD 7% GST_____

STATE TAX_____
*(NJ, NY, OH, MN, CA, IL, IN, PA, & SD
residents, add appropriate local sales tax)*

FINAL TOTAL_____
*(If paying in Canadian funds,
convert using the current
exchange rate, UNESCO
coupons welcome)*

☐ **BILL ME LATER:** (Bill-me option is good on
US/Canada/Mexico orders only; not good to
jobbers, wholesalers, or subscription agencies.)
☐ Check here if billing address is different from
shipping address and attach purchase order and
billing address information.

Signature_____

☐ **PAYMENT ENCLOSED: $_____**

☐ **PLEASE CHARGE TO MY CREDIT CARD.**

☐ Visa ☐ MasterCard ☐ AmEx ☐ Discover
☐ Diner's Club ☐ Eurocard ☐ JCB

Account # _____

Exp. Date_____

Signature_____

Prices in US dollars and subject to change without notice.

NAME_____

INSTITUTION_____

ADDRESS_____

CITY_____

STATE/ZIP_____

COUNTRY_____ COUNTY (NY residents only)_____

TEL_____ FAX_____

E-MAIL_____

May we use your e-mail address for confirmations and other types of information? ☐ Yes ☐ No
We appreciate receiving your e-mail address and fax number. Haworth would like to e-mail or fax special
discount offers to you, as a preferred customer. **We will never share, rent, or exchange your e-mail address
or fax number.** We regard such actions as an invasion of your privacy.

Order From Your Local Bookstore or Directly From
The Haworth Press, Inc.
10 Alice Street, Binghamton, New York 13904-1580 • USA
TELEPHONE: 1-800-HAWORTH (1-800-429-6784) / Outside US/Canada: (607) 722-5857
FAX: 1-800-895-0582 / Outside US/Canada: (607) 771-0012
E-mail to: orders@haworthpress.com

For orders outside US and Canada, you may wish to order through your local
sales representative, distributor, or bookseller.
For information, see http://haworthpress.com/distributors

(Discounts are available for individual orders in US and Canada only, not booksellers/distributors.)
PLEASE PHOTOCOPY THIS FORM FOR YOUR PERSONAL USE.
http://www.HaworthPress.com   BOF06